A portrait of the festivals, specialties, places, and people
behind the state's great food traditions, with over 150 recipes

A COOK'S TOUR OF MINNESOTA

Ann L. Burckhardt

Minnesota Historical
Society Press

The Minnesota Historical Society Press is a member of the Association of American University Presses.

Manufactured in the United States of America

10 9 8 7 6 5 4 3 2 1

♾ The paper used in this publication meets the minimum requirements of the American National Standard for Information Sciences—Permanence for Printed Library materials, ANSI Z39.48-1984.

Front cover photograph:
Kindra Murphy, Minneapolis

International Standard Book Number
0-87351-467-X (cloth)
0-87351-468-8 (paper)

Library of Congress Cataloging-in-Publication Data

Burckhardt, Ann, 1933–
  A cook's tour of Minnesota /
  Ann L. Burckhardt.
     p. cm.
Includes index.
   ISBN 0-87351-467-X
   (cloth : alk. paper)
   ISBN 0-87351-468-8
   (pbk. : alk. paper)
   1. Cookery, American.
   2. Cookery—Minnesota. I. Title.
TX715.B9497 2003
641.59776—dc21
                    2003011666

A COOK'S TOUR OF MINNESOTA

For Jean,

Read... cook... enjoy!

Ann L. Burckhardt

CONTENTS

viii **Preface**

CELEBRATIONS AND FESTIVALS

1
2 Bake-Off: The Grandmama of All Recipe Contests

2
8 Festival of Nations: Eat Your Way Around the World

3
13 Cinco de Mayo: Start Summer with a Fiesta

4
19 New Ulm's Heritagefest: Discover Germany in Minnesota

5
24 Powwow Primer: Jingle Dancers, Frybread, and More

6
31 Celebrating Pie: Braham Pie Day

7
37 Remembering St. Paul's Rondo: Rondo Days

8
43 Minnesota State Fair: Feeding the Fair's Thousands

9
49 Family Reunions + Feasting = Hmong New Year

10
55 Christmas Festival with Norwegian Buffet

SAVORY SPECIALTIES

11
62 Berry Picking at the Farm

12
67 The Butter Is the Best at Land O'Lakes

13
73 Cabin Time... and the Cookin' Is Easy

14
78 Betty Crocker Takes the Cake: A View from Her Kitchen

15
83 Seeing Red: Ken Davis Bar-B-Q Sauce

16
89 Wild Fruit—To Spread, Pour, and Sip

17
94 Schwan's Ice Cream—A Sweet Story

18
99 Soybeans: Good for You and for Animals Too

19
104 SPAM—Nothing Short of a Phenomenon

20
111 Gobble, Gobble, Gobble—The Whole World Eats Minnesota Turkey

21
116 Watkins Vanilla: A Favorite Flavor, a Fashionable Scent

22
123 Wild Rice: Minnesota's Grain of Choice

MEMORABLE PLACES

23
130 The American Swedish Institute: Mansion Museum Preserves Culture

24
135 BC Gardens—Woman-Powered and Community-Supported

25
141 Carlson's Apple Orchard and Bakery—Minnesota Apples Everywhere

26
147 Forest History Center—One Last Lumber Camp

27
151 Fine Food at Kavanaugh's Sylvan Lake Resort

28
157 Summer Fun—and a New Language Too

29
163 Schumacher's Hotel in the Heart of New Prague

30
169 Ironworld—How to Tour the Iron Range in Two Easy Hours

NORTH STAR COOKS

31
176 Leeann Chin: Mother, Caterer, Teacher, Restaurateur

32
182 Hockey Mom Beth Dooley Puts Health on the Menu

33
188 Marie Vogl Gery, Breakfast Queen

34
193 Al Sicherman, a.k.a. Mr. Tidbit

35
199 Grais Notes on Minnesota Jewish Cooking

36
205 Ginny Hoeschen: Live from the Test Kitchen

37
210 Lynne Rosetto Kasper and Her Splendid Table

38
215 Bea Ojakangas: Cookbook Writer Is a Favorite Finn

39
220 State Fair Judge Jan Stroom Finds the Best

40
226 Eberhard Werthmann: The Dean of Cooking Teachers

232 Appendix

240 Recipe Index

PREFACE

The people of Minnesota and their food—that's what this book is about. The chefs and their specialties. The dining hall cooks and the judges at the Minnesota State Fair and how they work during those ten busy days. The dominant ethnic groups and how they share old country foods with new neighbors. The farmers and uses for their products, be it beans or berries, tomatoes or turkeys. The entrepreneurs and the foods they market. The food experts and how they share their knowledge. The hockey moms and how they feed their budding athletes. The behind-the-scenes home economists and their work in test kitchens and for recipe contests.

I count myself fortunate to have been an active participant in the food scene in Minnesota for over forty years. Minnesota is a food-lover's haven. Here in the Twin Cities there is a constantly expanding restaurant scene. Around the state there are several leading national food companies and colleges where cutting-edge food research is going on. And everywhere there are home cooks—men and women who delight in preparing lovely meals for family and friends.

Memories of my early food experiences here in the Cities are vivid: Popping corn with my roommates in our apartment kitchen, then tucking bags of it under our arms as we walked downtown—nearly three miles!—to go to a matinee movie. Lunching at the popular Minneapolis cafeterias—the Forum, Richards Treat, and Becky's, watching my working-girl's budget. Being introduced to the famous Cuckoo Pie (it was really chicken) at the original Radisson Hotel and to roast suckling pig at Jax, this latter at a celebratory dinner hosted by General Mills.

Though ethnic eateries were few in the 1960s, we planned our evenings around giving them a try. We sampled German food (and dark beer) at Sheik's Restaurant, French food at Chateau de Paris (in the Dyckman Hotel), Mexican at La Casa Coronado, and Italian at Café de Napoli. But the big-deal place to go was Charlie's Café Exceptionale, the place I first tasted oysters Rockefeller. Now Twin Cities residents and, increasingly, those living in greater Minnesota as well, can spin a globe, choose a cuisine, and go out to sample it.

Sampling the fare at new restaurants is fun, and so is trying new food products. Just-introduced convenience products were my beat at the *Star Tribune* for years. So it was in my line of duty to prepare new offerings from food manufacturers, large and small. If the company was based in Minnesota, it was of even greater interest to our readers. The same was true of the new cookbooks I regularly reviewed—if it was written by a Minnesotan, it went to the top of the heap.

At bottom, food stories are people stories. They describe how people use food—in religious or family celebrations, as a gesture of friendship or generosity, even as a display of wealth. Stories about how a particular cuisine can become the focus of someone's life or how preparing a food together can forge a bond from one generation to another are the stories of our history, both as individuals and as part of the community of this great state. People's stories and food have been the passions of my life, and I'm honored to share these stories of Minnesotans and how the food they grow, prepare, sell, and serve shapes their lives—and ours.

CELEBRATIONS AND FESTIVALS

2 Bake-Off: The
   Grandmama of All
   Recipe Contests

8 Festival of Nations:
   Eat Your Way Around
   the World

13 Cinco de Mayo: Start
   Summer with a Fiesta

19 New Ulm's
   Heritagefest:
   Discover Germany in
   Minnesota

24 Powwow Primer:
   Jingle Dancers,
   Frybread, and More

31 Celebrating Pie:
   Braham Pie Day

37 Remembering
   St. Paul's Rondo:
   Rondo Days

43 Minnesota State Fair:
   Feeding the Fair's
   Thousands

49 Family Reunions +
   Feasting = Hmong
   New Year

55 Christmas Festival
   with Norwegian
   Buffet

1
BAKE-OFF
THE GRANDMAMA OF ALL RECIPE CONTESTS

The Pillsbury Bake-Off contest, created in Minneapolis in 1949 to celebrate Pillsbury's eightieth birthday, has become the most famous national baking-and-cooking contest ever. The popular contest marches on, continually reinventing itself while adding new recipes to the American repertoire.

Meticulously organized and run by a corps of Minnesotans, the country's best amateur cooks compete for the coveted grand prize. Cooks from around the state have won the top prize six times. Always a Bake-Off watcher, I served as a judge for the contest in 1982 and as a researcher in 2000. And I attended in 1986 and 1990 to report on the winners for the *Star Tribune*.

Philip Pillsbury, then-CEO of the Minneapolis milling company founded by his great-grandfather, gets credit for the Bake-Off contest idea. It was a period of postwar prosperity and the Pillsbury leadership felt that "devoted, industrious home cooks" ought to be given recognition along with some glamour. Their idea: a national recipe competition culminating in a gala weekend at which the winning foods would be chosen. The recipes would, of course, be made with Pillsbury's Best Flour. The Pillsbury staff sorted an avalanche of entries in what was first called the "Grand National Recipe and Baking Contest."

One hundred cooks from all over the nation were picked to compete for hefty cash prizes. The hundred finalists were feted at the most glamorous place in the country, New York City's Waldorf-Astoria Hotel. Competing in the contest often meant the first train ride or the first stay in a hotel for some of the home cooks. And when they got to New York, they were treated to luxuries such as room service with breakfast in bed and dinner with pheasant under glass.

During the cooking and judging for this first competition, former First Lady Eleanor Roosevelt and radio personality Art Linkletter mingled with the

The cooks go marching in, led by the late Philip Pillsbury, the man credited with starting the famed Bake-Off. The year: 1984; the place: San Diego.

finalists—ninety-seven women and three men. The press, among them Mary Hart, longtime women's editor of the *Minneapolis Tribune*, also stayed at the Waldorf. The contestants loved every minute of it. And so did the writers, who published the personal stories of the contestants along with the winning recipes. No-Knead Water-Rising Twists, baked by Theodora Smafield (of Detroit, Michigan), won the $25,000 grand prize plus an additional $25,000 for having submitted with her original entry a special token from her grocer. The event was such a great success that Pillsbury decided to do it all over again the next year.

The company continued to hold the Grand National yearly, although, during the 1950s, it began to be called the "Pillsbury Bake-Off Contest." That became the contest's official name in 1966; they trademarked the name in 1972.

In 1978 the company realized the contest would still be a big deal even if it were held every other year. Entries come in before an October 1 deadline one year. The contest is held in late February the next year. The Bake-Off staff puts in six intensive weeks of work before picking the hundred lucky finalists.

In 1982, when I was a Bake-Off judge, the top prize was up to $40,000. The featured products were Pillsbury flour, cake mixes, and refrigerated biscuits and crescent rolls. Recipes were grouped into three categories: economy, ethnic, and snack. The ethnic category had the most contenders, reflecting the nation's growing interest in foods of other nations.

By 1999, when I worked as a researcher for the fiftieth-anniversary Bake-Off, sponsoring products included the refrigerated doughs, Progresso bread crumbs, Green Giant vegetables, and Old El Paso Mexican items. Missing were the flour and cake mixes. The categories that year were Casual Snacks and Appetizers, Yummy Vegetables, Easy Weeknight Meals, and Fast and Fabulous Desserts and Treats.

In 1996 the Bake-Off grand prize jumped to $1,000,000. That first million went to the first man to win the top prize, a California cook who created a fudge torte.

But enough of details, I have some Bake-Off stories to share.

An unusual name was supposed to attract attention to your recipe when entries were sorted. I'll always remember Hoot Owl Cookies, which my roommates and I sampled in 1956 when tester Jane Brintlinger (now Leck) brought them to our apartment from the test kitchens. Another time she brought bright yellow rolls called Golden Bananzas that were banana flavored *and* banana shaped. Really!

Some years, the winning Bake-Off recipe sounds so good folks can't wait to try it. That was the case in 1969 when Edna M. Walker of Eden Prairie won the grand prize with her Magic Marshmallow Puffs. The recipe calls for two cans of crescent rolls and Twin Cities stores soon ran out of them. I remember hearing that one woman drove south in search of the rolls and got all the way to Mason City, Iowa, before she found them.

In 1982, at the thirtieth Bake-Off, our team of nine judges picked an elegant cookie from Holland as the grand prize winner. Elizabeth Meijer, the Dutch immigrant who had entered it, happened to be seated near me at the awards telecast. I watched her surreptitiously as the earlier awards were made. Then emcee Bob Barker called her name for the grand prize. She was composed and confident as she came forward. She pronounced the cookie name in Dutch, said she had never entered a recipe contest before, and that she had entered only

The ballroom of the Statler Hilton Hotel, Washington, D.C., abuzz with the twelfth Bake-Off in 1960.

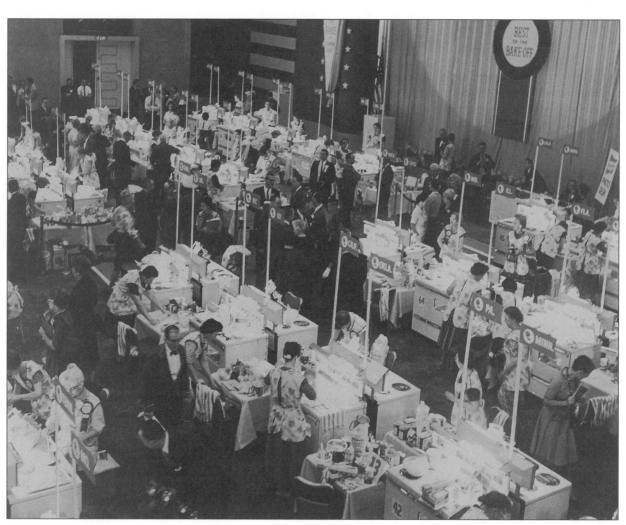

that one recipe. After the telecast, I sought her out. "You were so poised," I said. "Did you know you'd win?"

"Yes, I did," she admitted. "The photo on the big display showed my cookies with bisque angels. I love bisque angels and collect them. I took that as the sign that I would win, so I had my answer ready."

The contest takes place on what they call the Bake-Off floor, a huge room—often a ballroom—in which a workspace is set up for each cook. Reporters, like me, go from range to range, flashbulbs pop, gofers hurry by. The celebrity emcee, accompanied by a camera crew, moves about interviewing contestants for the telecast. Amid this chaos, each finalist must prepare two perfect batches of his or her recipe, one for judging, one for a display table. (They get ingredients for three batches—just in case.)

In 1990 I was covering the thirty-fourth Bake-Off for the Taste section of the Minneapolis *Star Tribune*. The plane winging to Phoenix, Arizona, was filled with Bake-Off contestants. The red-haired woman across the aisle introduced herself as Sue Zappa of St. Paul. Then her husband leaned across her to shake my hand. "You know," he said, grinning, "I'm her taster. She has diabetes, so she couldn't taste her cheesecake when she was working on it. I got cheesecake every night."

Through the years, the Bake-Off has become a reflection of our changing lives. More men are cooking for their families, thus the number of male contestants has grown. Many women work full-time outside the home, so quicker and easier recipes are developed. And ethnic food steadily gains in popularity, meaning that the special cheeses and other ingredients needed for these dishes are more widely available. What more could a contest offer? A million dollars—and a chance to help set a trend!

Here are the two recipes mentioned plus an oft-requested bar recipe and a Minnesota-special main dish, all from *Pillsbury Best of the Bake-Off Cookbook, 350 Recipes from America's Favorite Cooking Contest* (1996).

MAGIC MARSHMALLOW CRESCENT PUFFS

MAKES 16 ROLLS

For puffs:

¼ cup granulated sugar

2 tablespoons all-purpose flour

1 teaspoon cinnamon

2 (8-ounce) cans refrigerated crescent dinner rolls

16 large marshmallows

¼ cup butter or margarine, melted

For glaze:

½ cup powdered sugar

½ teaspoon vanilla

2 to 3 teaspoons milk

¼ cup chopped nuts, optional

A prizewinning breakfast treat from Edna N. Walker of Eden Prairie. The crescent dough is wrapped around marshmallows that melt during baking forming a sweet, hollow puff. I sometimes make a half recipe for coffee time with neighbors. To save calories, I skip the glaze.

Preheat oven to 375°F. Spray 16 muffin cups with nonstick cooking spray. In a small bowl, combine sugar, flour, and cinnamon.

Separate dough into 16 triangles. Dip 1 marshmallow in melted butter; roll in sugar mixture. Place marshmallow on shortest side of triangle. Roll up, starting at shortest side of triangle and rolling to opposite point. Completely cover marshmallow with dough; firmly pinch edges to seal. Dip one end in remaining butter; place butter side down in ungreased large muffin cup or 6-ounce custard cup. Repeat with remaining marshmallows.

Bake for 12 to 15 minutes or until golden brown. (Place foil or a cookie sheet on oven rack below muffin cups to catch any spills.) Immediately remove from muffin cups; cool on wire racks over waxed paper. In small bowl, blend powdered sugar, vanilla and enough milk for desired drizzling consistency. Drizzle over warm rolls. Sprinkle with nuts.

OATMEAL CARMELITAS

MAKES 36 SERVINGS

For crust:

2 cups all-purpose flour

2 cups quick-cooking rolled oats (not instant)

1 ½ cups firmly packed brown sugar

1 teaspoon baking soda

½ teaspoon salt

1 ¼ cups butter or margarine, softened

For filling:

12.5-ounce jar (1 cup) caramel ice cream topping

3 tablespoons all-purpose flour

6 ounces (1 cup) semisweet chocolate chips

½ cup chopped nuts

Next time you have to bake bars for a church or club event, try this combination from Erlyce Larson of Kennedy, Minnesota, a finalist in the eighteenth Bake-Off in 1967. They are one of Pillsbury's most requested recipes.

Preheat oven to 350°F. Grease 13 x 9-inch pan.

In large bowl, blend flour, oats, sugar, soda, salt, and butter at low speed on electric mixer until crumbly. Press half of crumb mixture, about 3 cups, in bottom of greased pan. Reserve remaining crumb mixture for topping.

Bake for 10 minutes. Meanwhile, in a small bowl, combine caramel topping and 3 tablespoons flour. Remove partially baked crust from oven; sprinkle with chocolate chips and nuts. Drizzle evenly with caramel mixture; sprinkle with reserved crumb mixture.

Bake for an additional 18 to 22 minutes or until golden brown. Cool completely. Refrigerate 1 to 2 hours until filling is set. Cut into bars.

ALMOND-FILLED COOKIE CAKE

MAKES 24 WEDGE-SHAPED SERVINGS

The Dutch treat that won the 1982 grand prize for Elizabeth Meijer, Danbury, Connecticut.

For crust:

2⅔ cups all-purpose flour

1⅓ cups sugar

1⅓ cups butter, softened
(do not use margarine)

½ teaspoon salt

1 egg

For filling:

1 cup finely chopped almonds

½ cup sugar

1 teaspoon grated lemon peel

1 egg, slightly beaten

4 whole blanched almonds

Preheat oven to 325°F. Place baking sheet in oven to preheat. Grease 9- or 10-inch springform pan.

In a large bowl, blend flour, 1⅓ cups sugar, softened butter, salt, and egg at low speed on electric mixer until soft dough forms. If desired, refrigerate dough for easier handling. Divide dough in half; spread half in bottom of greased pan to form crust.

In a small bowl, combine chopped almonds, ½ cup sugar, lemon peel, and slightly beaten egg; mix well. Spread over crust to within a half-inch of sides of pan.

Between 2 sheets of waxed paper, press remaining dough to 9- or 10-inch circle. Remove top sheet of waxed paper; place dough over filling. Remove waxed paper; press dough into place atop filling. Make a four-petaled flower in the center of the top crust with the 4 whole almonds.

Place cake on preheated cookie sheet. Bake for 65 to 75 minutes or until top is light golden brown. Cool 15 minutes; remove sides from pan. Cool completely. Cut into thin wedges.

WILD RICE AND HAM COUNTRY TART

MAKES 8 SERVINGS

Robert Holt of Mendota Heights created this 1990 runner-up winner when he was looking for a way to combine wild rice with other favorite ingredients. Try it for brunch or a light supper.

1 refrigerated pie crust
(half a 15-ounce package)

For filling:

1 cup cubed cooked ham

½ cup cooked wild rice,
drained

⅓ cup finely chopped red bell
pepper

¼ cup thinly sliced green
onion tops

1 (4.5-ounce) jar sliced
mushrooms, well drained

For custard:

3 eggs

1 cup dairy sour cream

1 tablespoon country-style
Dijon mustard

½ teaspoon salt

⅛ teaspoon pepper

For topping:

8 ounces (2 cups) shredded
Swiss cheese

11 pecan halves

Preheat oven to 425°F. Have ready a 10-inch tart pan with removable bottom or 9-inch pie pan.

Prepare pie crust according to package directions for one-crust baked shell. Place prepared crust in pan; press in bottom and up sides of pan. Trim edges if necessary. Do not prick crust.

Bake for 10 to 12 minutes or until crust is very light golden brown. Remove from oven. Reduce heat to 400°F.

In medium bowl, combine all filling ingredients; set aside. In small bowl, beat eggs until blended. Add sour cream, mustard, salt, and pepper; stir until smooth.

Sprinkle 1 cup of the cheese over bottom of baked shell. Spread filling mixture over cheese. Pour custard mixture over filling; sprinkle with remaining 1 cup cheese. Arrange pecan halves on top.

Bake for 30 to 35 minutes or until knife inserted in center comes out clean. Let stand 10 minutes before serving.

2 FESTIVAL OF NATIONS

EAT YOUR WAY AROUND THE WORLD

The people-watching is just great at the annual Festival of Nations. The music and dancing are terrific too. Oh, and did I mention the food? Yes, it's wonderful.

There's excitement in the air the minute you step into the Roy Wilkins Auditorium at RiverCentre in St. Paul. The ceiling is hung with flags of the many nations represented by the performers, artisans, gift vendors, and cooks.

A few years ago I attended the Festival on a May Sunday and the place was throbbing. "Drums, drums, drums" was the noon program by a troupe of Trinidadian musicians. The three drummers on the big stage—entertainment changes hourly—had distributed sticks to folks near the stage. The beat of the drums was impossible to resist. A young woman and the toddler on her lap were both beating out a rhythm with the plastic sticks. A woman in a European holiday costume was drumming too, the flower in her hair bobbing along.

But the smells from the nearby "Ethnic Cafés"—thirty-three of them— could not be ignored. At the entrance, two couples, walking from the huge entertainment area to this equally huge

A costumed server in the Greek café at the Festival of Nations offers some kibbeh, a triangular treat of meat, bulgur wheat, and pine nuts popular across the Mediterranean.

café section, stopped stock-still. Mouths open, they stared up and down at the colorful facades of the cafés lining the room, the hundreds of tables in the center of the room. They looked at each other: "Wow," their looks said.

Strolling up and down the aisles, I assessed the offerings. At the Turkish café, a mustachioed man and two pretty young girls were setting out their offerings: bean salad, *borek* (a cheese-filled pastry), *baklava*, lemonade, and dark, thick coffee. The girls, in Turkish costume, presented quite a contrast: one with the dark hair and eyes one might expect in a Turkish booth, her friend with blond hair and blue eyes.

I was ready for lunch. Such an array of foods! I decided against Chinese or Italian, foods readily available to me at most malls. I eased my hunger with a bowl of steaming *bigos* (Polish kraut and meat stew) served with a piece of very good rye bread. And dessert? Apple strudel from Bavaria? A mango shake from Oroma? Cossack Kisses (macaroons) from the Ukraine? I settled on a delicious deep-fried honey puff called *loukoumades* from the Greek café.

The Festival of Nations has been growing steadily for years, right alongside its sponsoring organization, the St. Paul-based International Institute of Minnesota. "The institute started with English classes for new arrivals, then

Cor Linders of North Oaks (left) and Wallina Dibble of New Hope, in traditional Dutch costume, offer this inviting cream puff.

added naturalization," explains Gloria Kurkowski of St. Paul, retired ethnic resources director of the institute. The immigrants studying there held parties at the institute. These parties, complete with costumes and food, led to the first festival in 1932.

"The festival is often a reunion for immigrants," says Gloria. "You hear lots of native tongues. You see friends clasping hands and embracing." And the celebration is wonderful visibility for the institute, which fosters many ethnic organizations.

The weekend-long festival is an excellent way for various ethnic groups to earn money, according to Gloria. An event with food and activities at their church or a community hall might draw several hundred people, but the festival draws thousands.

"The Festival of Nations brings people together from all over the Twin Cities, all over Minnesota," says Gloria. "It has survived through bus and streetcar strikes. Now they set the date five years in advance because it cannot conflict with either Easter or with Cinco de Mayo."

Gloria and her family exemplify the way the institute and the festival benefit newcomers to this country. Her Polish mother and father took English classes at the International Institute and were naturalized there (it no longer provides naturalization services). Gloria met her Polish husband, Norman, at the institute, and went on to work there twenty years. The two work as volunteers every day during the festival. In 2002, Gloria arranged the display of the institute's five hundred ethnic dolls, a fascinating and impressive collection. "Dolls are a good way of preserving costume designs," she explains.

"The dance groups that perform at the festival are a wonderful way for small children to be in touch with their ethnic roots," adds Gloria. "The kids who dance at the festival later work in the bazaar or exhibits. They learn the geography and history, even the language."

If you enjoy world cultures—music, dance, art, and food from around the globe—and great people-watching, check the event calendars for the Festival of Nations, which is usually held in late April or early May.

A troupe of Irish dancers taps out a lively rhythm on the festival stage.

POLISH BIGOS

2 to 3 pounds pork loin,
  chops, or ribs
1 pound Polish sausage
6 large carrots
2 large onions
1 quart refrigerated sauerkraut
  (sold in plastic bag)
½ cup water
1 tablespoon caraway seeds

Gloria Kurkowski learned to speak and to cook Polish as a child. This is her version of the hearty stew. For the 2002 Festival of Nations, eleven members of PACIM (Polish American Cultural Institute of Minnesota) made sixty gallons of the stew in the kitchen at Marian Pierzchalski's Gasthof restaurant in northeast Minneapolis. Their recipe's diverse ingredients included pork, beef, game, dried Polish mushrooms, onions, cabbage, tomatoes, sausage, and apples. Make bigos ahead of time, if possible, because it tastes even better the second day.

Preheat oven to 350°F. Place pork in a roaster, cover and roast until very tender, about 1 hour. Meanwhile, slice Polish sausage into ¼-inch rounds. Pare carrots; cut into ¼-inch slices. Peel onions; cut into ½-inch dice. Drain sauerkraut.

Remove pork from oven. As soon as it is cool enough to handle, remove meat from bones. Cut or shred meat into small pieces. Return meat to roaster. Add sliced Polish sausage, drained sauerkraut, and water. Cover and bake another 30 minutes.

Add carrots, onions, and caraway seeds and mix well. Cover and bake 2 hours more, stirring occasionally.

BORSCHT

2 potatoes, peeled
1 onion
1 carrot
1 tomato
Whole beets from 16-ounce
  can, drained
1 quart water
1 tablespoon vegetable oil,
  such as canola
5 whole peppercorns
3 bay leaves
Sour cream
Minced parsley or dill

An easy version of the famed soup identified with the former U.S.S.R. A meaty version is often served at the Ukrainian café during the festival. Delicious cold during hot weather. Using canned beets (rather than cooked fresh) saves time and cleanup.

Cut the potatoes into ½-inch dice. Mince the onion, grate the carrot, and chop the tomato. Finely chop the beets, using a food processor, if possible. Beets can also be grated.

Put the water and diced potatoes into a soup kettle, bring to boiling. Cook 5 to 10 minutes, or until potatoes are almost tender.

Meanwhile, heat the oil in a small skillet. Add the minced onion and stir-fry briefly. Add the grated carrot and stir-fry it with the onion.

Add the beets, tomato, carrots, and onion to the potatoes in the kettle. Stir in the peppercorns and bay leaves. Simmer 5 minutes, then remove from heat. Cover with lid and set aside until ready to serve, about 10 minutes.

Serve in bowls topped with dollops of sour cream and a sprinkling of parsley or dill.

For pastry:

2 cups flour

¼ teaspoon salt

½ cup butter

7 to 8 tablespoons cold water

For filling:

10–12 ounces Monterey Jack
cheese

Melted butter for brushing

CHEESE EMPANADAS

MAKES 12 SERVINGS

These rich turnovers are adapted from the recipe served at the festival by Luz Cifuentes, her sister, Fran, and her mother Inez, of St. Anthony. Their version is fried in deep fat, a technique I find both difficult and dangerous, so I worked out a way to bake them in the oven.

Stir together flour and salt in a large bowl. Cut in butter (using pastry cutter or two knives) until crumbly. Using a fork, mix in cold water until flour is moistened. Cut dough in half; roll each half into a ball and flatten it. Wrap one ball in plastic wrap and refrigerate.

Let other ball of dough rest while cutting 12 slices of cheese about 4 inches in length x 1 inch in width with a thickness of about ⅓ inch. On lightly floured surface, pat out resting dough into a six-inch disc. Using a sharp knife, cut disc into six equal wedges. One at a time, work wedge of dough into a circle, then, with rolling pin, roll dough thin forming a circle about 7 inches in diameter. It's not easy to roll a perfect circle, so hold a 7-inch plate over the pastry and cut with sharp knife to improve shape of circle.

Put one slice of cheese on the circular dough shape and fold the circle in half. With your fingers, push the edges shut, as if to seal it. Then, starting at one end of the just-meshed edges, fold the edges inward, as if you are resealing the edges. This is important to keep the cheese from squeezing out. Repeat with remaining pastry dough and cheese, forming 12 empanadas.

Meanwhile, preheat oven to 375°F. Place empanadas on two baking sheets covered with kitchen parchment paper or lightly greased. Bake 12 to 20 minutes, or until golden brown. After baking, transfer to a wire rack and brush lightly with melted butter (this simulates the deep-fried eating quality). If desired, sprinkle empanadas with salt or powdered sugar.

6 tablespoons butter

½ cup granulated sugar

1 ½ tablespoons powdered
cocoa

1 ½ cups ground crumbs of
plain cookies or vanilla
wafers

1 cup ground almonds

½ cup chopped almonds

3 tablespoons rum

Powdered sugar for rolling

ALMOND SALAMI

MAKES 50 TO 60 SLICES

Cilla Grauzer of Minnetonka makes a variety of European sweets sold at the International Pastries section of the Village Square Café. This no-bake cookie, which keeps a long time in the refrigerator, is very easy to make. This rolled confection looks vaguely like the sausage called salami, hence the name.

Soften butter and mix with granulated sugar, cocoa, cookie crumbs, ground almonds, chopped almonds, and rum.

Roll mixture (with the help of a piece of waxed paper) into two 2-inch diameter logs, then roll them in powdered sugar.

Wrap in waxed paper and refrigerate until firm, about 2 hours.

To serve: slice ¼-inch thick slices, keeping whatever is left of the unused roll refrigerated until needed.

3 CINCO DE MAYO

START SUMMER WITH A FIESTA

On the first weekend of May, the District del Sol, the business corridor along Concord Street on St. Paul's West Side, comes alive as Hispanics celebrate their heritage with music, dance, and food.

The festivities feel very much like Fourth of July *à la Mexicana,* but May 5 is not Mexican Independence Day. That's September 16. Cinco de Mayo is the anniversary of the Battle of Puebla. That is the day French troops, sent by Napoleon III, were defeated by under-equipped Mexican troops led by the fierce General Zaragoza and Colonel Diaz. Although the Mexicans did not win the war and France did rule Mexico for a time, the May 5 victory became a day to celebrate.

Though Cinco de Mayo has been celebrated in St. Paul's West Side since the 1960s, the first official Cinco de Mayo Fiesta on Concord Street was held in 1983. Business owners and community leaders thought a spring festival would attract visitors to the area and strengthen existing businesses. It worked. In 2002, St. Paul's Cinco de Mayo was the major Hispanic/Latino event in Minnesota, ranking among the ten largest May 5 festivals in the nation.

Attendance was about 85,000 on May 3 and 4, 2002. The Saturday morning parade, some eighty units strong, was the big draw—"the highlight"—said Julie Eigenfeld, former executive director of Riverview Economic Development Association (REDA), under whose auspices the event is held. (Michael A. DeTomaso is now the executive director.)

One of the eighty spirited units in the Cinco de Mayo Saturday morning parade.

REDA provides assistance to District del Sol, with its distinctive painted murals. It works with businesses ranging from mom-and-pop shops to much larger companies in the nearby industrial park. REDA helps area businesses thrive, sponsoring group promotions and providing technical help, like building rehabilitation and employee training, and networking opportunities.

"At Cinco de Mayo, we try to have activities that people can participate in," offered Julie. "In 2002, it was the salsa tasting. Nearly fifteen hundred people tasted eleven different salsas from seven Twin Cities restaurants and marked their ballots. Top prizes went to Boca Chica Restaurante for 'Hot,' El Burrito Mercado for 'Most Unique,' and Maria's Café for 'Mild.'" Boca Chica and El Burrito are in District del Sol; Maria's Café, owned by a Colombian family, is on Franklin Avenue in Minneapolis.

Families find lots to do at the fiesta. The Low Rider Car Show Friday night features brilliant paint jobs on the hoods, expert mechanics under the hoods. Live entertainment—including both mariachi music and flamenco dancing—alternates with electric music beats on four stages Saturday. There is also a Health and Wellness Village.

The flamenco, a dance originated by Spanish gypsies and ably performed by Minnesota Hispanics, thrills those at the fiesta.

A friend and I were on hand for the 2002 opening ceremony with the Danza Mexic Cuauhtemoc. Concord was closed, the crowd was large, and we wound up standing behind the energetic dancers. They wore Aztec costumes and headdresses, but it was easy to see that a few performers were as blond as others were dark. Anyone who wants to learn the dances is welcome, Julie explained later.

The food offered by the many vendors is diverse, too. "The guy selling gyros (spicy meat in pita sandwiches) does very well," Julie reported. Sizzling *fajitas*, hard and soft tacos, and hot corn on the cob slathered with butter and sprinkled with chili powder, vie with foot-long hot dogs for buyers' attention. Happily for those festival-goers with tired feet, District del Sol restaurants are all open for sit-down dining during the celebration as well.

Coming to the Cinco de Mayo Fiesta is an ideal way to visit one of Minnesota's largest Hispanic communities when it's all dressed up for company. And the date couldn't be easier to remember—the first Friday and Saturday in the month of May.

I asked Gloria Coronado Frias for help with authentic recipes for Cinco de Mayo. Gloria's family owns and operates the popular Boca Chica Restaurante in the heart of District del Sol in St. Paul's West Side. Her parents, Don Arturo and the late Dona Elvira Coronado, introduced many Minnesotans to Mexican fare at their gone-but-not-forgotten Casa Coronado in downtown Minneapolis.

A vendor offers the two-tortilla taco that's easy to fold and eat after it's filled.

Gloria recommended using the tostada, salsa, and enchilada recipes from *Cooking the Mexican Way*, by her sister, the late Rosa Coronado Collyard. The fajita and synchronizada recipes are from my personal files.

½ cup vegetable oil
12 (7-inch) corn tortillas
1 pound ground beef
½ cup chopped onion
1 (10-ounce) can diced
  tomatoes and green chiles
½ teaspoon each garlic salt,
  leaf oregano, and ground
  cumin
¼ teaspoon chili powder
¼ teaspoon dried sweet basil
1 (15-ounce) can refried beans
2 cups finely shredded lettuce
2 large ripe tomatoes, diced
1 cup or more shredded
  cheddar cheese
Salsa Cruda (recipe follows)
  or bottled salsa, mild or hot
  as desired

BEEF TOSTADAS

MAKES 6 SERVINGS

For a more colorful presentation, add guacamole (green) and sour cream (white) to the top of the tostada, with the salsa (red), so that you have the colors of the Mexican flag.

Heat oil in a medium frying pan (cast iron works best) over medium heat. Using tongs, submerge tortillas, one or two at a time, in hot oil and fry until crisp. Drain on paper towels.

Cook beef and onion in a skillet until meat is brown. Drain excess fat from beef and onions. Stir in canned chiles and tomatoes, garlic salt, oregano, cumin, chili powder, and basil. Simmer, uncovered, 15 minutes. Heat beans and prepare remaining vegetables and cheese.

Spread each tortilla with warm beans. Cover beans with two heaping tablespoons of meat mixture. Top with lettuce, tomato, and cheese. Each person adds salsa to their tostadas.

6 medium-size ripe tomatoes,
  finely chopped
½ cup finely chopped jalapeno
  or serrano chiles
⅓ cup minced onion
1 teaspoon salt

SALSA CRUDA

MAKES 2 CUPS

The name means "raw sauce," that is, uncooked. In many Hispanic homes, the family's version of this sauce is made fresh every day.

Be careful to wear rubber gloves when handling hot chiles. Keep your hands away from your eyes, too, to prevent a chile burn.

Mix the chopped tomatoes, chiles, onion, and salt in a bowl. Cover and refrigerate overnight to allow flavors to blend.

2 tablespoons vegetable oil
8 (7-inch) corn tortillas
3 (10-ounce) cans mild or hot
   enchilada sauce, heated
Chicken and Cheese Filling
   (recipe follows)
Sour cream

CHICKEN ENCHILADAS

MAKES 4 SERVINGS

When you have leftover roast turkey or pork roast, shred it to use in place of chicken in this versatile main dish. The chicken for the filling needs to be prepared ahead of time.

Preheat oven to 350°F. Heat oil in a large skillet and fry each tortilla for only a few seconds. Tortillas should be limp and soft. Remove tortilla with tongs and dip in the heated enchilada sauce, making sure it is well coated. Place tortilla on a cutting board and put about ⅓ to ½ cup Chicken and Cheese Filling in the center. Roll up and place in a baking pan with the opening face down.

When all tortillas have been filled and placed in the pan, cover them with the remaining sauce. Bake for 15 to 20 minutes, or until sauce is bubbly. Serve each enchilada with a spoonful of cold sour cream.

2 large chicken breasts
2 teaspoons vegetable oil
1 large onion, chopped
1 large green pepper, seeded
   and chopped
½ teaspoon dried leaf oregano
½ teaspoon dried sweet basil
2½ cups (10 ounces) grated
   Monterey Jack cheese

CHICKEN AND CHEESE FILLING

Simmer chicken breasts in 3 cups water for 25 to 30 minutes or until tender.

While chicken cooks, heat oil in a frying pan. Stir-fry onion, green pepper, oregano, and basil until onion and pepper are soft.

Drain chicken. When it has cooled enough to handle, remove bones and use your fingers or two forks to shred chicken. Stir chicken into onion mixture. Spoon on about 3 tablespoons each of chicken/onion mixture and Jack cheese in center of a fried tortilla that has been dipped in sauce. Roll up and place in pan.

(Recipes courtesy Lerner Publications Company, from *Cooking the Mexican Way* by Rosa Coronado (Collyard). Copyright © 2002 by Lerner Publications Company, a division of Lerner Publishing Group. Used by permission. All rights reserved.)

1 cup salsa or picante sauce (hot, medium, or mild)

3 tablespoons vegetable oil, divided

1 tablespoon chili powder, optional

2 cloves garlic, minced

1 pound sirloin steak

1 cup red bell pepper strips

1 cup green bell pepper strips

1 cup sliced onion, preferably sweet

8 (8-inch) soft flour tortillas

Sour cream, guacamole, chopped fresh cilantro, refried beans, grated Monterey Jack cheese, and/or more salsa or picante sauce for toppings

STEAK FAJITAS

MAKES 4 SERVINGS

This meal-in-a-tortilla can leave you with sticky fingers, but, oh, is it good.

Stir together salsa, 1 tablespoon of the oil, chili powder, and garlic in a large bowl. Mix in steak and cover bowl. Refrigerate all day or overnight, stirring once or twice.

Heat remaining oil in large skillet over medium-high heat. Add red and green peppers and onion. Cook 5 to 6 minutes or until peppers are tender and onions are golden. Set aside covered to keep warm.

Heat broiler. Remove beef from bowl and discard salsa mixture. Broil beef 6 to 8 minutes, turning once. Meanwhile, warm the tortillas by wrapping in foil and placing in a low-temperature oven (some tortilla packages give directions).

To serve, slice beef into thin strips and fill warm tortillas with beef and vegetable mixture. Pass bowls of toppings so people can choose their favorites.

---

2 (6-inch) corn tortillas

1 round slice luncheon meat, such as ham, bologna, or salami

1 thin slice cheese, such as Monterey Jack, mild cheddar or American, cut to fit tortilla

Vegetable oil for frying

Salsa or picante sauce for dipping, optional

SYNCHRONIZADAS

MAKES 1 SERVING

I learned to make this super-simple snack at a cooking school in Leon, Mexico. It is the forerunner of the popular quesadilla. Serve it as an after-school treat or as an accompaniment to soup or salad. Once you get the hang of it, you'll be adding all sorts of goodies to these little sandwiches, like slivers of green chilies, roasted red peppers, apple, or ripe avocado, maybe even whole kernel corn.

Start with a corn tortilla. Top it with the meat, then the cheese and the second tortilla. Heat a nonstick or cast iron skillet over medium heat. Brush skillet with a little of the oil. Place your meat-and-cheese tortilla sandwich in the skillet. Cook, turning once, until tortillas cheese begins to melt. Cut into wedges. Serve with a little bowl of salsa.

4 NEW ULM'S
HERITAGEFEST
DISCOVER GERMANY IN MINNESOTA

Gemütlichkeit (German for "warm cordiality") abounds the second and third weekends of July when New Ulm hosts its popular Heritagefest. Thousands of visitors from all over the state and around the world come for the Old World celebration. That German oompah music is infectious. Folks dance all over Brown County's fairgrounds, stopping only for a cooling drink or a German treat.

As many as eight European musical groups have played at the 'Fest. Their performances were on three huge tented stages at the fairgrounds, which fills

eight blocks close to downtown. The entire event is held outdoors, with the exception of the new, air-conditioned *Fest Halle.* Besides the lively music of the bands, there are festive folk songs by New Ulm's Concord Singers. The group, thirty-seven strong, is considered America's foremost amateur German-language chorus. They entertain happily—exuberantly. The men, clad in lederhosen, sing all six nights of Heritagefest at the Keg Opening ceremonies.

This happy accordion player is just one of the many men and women who provide nonstop music at Heritagefest.

Comical characters can be seen all over the festival grounds. The Heritage-fest *Narren* are masked, costumed figures billed as "the relatives everybody has but nobody wants." The first Narren, Hattie and Gretchen, appeared in 1989, when Rita Waibel and Avonna Domeier, both of New Ulm, put on masks from Germany, donned sunbonnets and braids, and became prairie *einwanderin.* The Narren troupe now numbers eleven including Sepp, the unmusical musician, and Tilly, the feather lady. The appearances of German gnomes called *Heinzel-mannchen* and the Morel Mushroom characters add to the merriment. All these characters join yodelers, marching bands, and colorful floats for the Heritage-fest parade on Sunday of the second weekend of the event.

Entertainment is continuous at Heritagefest—eating can be, too. The mostly ethnic menu is heavy on walk-along foods such as sandwiches and snacks. For hot days—typical for July—there are some sixteen drinks to choose from. Besides domestic and imported beers, you can order Bavarian *eiskaffee,* raspberry iced tea, and Lynchburg lemonade. Vendors give a German accent to minidonuts and sno-cones, calling them *pfannkuchen* and Alpin ice.

"This is a celebration of our German heritage," says Kathleen Backer, who manages the event working closely with its board of directors. "The community forms the backdrop. We have interesting architecture, historic sites, and specialty shops. People really enjoy it." Most visitors take time to visit the renowned Schell's Brewery south of town to take a tour and sip a sample.

Heritagefest also attracts bus tours, which are sponsored by banks or community education programs. The Minnesota Office of Tourism has selected Heritagefest as a top annual group tour festival.

Heritagefest grew out of a get-together called Polka Days, according to Kathleen. The first Heritagefest was held in 1975. Service groups, such as Rotary, provide volunteer support for ticket sales and security, for example. The groups enter into contracts with the management of Heritagefest and when the festival makes money—and it usually does—these groups share the profits. "It's a win-win situation," notes Kathleen.

"Weather is the variable," Kathleen continues. "In 2001 it was so hot for so long that the second weekend wasn't as big as we had hoped. If there's a storm warning, or threatening weather, we can move things indoors." Despite the heat in 2001, hungry folks at the festival ate over 30,000 *landjaegers,* the plump German sausages that require an extra-large bun.

The future of Heritagefest looks bright. New Ulm has passed a half-cent sales tax for capital improvements, and topping the list is a new multipurpose

A young visitor gets a pat on the back from a lady Narren, one of the comical masked, costumed figures—billed as "the relatives everybody has but nobody wants."

The clop-clop of horses pulling a vintage Schell's Beer delivery wagon, decked with flowers, is part of Heritagefest's exuberant parade.

Fest Halle on the fairgrounds with three thousand seats. When it's ready, weather—wet or hot—won't bother Heritagefest organizers or revelers.

These recipes for foods served at Heritagefest are adapted from the *Duetsch-Bohmische Kuche,* Editions No. 1 and 2. The books were published by the German-Bohemian Heritage Society, New Ulm, Minnesota.

HOT GERMAN POTATO SALAD

MAKES 6 TO 8 SERVINGS

6 medium potatoes, boiled in jackets
6 slices bacon

For dressing:
¾ cup chopped onion
2 tablespoons flour
1 ½ tablespoons sugar
1 ½ teaspoons salt
½ teaspoon celery seeds
Dash of pepper
¾ cup water
⅓ cup cider vinegar

The perfect accompaniment for ham, baked spareribs, or frankfurters.

Peel potatoes while still warm and slice thin. Fry bacon slowly in skillet; then drain; crumble when cool.

Fry onion in bacon fat until golden brown. Blend in the flour, sugar, salt, celery seeds, and pepper. Cook over low heat, stirring until smooth and bubbly. Remove from heat. Add water and vinegar. Return to heat and bring to boil, stirring constantly. Boil 1 minute. Carefully stir in the sliced potatoes and crumbled bacon; stir until potatoes are well coated with vinegar mixture. Remove from heat, cover, and let stand until ready to serve—not longer than 20 minutes.

SCHMIERKUCHEN

MAKES 2 KUCHENS, 6 TO 8 SERVINGS EACH

1 pound loaf frozen sweet dough, thawed*

Topping for kuchen:
2 cups small-curd cottage cheese
2 tablespoons granulated sugar
2 tablespoons cornstarch
¼ teaspoon salt
¼ cup half-and-half
1 teaspoon vanilla
2 egg whites, beaten
Raisins
Cinnamon sugar

*Overnight thawing in the refrigerator works well.

This toothsome version of cheesecake is served as a midmorning treat or as dessert. This is my updated version of Colleen Kastanek's recipe. She wrote: "After church on Sunday, my Grandma Eleanor Gulden would wait for us to stop by her house where she'd have at least coffee, Smear Kuchen [the anglicized spelling] and sugar cookies, if not sultz (homemade pork luncheon meat), cheese, and a number of other 'snacks' to tide us over until we got back home. It was a six-mile trip!"

Combine the cottage cheese, sugar, cornstarch, salt, half-and-half, vanilla, and egg whites.

Preheat oven to 350°F. Divide dough in half and shape into two balls. Coat two 9-inch pie pans with nonstick cooking spray. Roll out each ball of sweet dough to fit bottom and sides of prepared pan. Dough starts to contract very quickly after rolling, so work quickly. Spread half of cottage cheese filling in even layer on each crust. Sprinkle filling generously with raisins, then sprinkle with cinnamon sugar.

Bake 25 to 30 minutes, or until crust is golden and filling is set.

SAUERKRAUT WITH APPLES AND POTATOES

MAKES 8 TO 10 SERVINGS

1 small onion, grated (⅓ cup)

¼ cup butter

2 tablespoons brown sugar

½ teaspoon salt

1 teaspoon vinegar

1½ cups apple cider or juice

1 cup chicken broth

1 small potato, peeled and grated

1 quart sauerkraut, washed and drained

1 cup diced peeled apples

To turn this side dish into a main dish, add cut-up smoked pork chops and/or sliced bratwurst, cooking the mixture 1 to 1½ hours in all.

Cook onion in butter until tender. Add brown sugar, salt, vinegar, apple cider, broth, grated potato, and drained kraut.

Cook, covered, 30 to 45 minutes. Add diced apple and cook another 15 to 20 minutes.

SPAETZLE

MAKES 6 TO 8 SERVINGS

4 eggs

1 cup water or milk

1 teaspoon salt

2½ to 3 cups flour

2 tablespoons butter

Just the thing to serve with gravy made after roasting pork or beef. Also delicious tossed with melted butter and topped with buttered crumbs. So popular that a boxed mix is now available for the little dumplings.

Beat eggs and water or milk together. Add salt and flour. Beat vigorously with wooden spoon. Batter should be thick and smooth.

Bring a large kettle of water to a boil over high heat. Choose one of these methods to shape spaetzle. (1) Easiest but requires special equipment: Push about one-fourth of the batter through a spaetzle maker forming dumplings about 1-inch long. (2) By hand—quite time-consuming: Using two wet teaspoons, scoop up rounds of batter and drop into boiling water.

(3) Colander method: Put batter into colander with large holes; press batter through holes with a rubber spatula.

Cook spaetzle in boiling water, stirring occasionally, until they float to surface (5 to 8 minutes, depending on size). Remove using a slotted spoon; keep warm. Repeat shaping/cooking process until all batter is used. Toss spaetzle with melted butter just before serving. (Note: Extra spaetzle freeze and reheat nicely.)

5 POWWOW PRIMER

JINGLE DANCERS, FRYBREAD, AND MORE

As they enter the powwow grounds, they step from one world to another, from modern to ancient, from the material to the spiritual. These Minnesotans—be they Ojibwe (Chippewa) or Dakota (Sioux)—live within two different worlds: today's technical world and yesterday's natural world.

Their powwow transportation, once a horse, is now horsepower under the hood of an SUV or a van. Their powwow weekend home is generally not a tipi, but its twenty-first-century equivalent: a sleek, brightly colored nylon tent. They step into their tents in jeans and T-shirts and emerge in feather head-dresses, fringed leather, elaborate shawls or dresses covered with jingles.

Native American women make the traditional circle of the powwow ground that begins the program at Shakopee.

The location of the Cass Lake Memorial Powwow Grounds adds to the striking contrast between present and past. First you come to the Palace Casino, a glitzy monument to gambling, alluring with blinking lights and spinning tables. Wonderful photographs of powwow dancers decorate the hall that links the casino to the Palace hotel and restaurants. Back outside you see the signs for the powwow grounds: where to park, where to walk. The area is surrounded by pines and birch, and not far away, loons call out over Big Wolf Lake. There's a woodsy campground and beyond it, the arena.

The powwow arena is a set of concentric circles. At the very center is a canopied shelter that protects the musicians and their equipment from the July sun or rain showers. Elders and powwow officials may join the musicians there. The next circle is the dance area, with space for rows and rows of dancers. Those watching the proceedings can stand, sit on bleachers, or find seats in one of several roofed buildings. My friend and I are early enough to get tiered theater-style seats in one of these buildings—ah, to be out of that sun. Vendors—sixteen offering food, others selling native crafts and art—complete this third circle of the arena.

A dancer in full regalia competes in the arena at the Shakopee powwow.

We watch the dances and, between dances, the little scenes along the sidelines—grandparents with squirming grandkids, teenagers teasing and poking, and old men, heads together, chatting, chuckling. But I didn't really understand what was happening in the arena, and the Cass Lake elders were too deeply involved in the big event to answer a lot of questions. I badly needed some sort of program to put me in the know.

After my visit to Cass Lake, I researched Julia White's, *The Powwow Trail*, and other books and Internet resources, and put together this minicourse.

During the dancing, the arena is sacred ground and is blessed and prayed over as such. As a guest, you are watching ancient ceremonies, traditions that have endured through many adversities. No alcohol or drugs are allowed on the grounds. Nor do audience members walk across the arena between dances.

The vivid costumes that the powwow dancers wear are called regalia (what an exciting word!). These items of clothing are treasured possessions, often made by family members.

Girls and women perform as shawl dancers or jingle-dress dancers. The fringed, symbol-covered shawls, extended across the dancer's outstretched arms, swing as she takes her dance steps. Rows and rows of jingles (cone-shaped bells shaped from snuff-box lids) decorate the jingle dresses, attracting everyone's attention. Beautifully beaded accessories complete these costumes.

Men and boys perform as hoop dancers or grass dancers. Hoop dancers deck their bodies with beadwork that will be seen to advantage as they swirl several hoops

This cook pats out rounds of dough while fry bread bubbles in the skillet. A washtub-size batch of dough awaits her busy hands.

at once. The swaying and stomping of grass dancers recalls the swaying of grass as the wind moves across the land. Long ribbons and strands of yarn have long since replaced the tall grass that such dancers once wore.

Dancing these traditional dances is both enjoyable exercise and a way to totally involve oneself in one's heritage. Powwow dancing is also an absorbing parent-child activity, with little children moving to the beat alongside their mother or father in the arena.

Hundreds of years ago, the word powwow meant a shaman or spiritual leader. Later, the word was used for gathering places, landmarks where significant spiritual events took place. Today, the powwow is a highly visible Native American celebration, as likely to be held on a college campus as on a reservation. Every state has one.

Some food vendors, artists, and artisans follow the powwow trail, making their living by selling their wares at a series of powwows across a state or a region.

Everything I read about powwows reiterated that fry bread is *the* food for the celebration. At Cass Lake, our lunch is an Indian taco the likes of which I'd never seen. Hot, thick fry bread covers the plate and, in turn, is covered with a meat-rich chili, then topped with chopped tomatoes and lettuce, shredded cheese, and sour cream. A dollop of salsa crowns the creation. I couldn't begin to eat it all. A man sharing our picnic table comments that every cook's fry bread is different. "But they're all good," he hastens to add.

My first attempt at making fry bread (using a recipe from my cookbook library) was a flop. Too much baking powder—ack! It was time to call Gypsi Lemoine of Cottage Grove, a yoga classmate, who offered to help me explore Indian food.

Making fry bread, like making so many ethnic foods, is best learned from someone who can show you the technique. Gypsi, a nurse/healer and mother of three, learned the technique from a Red Lake friend. And she has helped with the monthly Taco Sundays at the Office of Indian Ministry in Minneapolis. She and her daughters are part of the congregation that meets at the Office. "The altar cloth is a buffalo skin. And we all sit around in a circle," she says.

We have the flour, the oil, and all the other ingredients lined up on her work counter when Gypsi excuses herself. Returning to the kitchen, she presses a pinch of tobacco into my hand. "I forgot to tell you to bring some tobacco. It's traditional to give tobacco to the one who will help you. And I've picked some fresh sage. The smoke from the sage will purify and cleanse. The tobacco is sacred; we pray with tobacco." Gypsi did not learn that she was descended from a *métis* (French for "mixed blood") until she was grown. She is a serious student of Native American spirituality, learning about sweat lodges, pipe ceremonies, and other sacred practices.

Gypsi is very careful with the oil for the fry bread. She explains that hot oil had caused a fire in her house some years ago. And she is wary about the dietary effects of the bread. "Before the white settlers arrived, and before we got government commodities—the white flour, the fat—there was no diabetes among the Indians," she says.

"You think fry bread is good dipped in sugar," she says, holding up a chunk of the just-fried bread. "You should taste it topped with a mixture of wild blueberries and maple syrup. They cook it up like a sauce. It's so good."

Another traditional food that Gypsi and her family like is buffalo. They purchase the lean meat in quantity and have it in the freezer. She prefers the flavor of buffalo to beef.

Watching the Cass Lake Powwow and meeting with a knowledgeable Indian woman have given me a glimpse of the rich trove that is the Minnesota Native American culture.

The Cass Lake Memorial Powwow Grounds, as part of the Leech Lake Indian Reservation, is situated near towering pines and many lakes.

FRY BREAD

5 cups all-purpose flour

2 teaspoons baking powder

½ cup sugar

½ teaspoon salt

⅛ cup plus 2 tablespoons nonfat dry milk powder

Water as needed

Vegetable oil for deep-fat frying

Granulated sugar

Gypsi Lemoine of Cottage Grove shared these directions. The bread dough can also be used for making Prairie Dogs: a wiener wrapped in fry bread dough and fried.

Measure the flour, baking powder, sugar, and salt into a deep bowl; stir to combine. Place the ⅛ cup nonfat dry milk in a 2-cup measuring cup. Add water to make 1⅓ cups liquid.

Make a well in the center of the flour mixture and pour about 2 tablespoons of the liquid into it. Using your right hand and working in a circular motion, begin to draw flour from the sides of the well. Continue mixing round and round, adding liquid 2 tablespoons at a time until all the flour is moistened. You will probably need to dissolve the remaining 2 tablespoons dry milk in another ⅓ cup or so of water, continuing to add liquid until you have formed a stiff dough. Round up dough into a ball. Cover bowl.

Fill an 8-inch cast iron skillet with vegetable oil and start heating over medium heat. Place bowl of dough at back of stove near warming oil for about 10 minutes.

Meanwhile, make a stack of paper towel sheets for blotting the hot fried bread.

When oil is hot—it will be moving in the skillet (if you have a deep-fat thermometer, it should be 360°F), start shaping breads. Take a clump of dough and roll into a ball, then pat and slap the ball back and forth between the palms of your hands shaping a disc of dough. With your finger, poke a hole in the dough. Working quickly, place the dough in the hot oil. Fry the bread, turning once, until puffed and golden. If you have one, place a frying screen over the skillet during cooking.

Lift bread out of oil with tongs or slotted spoon. Place on paper towels to blot excess oil. Repeat the shaping and frying until all the dough has been used. When bread is cool enough to handle, serve with sugar for dipping. Finished bread should be chewy, not crisp. If yours is crisp, it has been patted too flat.

INDIAN TACOS

Fry Bread (recipe above)

Taco meat (ground meat seasoned with chili powder, salt, and pepper)* or chili

Shredded lettuce

Chopped tomato

Shredded cheese

Salsa and/or sour cream

*See page 102 for a taco meat recipe.

Place warm fry bread on medium plate. Top with generous portion of taco meat or chili. Garnish with lettuce, cheese, chopped tomato, and salsa and/or sour cream.

Variation: Add a layer of hot beans atop the meat or chili.

JERKY

1 to 2 pounds venison steak, buffalo steak, or beef flank steak
½ cup soy sauce*

*If you like the flavor of Worcestershire sauce, substitute that for about 2 tablespoons of the soy sauce.

This is the modern-day version of the salted, dried meat that Native Americans carried with them as they hunted or moved to a new area. Though the original was made with a salt mixture, using soy sauce makes it easier to distribute the seasoning.

Partially freeze meat for easier slicing. Have ready a rack in a 2-inch deep oven pan.

Slice meat with the grain into pieces ½-inch thick and 3 to 4 inches long. Dip the meat strips in soy sauce. Arrange on the rack far enough apart for easy turning.

Dry meat in 160 to 170°F oven 10 to 12 hours, turning once after half the time. Finished jerky will be dark and fibrous.

BUFFALO BURGERS

MAKES 4 SERVINGS

1 pound ground buffalo
¼ teaspoon black pepper
1 teaspoon Worcestershire sauce
4 teaspoons ketchup
1 teaspoon salt
1 teaspoon mustard
2 teaspoons prepared horseradish

This easy recipe is from the 1993 Minnesota Grown Farmer to Consumer Directory, which includes listings of farmers who raise buffalo and sell buffalo meat. Minnesota's Department of Agriculture publishes the directory every year and distributes it free of charge.

Combine buffalo, pepper, Worcestershire sauce, ketchup, salt, mustard, and horseradish. Shape mixture into four patties.

Grill burgers over low coals about 5 minutes on each side. Serve as you would any burger—in buns with mayonnaise, lettuce, and tomato. (Note: If it is necessary to keep burgers warm after cooking, pour a little beef broth over them because they can get tough and dry.)

CELEBRATING PIE

BRAHAM PIE DAY

"Come and have pie" was the simple idea for the original Pie Day back in 1990. And it still is today. Pie Day was Phyllis Londgren's brainchild and she tells it well: "I was a retired schoolteacher working as a Kelly Girl at the Braham city hall. It was 1990 and Rudy Perpich was in office. A letter came announcing a 'Celebrate Minnesota' campaign. Towns could apply for a small grant to hold a civic celebration after July 1. Well, since people always stopped in Braham for pie on the way to Duluth, the town was associated with pie. A legend was running the Park Café and that's where people stopped. Though [Interstate] 35W had killed that practice, people still thought of Braham and pie.

"We got the grant. We baked the pies and people came and had pie. The eleven churches in the area made the pies, serving in relays from 9 A.M. to 5 P.M. Everyone enjoyed it so much we decided to do it a second year. From there, it just took off."

Now Braham Pie Day is a full-fledged, daylong celebration with contests of all sorts, music, demonstrations, and art and craft booths, with coverage on local and national TV and in books on Minnesota's festivals and culture. Folks for miles around reserve the first Friday in August for a visit to Braham and a slice or three of delicious pie.

"Got pie?" was the question on a T-shirt sold at Braham's 2002 Pie Day. You bet they had pie. The pie total was 580 fruit pies plus 280 cream and/or unbaked pies, according to Valorie Arrowsmith of the Pie Day committee.

On the day I attended, pie lovers were getting in line by 10 A.M. for a wedge of one of the fruit pies being served under the big tent in the town park. It was a perfect Minnesota summer day, bright enough to wear sunglasses, but not so hot that the ice cream on your pie would melt too quickly. And folks just kept

The Braham "Peach Ladies" prepare peaches for pie-baking day.

coming all day long. By 6:15 that evening the fruit pies were all gone. There were still pies at Park Café, where the cream and unbaked pies were kept under refrigeration. Between five and six thousand people came from towns around Braham and from all over the state, Valorie reported later.

Pie day is run—smoothly and efficiently—by a small army of volunteers, dedicated men and women happy to share their love for Braham and for pie. It takes 100-plus volunteers just to bake those 580 fruit pies, a task carried out at Braham Area High School a few days before the big event. The kitchen there is spotless, Phyllis announced. The crust is made with lard and vinegar. Exactly 6.6 ounces of pastry is rolled out for each crust. The initial of the fruit in the filling is cut into the crust. (Could you have guessed that R-B-R is Raspberry-Blueberry-Rhubarb?) The volunteers bake and freeze.

On the big day, the pies ride on racks on a pickup truck from the school to the big serving tent downtown. There they go into two screen-covered pie safes—sixteen pies per safe. Each pie sits on a piece of ice (as ice melts, the water drips out below). Servers cut each pie into seven exactly-equal wedges following a guide used to mark the portions.

After buying their pie—most people add ice cream—and beverage, customers head to tables and chairs set up between the pie and entertainment tents. As my friend and I enjoyed our fruit pie (I had raspberry-blueberry-rhubarb, which was sweetened just right), we listened to Kevin Carlson's singing. Billed as the Swedish-Irish tenor from New York, he has a fine voice and a global repertoire of familiar songs. We also watched a young mom perform a Pie Day balancing act: her right hand guided her toddler's stroller while she carried two plates of pie à la mode in her left hand.

Music, prize drawings, and Pie Day events alternated in the entertainment tent next door to the pie tent. There was an impromptu style show of garments from the Tusen Tack thrift store (which raises money for the Braham food shelf) across the street. (This building bears Caprice Glaser's mouth-watering mural of a huge two-crust pie.) There was the Pie-Alluia Chorus performing the "Pie Song." And there was the Junior Pie Eating Contest, soon followed by the Senior Pie Eating competition.

There was also a reading from *American Pie: Slices of Life (and Pie) from America's Back Roads* by author Pascale LeDraoulec. She read from the chapter she had written on Pie Day after coming to town to see the pie mural, one of many pie-tasting stops on a cross-country trip in 2000. Her station wagon, she said, bore the bumper sticker: IBRK4PI (I Brake for Pie).

The Pie Baking Contest—always a highlight—was of particular interest in

Eager participants in the Junior Pie Eating Contest dive in face first.

A young trio serves pie with a smile at Braham Pie Day.

2002 because NBC had sent a film crew from Los Angeles to follow first-time contestants. A new program to be called *Life Moments* was in the works and the producers thought Braham Pie Day sounded like fun, especially since a team from Betty Crocker's test kitchen was judging. Two of the three novice bakers featured in the TV segment won the second prizes in their categories.

But not all the pie eating was done under the big top. The Park Café was packed full of pie lovers. When they opened for business that morning, they had forty different flavors from peanut butter to pina colada. Banana cream pie is by far the most popular, according to the café crew. With the oven capacity to bake twelve pies at a time, they continued baking all during Pie Day.

Between slices of pie, you can stroll the craft area. Here the streets that separate the individual tents have pie-appropriate names, like Cherry Lane, Apple Alley, and Cookie Crumb Crest. And Judy Olson Parkway, named for 2001's winning pie baker.

The recipes for these yummy pies are from *Braham's Pie Cookbook* published in 1993.

1 9-inch unbaked pie crust

For sauce:

1 ½ (1-ounce) squares
    unsweetened chocolate
½ cup water
⅔ cup granulated sugar
¼ cup butter
1 ½ teaspoons vanilla

For batter:

1 cup all-purpose flour
¾ cup granulated sugar
1 teaspoon baking powder
½ teaspoon salt
¼ cup margarine, softened, or
    soft shortening
½ cup milk
½ teaspoon vanilla
1 egg

For topping:

½ cup finely chopped walnuts

COLONIAL INNKEEPER'S PIE

MAKES 8 SERVINGS

Lois Callguire, St. Paul, submitted this unusual dessert for the pie book. I clearly remember taste-testing it before it was featured in Betty Crocker's Guide to Easy Entertaining *in 1959. Cake batter is poured into the pie crust, then a warm chocolate sauce is poured over the cake batter. After baking, the sauce is beneath the cake.*

Cover pie shell with plastic wrap while preparing the sauce and batter.

Melt chocolate with water; add sugar. Bring to a boil, stirring constantly. Remove from heat; stir in butter and vanilla. Set aside.

Preheat oven to 350°F. Stir flour, sugar, baking powder, and salt together. Add shortening, milk, and vanilla. Beat 2 minutes at medium speed with electric mixer or 300 vigorous strokes by hand. Scrape sides and bottom of bowl constantly. Add egg. Beat 2 more minutes, again scraping bowl constantly. Pour batter into prepared pie shell. Stir sauce and pour carefully over cake batter. Sprinkle top with nuts.

Bake 50 to 60 minutes or until toothpick inserted in center comes out clean. If desired, garnish with whipped cream.

4 ounces Baker's German's
    sweet chocolate*
⅓ cup milk, divided
3 ounces cream cheese,
    softened
8-ounce carton whipped
    topping such as Cool Whip,
    thawed
2 small Heath bars, chopped
9-inch graham cracker crumb
    crust

*This chocolate is named after
    the man who devised the
    formula, one Samuel German.

CRUNCHY CHOCOLATE
CHIFFON PIE

MAKES 7 SERVINGS

Irene S. King, Detroit Lakes, entered this treat, the type of dessert I call "freeze with ease."

Microwave chocolate and 2 tablespoons of the milk in large microwave bowl on high/full power 1 ½ to 2 minutes or until chocolate is almost melted, stirring halfway through the heating time. After removing from microwave, continue stirring until chocolate is completely melted.

Beat in cream cheese and the remaining milk until well blended. Refrigerate about 10 minutes to cool. Gently stir in whipped topping, stirring until smooth. Add chopped Heath bars. Spoon into crust. Freeze until firm, about 4 hours or overnight.

At serving time, garnish with chocolate shavings or curls, if desired.

1 9-inch unbaked pie crust,
homemade or store bought

For filling:

About 4 cups drained, canned
peach slices (two 15-ounce
cans)

½ cup granulated sugar

2 tablespoons minute tapioca

1 teaspoon lemon juice

For topping:

¼ cup butter, softened

½ cup all-purpose flour

¼ cup brown sugar

½ cup chopped pecans

PEACH PRALINE PIE

MAKES 7 SERVINGS

Everyone back at home enjoyed this peachy-keen pie when I tested it. The recipe is from Judy Boucher of Chisago City.

Preheat oven to 350°F (325°F if using a glass pan).

Combine peach slices, granulated sugar, tapioca, and lemon juice. Let stand while you prepare topping.

Mix butter, flour, brown sugar, and pecans with pastry blender, two knives, or your clean hands until crumbly. Sprinkle one-fourth of brown sugar mixture on the bottom of the unbaked pie shell. Spoon the peach mixture on top. Sprinkle the rest of the topping on the peach mixture, distributing evenly. Bake for about 50 minutes or until topping is golden brown and filling is set.

¾ cup granulated sugar

½ cup buttermilk baking mix,
such as Bisquick

2 tablespoons butter or
margarine, softened

13-ounce can evaporated milk

2 teaspoons vanilla

2½ teaspoons pumpkin pie
spice

15-ounce can pumpkin

2 eggs

IMPOSSIBLE PUMPKIN PIE

MAKES 8 SERVINGS

Ruth Magnuson of Ham Lake shared this fall special. She wrote "no crust needed—it makes its own."

Put sugar, baking mix, butter, evaporated milk, vanilla, spice, pumpkin, and eggs into container of electric blender; blend thoroughly. Pour into lightly greased 10-inch pie plate. Bake at 350°F for 50 to 55 minutes or until knife inserted in center comes out clean.

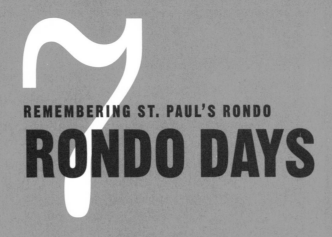

7
REMEMBERING ST. PAUL'S RONDO
RONDO DAYS

Rondo—it's a pioneer, it's a community, it's a celebration. And that celebration features satisfying soul and Caribbean food.

The pioneer was the namesake of a beloved, now-gone street in St. Paul. His name was Rondeau and he was French Canadian like many of his fellow voyageurs. After his time in the Minnesota fur trade, Joseph Rondeau settled down to farm in the fast-growing area that is now the Twin Cities. The area north and east of the St. Paul Cathedral, where Rondeau began farming in 1862, was later platted. The city fathers named the central street, which ran east and west

A drill team in the Saturday morning Rondo Days parade took the light shower in stride, despite the wet street.

Families often come to the Rondo Days celebration straight from church.

between the gold-domed capitol and the Midway area, for Rondeau (using the English spelling).

Rondo Avenue became the center of St. Paul's black community. And a thriving community it was in the days before and after the two great wars. There were well-kept homes on Rondo, along with stores and eating places. St. Paul was still compact in those days and residents of Rondo walked *their* street to work, to school, and to play. Long before the it-takes-a-village-to-raise-a-child idea became widely publicized, the families of Rondo were keeping an eye on one another's kids and grandkids. Rondo-raised adults, now parents and grandparents themselves, recall the way the neighborhood grapevine helped keep them on the straight and narrow.

Then, in the mid-1960s, the state began building Interstate 94, the multilane link between the centers of Minneapolis and St. Paul. Its route *was* Rondo. The bustling community was torn asunder. Businesses closed and homes were demolished or moved to other sites. Rondo residents protested, but succeeded only in getting the highway dug below street level, making it less visible to the now-divided community.

By 1984, an organization called Rondo Avenue, Inc., was started by a group of people who had grown up in Rondo, including Floyd Smaller and Roger Anderson. They launched a "Remember Rondo" campaign and began the celebration of Rondo Days. The event is held the third full weekend of August, typically a scorcher of a weekend. "It can be the hottest weekend of the summer. We're accustomed to that," says Henry Lewis, St. Paul, vice-president of Rondo Avenue, Inc. Indeed, the heat of the summer matches the heat of some of the foods served, particularly the Caribbean dishes.

A dinner for senior citizens typically starts the weekend. They are the Rondo home- and business-owners thirty-five-plus years later. For some, the meal at St. Peter Claver Catholic Church, on North Oxford in St. Paul, starts a weekend of reunion and reminiscence.

Something to smile about: fresh fried chicken from one of many vendors offering soul food and Caribbean specialties.

Bob's Fresh Lemonade Stand keeps customers lined up for "regular" or "jumbo" refreshment.

The highlight of Rondo Days is always the Saturday morning parade. Few within earshot can resist the beat of the drums ringing out from precision drill teams and drum and bugle corps marching along so smartly. "The Jolly Seniors from Martin Luther King Center always ride in the parade," reports Dorothea Burns, assistant director of the center, of which the community's longtime focus, the Hallie Q. Brown Center, is now a part. "Yes, we dress up, about twelve or fifteen usually. Oh, sure, it's hot, but we ride in an open wagon with a canopy over the top." Politicians on the campaign trail ride in the parade too. I wore my coolest sundress and a big floppy hat to check out the food booths, watch the families, and sip the chilled lemonade.

The parade presents an opportunity to pay homage to leaders from within the African American community. In 1991, Alan Page, the former Minnesota Viking player now serving on the Minnesota Supreme Court, was grand marshal. In 1995, two Taylors—unrelated though they were both reared in Rondo—shared the honor. David Taylor, a historian and dean of the General College at the University of Minnesota, and Janabelle Taylor, who worked at the Hallie Q. Brown Center starting in the 1930s, were praised for sharing widely the lessons they learned in Rondo.

In 2002, the parade led to a festival on the grounds of J. J. Hill Montessori Magnet School on Selby in St. Paul, in the north part of the old Rondo community. There was something for everyone: booths on insurance, education, and health; vendors of clothing and novelties; and a carnival with rides and games. Food vendors offered standard American festival fare, including the inevitable minidonuts and hot dogs, but also satisfying soul food, such as sweet potato pie and barbecue wings, and spicy Caribbean offerings, including jerk chicken and pigeon peas with rice. When darkness brought some cool air, there was dancing until midnight.

Rondo Days has become the weekend that one-time residents who now live in other states come home for a reunion with family and old schoolmates. And grandchildren now living in sprawling suburbs come in to sit beside their grandparents who recall for them the close-knit community that was Rondo.

Here are recipes for celebrating Rondo Days at your house.

4 lemons
3 cups water
½ cup granulated sugar
Ice

LEMONADE—THE REAL THING
MAKES 6 SERVINGS

Sellers at three lemonade stands were squeezing lemons constantly as participants tried in vain to get cool. No lemonade powders or concentrates here, thank you.

Roll lemons back and forth on work surface, pushing with the heel of your hand—this helps release juice. Cut lemons in half and squeeze juice using hand juicer or an automatic one. You should have about 1 cup lemon juice.

In pitcher, stir together lemon juice, water, and sugar. Keep stirring until sugar is dissolved. To serve, pour over ice in glasses or cups.

Variation: Use part oranges or part limes with lemons to give 'ade a different tang. If using part limes, more sugar may be needed.

1 (about 11-ounce) turkey leg
    per person
Favorite barbecue sauce,
    bottled or homemade
Disposable oven bag(s)

BARBECUED TURKEY LEGS
1 LEG = 1 SERVING

Vendors at events such as Rondo Days and the State Fair are able to buy precooked frozen turkey legs, then finish them over coals or on a big grill at the event. It's also very easy to roast the legs in the oven. Using oven bags simplifies cleanup greatly.

Brush each turkey leg generously with barbecue sauce. Prepare the oven bag for use as directed on the package. Place sauce-covered legs in oven bag(s). Roast in a 325°F oven 2 to 2½ hours, or until fork tender.

Pan-roasted legs: Arrange turkey legs in a large roasting pan. Roast at 325°F 1 hour, then apply barbecue sauce and roast another 1 to 1½ hours, basting with sauce as time permits.

SWEET POTATO PIE

MAKES 6 SERVINGS

3 large sweet potatoes
  (1 ¾ pounds)
6 tablespoons butter, melted
1 ¼ cups granulated sugar
½ cup milk
Pinch of ground cinnamon
Pinch of ground nutmeg
1 9-inch pie crust, homemade
  or store bought

Sweet potatoes, whether boiled and buttered, or turned into a toothsome pie, have long been part of the beloved soul foods, along with fried fish, collard greens, grits, pinto beans, cole slaw, potato salad, and corn bread.

Cook the potatoes in boiling water until fork tender; drain. Let potatoes cool.

Peel potatoes and put them in a large mixing bowl. Mash potatoes with a potato masher until no lumps remain. Stir in the butter, sugar, milk, cinnamon, and nutmeg, continuing to stir until you can see that the spices are well distributed. Pour the potato mixture into pie crust.

Preheat oven to 375°F (350°F for glass pan) and bake for 40 to 50 minutes, or until toothpick inserted in center comes out dry.

CARIBBEAN JERK CHICKEN

MAKES 4 SERVINGS

2 tablespoons salt
2 tablespoons garlic powder
1 tablespoon sugar
1 tablespoon ground allspice
1 tablespoon dried thyme or
  3 tablespoons fresh thyme
  leaves or 1 tablespoon dried
  thyme
1 ½ teaspoons cayenne pepper
1 ½ teaspoons freshly ground
  black pepper
1 ½ teaspoons ground sage
¾ teaspoon ground nutmeg
¾ teaspoon ground cinnamon
¼ cup olive oil
¼ cup soy sauce
¾ cup white vinegar
½ cup orange juice
Juice of 1 lime
1 Scotch bonnet pepper,
  seeded and finely chopped
1 cup chopped white onion
3 green onions, finely chopped
4 (6- to 8-ounce) chicken
  breasts

The thick, highly seasoned marinade, so popular in Jamaica and throughout the Caribbean islands, produces moist, flavorful chicken.

In a large bowl, combine the salt, garlic powder, sugar, allspice, thyme, cayenne pepper, black pepper, sage, nutmeg, and cinnamon. Beat in the olive oil, soy sauce, vinegar, orange juice, and lime juice. Add the finely chopped Scotch Bonnet pepper, white and green onions; mix well. Add the chicken breasts, cover and marinate in the refrigerator for at least 1 hour, longer if possible.

Preheat the broiler. Remove the chicken breasts from the marinade and broil for 6 minutes on each side or until fully cooked: juices run clear. Baste chicken with marinade a time or two during broiling.

8 MINNESOTA STATE FAIR

FEEDING THE FAIR'S THOUSANDS

For some, the Minnesota State Fair is a movable feast. For others, it's three square meals a day, just like at home. By movable feast I mean foods you can eat as you walk: foot-long hot dogs, fried cheese curds, big cinnamon rolls, rice cereal bars, and anything—everything!—on a stick.

Staubo's crunchy, deep-fried onion and green-pepper rings were part of that movable feast for ten years, 1975 through 1985. Iris Staubus of Woodbury tells it like it was. "My mom and dad—Bonnie and John Staubus, Sr.—tasted these fried

Long or short, a wiener in a bun has been a Minnesota State Fair favorite for a century.

green-pepper rings at a wedding reception and thought the rings would make a good food to sell at the fair. We found a great recipe and made an application for a booth. We got the OK in early June and lined someone up to build our booth. My three brothers—John, Tom, and David, ages seventeen to twenty-seven that first year—and I signed on to work during the fair. We lined up friends, too, anyone willing to help us.

"To get people to try our rings, we offered a sample for ten cents. Besides the green-pepper rings, we had onion rings because that's what people were familiar with. We fried them, then sacked them up, six to a bag. It was very labor intensive. It took two people frying, two people selling at the counter, and a fifth person filling the bowls of batter and fresh rings for those frying.

"Our parents stayed in a trailer in the campground doing all the cutting and mixing the batter. John, Jr., and his wife, Donna, ferried the supplies over from the folks' trailer in a cooler-cart. We stayed open late to serve people coming from the grandstand.

"After that first year, we all worked so hard, it was a wonder we were still speaking to each other. But the fair gets in your blood. It's exciting to be a part of it. No, we didn't make tons of money, but it really fostered camaraderie between family and friends."

People who want a just-like-home meal at the fair go to dining halls like the one operated by Hamline United Methodist Church, St. Paul, which has been operating for over a hundred years. Or to Epiphany Country Diner (on Underwood Avenue west of the Horticulture Agriculture Building), where workers from Epiphany Catholic Church, Coon Rapids, serve full meals to the fair's multitudes. The line of hungry folks starts at 6:30 A.M. and moves steadily all day.

Look for this sign, at Underwood west of the Hort Building, for full meal service at the fair.

Father Bernie (Bernard) Reiser himself is almost always on hand to greet those waiting in line at the diner. Though he wears priestly black at church, Fr. Reiser stays comfortable in a sport shirt at the fair. A clown in rainbow wig and white face may be there, too, cracking wise as people work their way to the door.

The time from entering that door to sitting down at the table is ten minutes maximum, according to Fr. Reiser. First, the order is taken by a hostess, who marks their order slip. Next is the caller, who shouts, "Ham dinner—adult," for example. Along the fifteen-foot food line, customers make choices about condiments, beverages, and the flavor of pie. "The food is put on the tray and carried to the table for them," he says.

Portions are generous, something that brings people back year after year, says Fr. Reiser. "The turkey is *really* a turkey dinner, all the trimmings." There's always plenty of food on hand, much of it in the freezer. Food for the diner is purchased from vendors, which keeps the meals consistent. "You can't have a hundred mamas making a hundred pies," says Fr. Reiser. "This way if there's a problem, you call the vendor."

Newsmen from WCCO Radio and Television frequent the diner. "[Popular radio host] Jergen Nash used to slip in and sit and read the paper," says Fr. Reiser. Coming to a dining hall is a good way to rest the feet after trekking through miles of exhibits. And sometimes rain drives people inside. Epiphany's policy is "eat first, pay later." "People are honest," says Fr. Reiser, with a smile. "Paying takes as much time as getting the food on the plate. That's why we have it at the end."

Between 100 and 125 workers come in each day to run the diner. Those on the early shift gather at the church parking lot in Coon Rapids at 5:30 A.M. to ride the church bus to the fairgrounds. At 6 A.M., after a word of prayer, they take their posts for the 6:30 opening. The second shift arrives at 2:30 P.M., handles the busy dinner hour and closes at 8 P.M. Each worker gets a meal. During the 2000 fair, the Epiphany crews served 25,796 customers (10,015 at breakfast plus 15,781 at lunch or dinner).

Fr. Reiser recalls the day a boy, thirteen or fourteen years old, was working in the dining hall kitchen alongside a surgeon, the two chatting amiably. "The kids get a sense of ownership working at the diner. They know it helps pay for bricks and mortar."

Epiphany opened its diner just two years after the congregation was founded. Fr. Reiser started the church in 1964 with seventy-two acres of land—no building. Today there are 4,500 members, a campus of buildings, and myriad activities. A St. Paul church offered Fr. Reiser the diner, which they were closing due to a

A full meal at a fair price—plus a chance to sit down—draws people to the Epiphany Diner.

Over a hundred workers serve over 25,000 customers at the Epiphany Diner during the state fair.

STATE FAIR CALORIE COUNTS

Apple = 81

Cookie from Sweet Martha = 110

Corn dog = 180

French toast, 2 slices = 240

Ice cream cone, 2 scoops = 340

Lemonade, 12 ounces = 150

Milk, whole, 1 cup = 150

Minidonut, 1 = 60

Onion rings, 5 = 240

Saltwater taffy, 1 piece = 50

Strawberry shortcake = 375

Texas toast, 1 slice = 170

Turkey dinner: turkey, gravy,
    stuffing, mashed potatoes, &
    green beans = 390

shortage of workers. He conferred with the state fair, which leases space to 300 food vendors—there are 1,200 vendors total—then took the idea to his parishioners.

New foods are added to the fair menu every year. The Epiphany Diner began serving Minnesota-grown ostrich meat in 1998. "It tastes like beef, yet it's almost fat free, a very low-cholesterol meat," Fr. Reiser explains. In 2000, they introduced vegetable lasagne and pancake on a stick (a breakfast item similar to a corn dog).

One year deep-fried candy bars were the "in" food for movable feasters, while another year macaroni and cheese on a stick was the much-talked-about snack.

Wondering what the newest fair treat is this year? Just tune in to TV shows telecast from the fair. They'll show you—even taste it for you. Then go on out to the fair and try it out for yourself. It's a Minnesota tradition.

Here are directions for preparing four Minnesota State Fair treats at home.

⅓ cup butter, melted

6 eggs

1 ½ cups milk (part half-and-half adds richness)

1 ½ tablespoons powdered sugar

1 teaspoon vanilla

½ teaspoon cinnamon

12 slices firm white bread*

*English muffin bread works well; so do raisin and whole wheat bread.

OVEN-BAKED FRENCH TOAST

MAKES 6 SERVINGS

It's wonderful to get to the fair early before the roads get dusty and crowded. That's why breakfast at one of the church dining halls, feasting on French toast or blueberry pancakes, is such a good idea.

Move oven racks to lowest and middle levels. Use kitchen paintbrush to generously grease two 15 x 10-inch jelly roll pans with melted butter. Preheat oven to 425°F.

Break eggs into wide bowl; add milk, sugar, vanilla, and cinnamon; beat well.

Dip bread one slice at a time in egg mixture, turning to coat well on both sides.

Place 6 slices in each pan. Brush tops of slices with remaining melted butter.

Bake 10 to 12 minutes, then switch positions of pans, top left to bottom right, and vice versa. Bake 8 to 10 minutes longer, or until toast is crisp. Serve hot with butter and syrup.

P.S. Leftover French toast freezes well and can be reheated in the toaster.

2 (1-pound) loaves frozen sweet bread dough

¼ cup butter, softened

3 to 4 tablespoons granulated or brown sugar

1 teaspoon ground cinnamon

½ cup raisins or chopped walnuts, optional

6 (8-inch diameter) disposable aluminum pans

Nonstick vegetable oil spray

Melted butter for brushing finished rolls

BIG BIG CINNAMON ROLLS

MAKES 6 BIG ROLLS

These rolls are only half as big as the plate-size rolls sold at the fair—yet they're big enough for two to share.

Place frozen dough loaves side by side in a plastic bag. Thaw in refrigerator 6 to 8 hours or overnight.

Still keeping loaves side by side, transfer to floured surface. Then punch dough down using the knuckles of both hands. With rolling pin, roll dough out as thin as you can—about 8 inches wide and 13 inches long. Spread dough thickly with softened butter. Sprinkle sugar, then cinnamon, generously over butter. If using raisins or walnuts, distribute them evenly atop cinnamon. Roll up jelly-roll style from

long side of dough. Cut roll into six equal slices.

Spray pans with nonstick vegetable oil spray. Place one slice of rolled dough in each prepared pan. Flatten each roll with the palm of your hand. Let rolls rise 30 minutes.

Flatten again and let rise another 30 minutes. Flatten a third time before baking.

Bake in preheated 350°F oven 35 to 40 minutes, or until golden brown. Remove from oven. Brush hot rolls with melted butter—this prevents rolls from getting too hard and crusty.

Ripe watermelon, red or
yellow
12-inch long bamboo skewers

WATERMELON ON A STICK

The hardest part of making these healthy treats is getting the stick in straight down the center. Serve these outdoors so folks can spit the seeds on the ground. Fresh pineapple can be cut and served on a stick this same way.

Using a long-bladed knife, cut melon flesh into rectangular pieces 1 ½ to 2 inches wide and 6 or 7 inches long, keeping to the fruit in the center (called the heart) or along the rind, leaving out the sections where seeds are the thickest.

Working slowly and carefully, push the point of the skewer into the piece of melon, striving to center it. You may need a few tries to get the knack—they're fun to eat whether the skewer has gone through straight or bit slanty.

Any watermelon remaining after cutting the pieces to put on the sticks makes a good slush: remove seeds, then blend in electric blender and dilute with chilled club soda or ginger ale.

1 cup (2 sticks) margarine,
butter, or butter-flavored
shortening, softened
1 cup firmly packed brown
sugar
½ cup granulated sugar
2 eggs
2 tablespoons milk
2 teaspoons vanilla
1 teaspoon baking soda
½ teaspoon ground cinnamon
½ teaspoon salt, optional
2 ½ cups rolled oats, quick or
old-fashioned, uncooked
1 ¾ cups all-purpose flour
2 cups (12-ounce package)
chocolate chips
1 cup chopped nuts (optional)

ALMOST MARTHA'S OATMEAL CHOCOLATE CHIP COOKIES

MAKES ABOUT 5 DOZEN

Martha Rossini Olson, a.k.a. Sweet Martha, sells fresh-baked cookies—piles of them— at the fair. In fact, they sell so well, she is manufacturing them and selling them frozen, ready to bake. Her recipe is, of course, top secret, but we did our best to come up with something close. For maximum chewiness, use the old-fashioned oats.

Preheat oven to 375°F. Beat margarine, brown sugar, granulated sugar, eggs, milk, vanilla, soda, cinnamon, and salt in large bowl with electric mixer on medium speed, or mix with spoon. Stir in oats, flour, chocolate chips, and, if using, nuts; mix well.

Before you bake a whole pan of cookies, try a test cookie: Bake one rounded tablespoonful of dough as directed—in this case on an ungreased baking sheet. If the cookie seems to spread out too much, stir 1 to 2 tablespoons of additional flour into the dough or cover the dough and refrigerate it 1 to 2 hours before you bake the cookies.

Bake 9 to 10 minutes for a chewy cookie or 11 to 13 minutes for a crisp cookie. Cool 1 minute on cookie sheets; remove to wire rack. Cool completely. Store tightly covered.

FAMILY REUNIONS + FEASTING =
HMONG NEW YEAR

No sooner was the Hmong community established in St. Paul than it launched New Year festivities. Recently I attended the twenty-fifth annual Minnesota Hmong New Year at St. Paul's RiverCentre November 24 through 26. Here people of all ages honor the custom of celebrating the end of the harvest season and the start of another year with family reunions, feasting, courting, dancing, and games.

Kathy Vang wore a bright-colored gown and an aluminum headdress as she played a ball-toss courting game at the Hmong New Year celebration.

The New Year is the only major holiday for the Hmong (pronounced "mung"), according to Ilean Her, a Laos-born Hmong and head of the Asian-Pacific Minnesotans Council, a state agency. The three-day celebration is held the weekend after Thanksgiving. Knowing the annual dates allows relatives to come from out of town to share the fun, she says. The event is sponsored by the Lao Family Community organizations of Minneapolis and St. Paul plus a variety of youth and women's organizations.

At New Year's time in Laos, it was traditional to kill a cow, Ilean explains. The Hmong cuisine in Laos was a vegetable-based cuisine and meat was very hard to come by. But

New Year's was the exception. "A whole cow is a lot of meat and, since there was no refrigeration, they had to eat it all," says Ilean. "Thus, the whole community came together to eat up the cow."

For the New Year here in Minnesota, the Hmong still like to slaughter a whole cow as part of their ceremonial practices. "The Hmong are industrious. They see a cow in a field, knock on the door, and ask how much the farmer wants for the cow," Ilean says. "Then they buy it, kill it, clean it there, and take the meat home. A cow is a lot of work. But now we have freezers."

"In Hmong tradition the chicken or rooster is sacred. The rooster crows at New Year's Day," explains Ilean. "And it is the rooster that takes you to the afterworld at the time of death. Also at the New Year's celebration each person is given an egg. That egg may simply be boiled or used in a soup." Shimmering traditional costumes, including distinctive headdresses, are worn for the New Year partying. "I have many New Year costumes because the colors and fabrics change with the fashion trends," adds Ilean. With 45,000 Hmong in Minnesota, the New Year can be a pretty big party.

Sixty percent of Minnesota's Hmong live in St. Paul. "We like St. Paul, not only because relatives and friends are here, but because it is easier to find decent housing and get services." Some of the industrious Hmong have found work in offices and factories, while others are doing what they did in Laos: farming. Many of the farmers actually live in the city but cultivate a few acres outside the urban center. They travel back and forth daily to plant, weed, and water, selling the harvested produce at farmers' markets throughout the growing season. In addition to the typical American produce, such as tomatoes and sweet corn, and the exotic Hmong produce, these stalls frequently display intricate traditional needlework done by the women of the family.

In Laos, the Hmong had an agrarian society, according to Ilean. "Money had no real value. People worked together. We may think of a clan as those who share the same last name, but, in practice, the clan is an entire village of thirty to forty families, cooperating and sharing. Everyone knew everyone else's children, therefore crime was low. People did fight, but very rarely. And moral crimes, such as adultery, were harshly punished."

Each Hmong family had its own small plot—the amount of land that they thought they could farm. But if they did plant more than they could handle, their neighbors would come to help them do the weeding. The vegetables and fruits they produced were shared by everyone. In this country, when the Hmong immigrants first congregated in cities, they started growing greens, such as cilantro and Thai basil and their traditional healing herbs. They used

Hmong families enjoy both traditional Laotian foods and modern American fare.

window boxes and planters along sidewalks until neighborhood plots could be found.

Ilean's family came to Clinton, Iowa, when she was seven years old. She went right into first grade, the only Hmong in her class. In 1985, when she was a junior in high school, her family moved to Minnesota to be near her father's family. Their family (including a younger brother born in the U.S.) has thrived in St. Paul. Ilean graduated first from Hamline University then the University of Minnesota Law School. Her father works in elder services, her mother for the city of Minneapolis.

When she teaches Hmong cooking to friends, Ilean explains that it's hard to distinguish Hmong foods from other Southeast Asian cuisines. "The food is very bland. We just season with MSG [monosodium glutamate] and salt. The main herbs are lemon grass and cilantro [also called fresh coriander or Chinese parsley]. We are famous for a chicken soup seasoned with herbs. This is the soup eaten by women after they have given birth."

The Hmong eat pork and chicken (a Hmong slaughterhouse, Long Cheng, near St. Paul, has been in operation about ten years) but, according to Ilean, beef is the meat of choice. They like big chunks of beef in a soup with ginger, lemon grass, and bay leaf. They also make an excellent beef salad. Ilean reports that her mother cooks beef variety meats, even using the bile ducts in an old-country stew. "The traditional foods remind them of their beloved country. And sometimes they are homesick."

Lemon grass, used by both Hmong and Thai cooks, has caught on with adventurous cooks. The grass looks something like celery with a slimmer, longer stalk and lends a distinctive lemon flavor to foods. Because lemon grass is very fibrous, I try to remove it after the flavor has been released, before the food is served.

The Hmong rarely use fish sauce as the Vietnamese and Thai do, but they do make a sauce from tiny red chili peppers. The fiery sauce is used for dipping meat or roasted vegetables.

Oriental eggplants fresh-picked from a Hmong farm garden.

The vegetables they used to grow in Laos are slowly gaining popularity here in Minnesota. One is the green "long bean," named for its twelve-inch-plus length. The beans are used just like our short beans. "When the seeds in the long bean are small, the cut-up bean is eaten fresh," says Ilean. "A few are allowed to mature and the seed is saved to be planted the next year." Oriental eggplants are also popular. They can be long and narrow, purple or white, but also may be small and round. Their flesh is like the familiar egg-shaped variety. June is the time to try cooking with fresh pea vines that can be added to any stir-fry. Then there are mustard greens in mid-summer—to stir-fry or to add (sparingly—they're strong) to salads.

Minnesota cooks are amazed at the size—and pungency—of the Oriental radish called daikon. It is often shredded or julienne-cut and added to tossed salads. One daikon can be three inches thick and up to ten inches long. The Hmong have also introduced Chinese broccoli (also called flowering cabbage). Dark green like broccoli and similar in flavor, this vegetable has a long stem with dark green leaves and tiny yellow or white flowers. You may need to visit the farmers' markets to buy and sample these Hmong vegetables (not all are readily available in supermarkets), and like many Minnesota food lovers, you might just add a stop to your local market as part of your regular summer weekend routine.

This first recipe and the one for beef curry with eggplant are from Mai Vang, Rosemount, who with her brothers and sisters and parents, raised a market garden of Hmong vegetables near the Koch Refinery (now Flint Hill Resources) outside St. Paul. The other recipes originally appeared in *The St. Paul Farmers' Market Produce Cookbook*.

STIR-FRIED BEEF WITH PEA VINES

MAKES 4 SERVINGS

1 pound sirloin beef steak, cut into thin, bite-size pieces

2 teaspoons soy sauce, divided

½ teaspoon sugar

1 teaspoon cornstarch

¼ teaspoon ground black pepper

1 teaspoon salt

3 teaspoons vegetable oil

1 teaspoon chopped garlic

1 pound pea vines, washed and cut into 1-inch sections

1 teaspoon oyster sauce

4 teaspoons water

1 teaspoon chopped green onion tops

Serve over generous portions of hot cooked rice. Your wok or skillet will be very full when you first add the vines, but they cook down quickly.

Place beef in large glass bowl. In small bowl, combine 1 teaspoon of the soy sauce, sugar, cornstarch, black pepper, and salt. Pour over beef and refrigerate 30 minutes.

Heat a Chinese wok or large skillet on stovetop over medium-high heat. Add 2 teaspoons of the vegetable oil. Rotate the wok to coat the sides with oil. Add garlic and fry until fragrant. Add the beef; stir-fry until brown, about 3 minutes. Remove beef from wok. Add remaining teaspoon oil to wok. When oil is hot, add pea vines and stir-fry for one minute. Stir in oyster sauce, the remaining teaspoon of soy sauce and water; heat to boiling. Stir in browned beef and heat to boiling again. Garnish with chopped green onion.

HMONG HOT PEPPER SAUCE

MAKES 1 ½ CUPS SAUCE

1 bunch green onions, chopped fine

½ bunch cilantro, minced

½ cup mint leaves, minced

½ inch of lemon grass (peel off outer layer), minced

3 leaves Oriental cilantro, minced*

Juice of 2 lemons

5 hot Thai peppers, minced

½ cup dry-roasted peanuts, ground almost to butter

2 teaspoons bottled fish sauce (nuoc nam or nam pla)

Salt

2 ½ teaspoons water, if needed

*Oriental cilantro has a narrow, jagged leaf something like a dandelion leaf; available in Asian markets and, in summer, farmers' markets.

In traditional homes, this sauce is made fresh every day. The peppers used in this sauce are the tiny, pointed red peppers called Thai peppers. Be careful not to touch your eyes or mouth with your hands while you are cutting up the peppers—their natural fire can burn tender flesh. If you have a food processor, use it to mince or process the ingredients, being careful to keep them separate.

Combine onions, cilantro, mint, lemon grass, Oriental cilantro, lemon juice, peppers, and peanuts. Add fish sauce. Stir ingredients together. Taste and, if you wish, add salt. If sauce is not juicy enough, add water. Store in refrigerator. Serve as a condiment with meats and/or vegetables.

4-inch piece daikon radish, peeled
2 teaspoons salt
2 medium carrots, peeled
2 cups ice water

For dressing:

1 tablespoon soy sauce
1 teaspoon sugar
1 tablespoon oriental dark sesame oil

DAIKON RADISH AND CARROT SALAD

MAKES 4 SERVINGS

Use a vegetable peeler to peel down the radish lengthwise, making long thin shreds. Put shred in a bowl and sprinkle with 1 teaspoon salt. Cover and refrigerate 1 hour.

Cut carrots in half lengthwise. Use a vegetable peeler to peel down the carrot half, lengthwise, making long thin shreds. In a large bowl, combine the ice water, remaining 1 teaspoon salt, and the carrot and radish shreds. Mix well. Cover and refrigerate 1 hour.

For dressing: Combine soy sauce, sugar, and sesame oil in a small bowl. Stir until sugar is dissolved. Cover and refrigerate until ready to use. Rinse radish and carrot to remove salt. Drain vegetables. Put into a bowl and toss with dressing. Chill before serving.

1 teaspoon vegetable oil
2 tablespoons red curry paste*
½ pound beef loin, sliced thinly
1 tablespoon fish sauce
1 teaspoon salt
1 teaspoon sugar
2 cups coconut milk or half-and-half
2 cups water
1 stalk lemon grass
1 cup diced Oriental eggplant
1 cup 1-inch pieces long beans
15 fresh Thai purple basil leaves, torn**
Hot cooked white rice

*This potent paste is available canned in Asian markets.

**Green Italian basil may also be used.

BEEF CURRY WITH ORIENTAL EGGPLANT AND LONG BEANS

MAKES 4 SERVINGS

In a large saucepan, heat oil over low heat. Stir-fry curry paste for 2 minutes. Add beef and stir-fry for 1 minute. Add fish sauce, salt, and sugar and cook for 2 minutes, stirring a few times. Add coconut milk or half-and-half, water, and lemon grass; mix well. Cover and simmer 20 minutes.

Add eggplant and cook 3 minutes, stirring. Add beans and cook over medium heat until eggplant and beans are tender, 15 to 20 minutes. Stir in basil leaves. Serve with hot rice.

10
CHRISTMAS FESTIVAL
WITH NORWEGIAN BUFFET

Jeg er sa glad hver julekveld,
For da ble Jesus født;
Da lyste stjernen som en sol,
Og engler sang sa søtt.

I am so glad each Christmas Eve,
The night of Jesus' birth;
The Star shone radiant as the sun,
And angels sang on earth.

Buntrock Commons, in the heart of the St. Olaf campus,
decorated for Christmas.

The words, "And angels sang on earth," always remind me of the St. Olaf choir and its former founder and longtime director, F. Melius Christiansen.

Our church choir sang the hymn when I was a teenager; we learned the Norwegian phonetically. Years later, it was a thrill to hear the renowned St. Olaf choir perform it at Christmas Festival at the college. My daughter and I were guests of the late Willmar Thorkelson, then the *Star Tribune* religion editor. We attended both the smorgasbord and the hugely popular concert at the college in Northfield.

This happy combination of traditional food and festive music continues every year at St. Olaf. Typically, Christmas Festival is the first weekend of December, with performances Thursday, Friday, and Saturday evenings at 7:30 P.M. and Sunday afternoon at 3:30 P.M. The 550 performers are all

St. Olaf students—roughly one-sixth of the student body in five choirs and the orchestra. As I watched the singers, I let my eyes roam from face to face, taking pleasure in their faith and fervor.

Going to the buffet and the concert is a wonderful way to open the holiday season. But you need connections to get in. "Tickets go to alumni, parents, faculty, and staff, and to students who participate," says Jean Callister-Benson, St. Olaf's director of stewardship.

"Though 3,000 people attend each concert, we always have to turn people away," she adds. "With four concerts, that's 12,000 people to park, feed, seat, and inspire." The music can be counted on for the inspiration; the rest is up to a whole corps of workers, with staffers like Jean on the scene.

If you're turned away, you can still hear the concert. It is broadcast live on the campus radio station, Classical 89.3 (formerly WCAL). And the annual concert is recorded and both cassette tapes and CDs are produced for sale.

The Christmas Festival dinner is really three buffets, all in Buntrock Commons, the sprawling stone student center dedicated in 1999. Guests of the college and donors dine in the lovely King's Room. Parents and alumni usually dine in the Ballroom, which seats three hundred. It opens at 4:30 P.M. and tables turn over two or three times, according to Jean. Concertgoers can also partake of the Scandinavian buffet in the cafeteria, alongside the students who can have the holiday meal or their regular "caf" fare.

Lutefisk, the butt of many a Minnesota joke (about its pungent smell and its

The St. Olaf choir sings Christmas music from around the globe.

being soaked in lye), is the most popular item on the Christmas buffet, says Jean. Also very popular are the warm fruit soup and *rommegrøt*, the cream pudding usually served with melted butter on top. There are different styles of eating lutefisk. "One man took the boiled potatoes, topped them with lutefisk, then added another layer of potatoes, covering it all with melted butter. He obviously enjoyed the plateful and went back for seconds," recalls Jean.

The menu also includes meatballs, carved ham, and peas and carrots. Breads include lefse, the potato-based flat bread, and *julekake*, a fruited yeast bread. "Our meatballs, seasoned with allspice and served in gravy, are for the growing numbers who didn't grow up on lutefisk," Jean explains. Trays of Christmas cookies provide something sweet to end with.

While lutefisk consumption lags here, it is growing in popularity in Norway. The humble fish is served in all the trendy restaurants in Oslo, according to Solveig Zempel, professor of Norwegian at the college and frequent traveler to Norway. She says that lutefisk had fallen out of favor in the old country, but about ten years ago, interest revived.

Solveig, who grew up in the Scandinavian community of Roseau, Minnesota, and is the daughter of Ella Rølvaag Tweet and the granddaughter of honored novelist O. E. Rølvaag, contrasts the Christmas meals of her girlhood with the St. Olaf feast. "Our family—my father ran a Ben Franklin store—had pork ribs for Christmas Day dinner. Another Christmas food was milk porridge, called *fløtegrøt*, made with milk and flour and served with cinnamon sugar and butter. The *fløtegrøt* was accompanied by *julekake*. We also had salty meats, various cheeses, herring cutlets, and little tins of pickled fish.

Students and concertgoers alike are served holiday fare at the sizable college cafeteria in Buntrock. Note the Norwegian flag at right.

"Christmas baking was important. We made *fattigmann*, rosettes, and *krumkake*. [For the uninitiated, *fattigmann* is a deep-fried, intricately shaped cookie; rosettes are crisp fanciful shapes, also deep-fried, then sugar coated; and *krumkake* are rolled or curled (like an ice cream cone) after being baked on a special iron.] My grandmother always put two tablespoons of brandy into the *fattigmann* dough, which made the cookies crisper."

Cardamom is much used at holiday time, in both cookies and breads. "Get the cardamom in the shell," advises Solveig. "No, don't get it ground. Grind the seeds yourself. I use a coffee grinder, but you could use a mortar and pestle.

"My mother served what she called immigrant/peasant food. Very plain food. And she served *får-i-kål*, which is a lamb and cabbage stew many consider the national dish of Norway. It is cooked in layers and seasoned with peppercorns."

Game is another food that Norse enjoy, both here and in the old country. "My cousin shares game—venison and moose—with my family. It is served with a wonderful game gravy enriched with gjetost." *Gjetost*, a slightly sweet, caramel-colored Norwegian cheese, is typically served at breakfast atop dense, flavorful whole grain breads.

When we met, Solveig was on sabbatical, translating fourteen diaries of a Norwegian pastor and his wife, written between 1879 and 1888. She has already published a book of translations, *In Their Own Words: Letters of Norwegian Immigrants*.

Being fluent in Norwegian, as Solveig and her colleague Margaret Hayford O'Leary are, means the cook has access to holiday recipes in native-language Norwegian cookbooks. Margaret showed me several beautiful cookbooks printed in Norwegian. Alas, all I could "read" was the pictures; the words with the crosshatched øs, were beyond me. And a researcher at heart, Margaret also brought me copies of articles about the St. Olaf Christmas buffet from the 50s and the 70s. The menu, they show, is time-honored, though there have been small changes. Lutefisk, meatballs, and ham were served at the first buffet in 1940. The spareribs, served for decades, have been replaced by pork roast, which is easier to handle, both for the cook and the diner. Lefse, baked by Northfield volunteers in years past, is now purchased in bulk. Margaret also explained why candles are typical décor for holiday meals such as Christmas Festival: "That's because, during December, it is dark by 3:30 in the afternoon in Norway."

Greg Colline, executive chef with Bon Appetit, shared the recipes for rice pudding, Christmas salad, and fruit soup. Bon Appetit is the catering company that holds the contract for St. Olaf's food service. The directions for lutefisk are adapted from that redoubtable Scandinavian source, Beatrice Ojakangas.

FOOD SERVED AT THE CHRISTMAS FEST

Figures from Bon Appetit executive chef Greg Colline, 2001

Lutefisk	750 pounds	Coined (sliced) carrots	320 pounds
Pork loins	700 pounds	Frozen peas	300 pounds
Pork gravy	160 gallons	Cranberry salad	450 pounds
Bone-in smoked ham	64 hams	Lefse	420 pounds
Meatballs	900 pounds or 14,400	Rommegrøt	120 gallons
Potatoes	1,300 pounds		

¾ cup white rice
1 teaspoon salt
4 cups milk, preferably whole
   milk
½ cup sugar
½ teaspoon almond extract
1 pint heavy whipping cream
About 4 tablespoons superfine
   or powdered sugar
½ cup chopped almonds,
   optional
Raspberry, strawberry, or
   lingonberry sauce for topping

RISKREM (RICE CREAM)

MAKES 6 SERVINGS

Cook rice, salt, and milk in top of double boiler over simmering water 1 to 1 ½ hours, or until rice is soft and mixture is thick.

Stir in the sugar and almond extract. Chill several hours or overnight.

Whip cream and 2 tablespoons superfine or powdered sugar with electric mixer on high speed until soft peaks form. Break up the chilled rice mixture with two forks or with a hand mixer on the low setting. Fold whipped cream into the rice. Fold in almonds, if using. Serve in individual bowls topped with fruit sauce.

2 pounds ready-to-cook
   (presoaked) lutefisk
Butter to flavor fish
Salt
Melted butter to serve with fish

LUTEFISK

MAKES 4 TO 6 SERVINGS

No book on Minnesota food would be complete without directions for cooking this famous fish.

Preheat oven to 350°F. Cut lutefisk in serving-size pieces. Select a baking dish or shallow casserole with a lid. Spray dish with nonstick vegetable oil spray. Place the fish pieces skin side down in prepared dish. Dot generously with butter. Season with salt. Cover with lid.

Bake 30 to 40 minutes, or until fish flakes. Serve immediately with melted butter. A cream sauce (white sauce made with half-and-half) may also be offered.

CHRISTMAS CRANBERRY SALAD

MAKES 8 SERVINGS

12-ounce bag whole fresh or frozen cranberries
¾ cup walnuts
1 cup sugar
1 ½ cups pineapple tidbits
Zest or grated rind from ½ orange

Place the cranberries and walnuts in the work bowl of a food processor fitted with the metal blade. Using the pulse setting, chop into small pieces. Be careful not to puree the cranberries. Transfer the cranberry mixture to a mixing bowl and add the sugar and pineapple. Mix well. Cover and chill overnight in refrigerator.

Serve in a pretty bowl garnished with the orange zest.

Variation: For an attractive presentation, serve the cranberry mixture in a lettuce cup. For a light dressing for the lettuce, pour some of the accumulated liquid off the salad and whisk 1 teaspoon of red wine vinegar into it. Drizzle this dressing on the lettuce then garnish with orange zest.

OLE FRUIT SOUP

MAKES 8 SERVINGS

2 cups plus 2 tablespoons dried plums (prunes) (14 ounces)
½ cup dried apricots
¾ cup golden raisins
¾ cup dark raisins
1 stick cinnamon
3 tablespoons quick-cooking tapioca (minute)
1 cup purple or white grape juice
¾ cup granulated sugar
¾ teaspoon lemon juice
Half an orange sliced into wheels
Half a lemon sliced into wheels

Though served warm at the buffet, this thick soup is delicious cold too.

Cut the plums and apricots in quarters (kitchen shears work well). Place in medium saucepan. Add the golden and dark raisins, cinnamon stick, and tapioca. Stir in the grape juice and let stand for 1 hour. Stir in the sugar and lemon juice. Bring to a boil and simmer 20 to 30 minutes, or until fruit is tender and the soup is thickened. Remove cinnamon stick. Serve warm garnished with orange and lemon slices.

SAVORY SPECIALTIES

62 Berry Picking at the Farm

67 The Butter Is the Best at Land O'Lakes

73 Cabin Time ... and the Cookin' Is Easy

78 Betty Crocker Takes the Cake: A View from Her Kitchen

83 Seeing Red: Ken Davis Bar-B-Q Sauce

89 Wild Fruit—To Spread, Pour, and Sip

94 Schwan's Ice Cream—A Sweet Story

99 Soybeans: Good for You and for Animals Too

104 SPAM—Nothing Short of a Phenomenon

111 Gobble, Gobble, Gobble—The Whole World Eats Minnesota Turkey

116 Watkins Vanilla: A Favorite Flavor, a Fashionable Scent

123 Wild Rice: Minnesota's Grain of Choice

11 BERRY PICKING
AT THE FARM

The breeze is on my face, the sun on my back. And the little basket on my arm is slowly filling with berries, the plump winter-hardy blueberries that have fascinated me for years.

Going berry picking is a wonderful, midwestern summer outing. As teenagers, my brother Bob and I joined our mother picking gooseberries in a tiny town called Volga City near my childhood home, Strawberry Point, Iowa.

In Strawberry, as we called it, our home—and most everyone else's—had a patch of the red berries in the backyard. In strawberry season, we happily ate the sweet berries three times a day. Mom made jars and jars of jam from the strawberries and gooseberries. During the winter, as Bob and I heaped our breakfast toast with jam, she'd warn: "Now that's spread, not pile."

During the early 1980s, neighbor Muriel Carney persuaded me to join her on a trip to Belle Plaine, Minnesota, to a strawberry farm. After a tiring morning squatting and kneeling to gather the ripe berries, I vowed to wait until the promised Minnesota blueberry farms opened for business before picking berries again. No kneeling with blueberries!

A bowl of blue gems. This is a recent variety by the name of Aurora.

That day came almost ten years later, when I visited Apple Brook Farms in Brooklyn Park. These were the brand-new Minnesota blueberries that I'd heard about in the early seventies. Back then, *Star Tribune* colleague Beth Anderson (now Erickson) was holding the monthly Taste recipe contest at her home. Judith Bell, Beth, and I divvied up the recipe finalists—something with berries—prepared the recipes at home, and gathered, with judges, to pick a winner.

One of the judges was a soft-spoken Canadian named Cecil Stushnoff. When the tasting was done, Dr. Stushnoff began telling us of his work with crosses of blueberry plants. The department of horticultural sciences at the University of Minnesota, already highly successful with winter-hardy apples, wooed Stushnoff from Canada to apply his expertise to blueberries.

Young North Blue bushes being tended in a nursery.

His first "blue" babies were introduced in 1983. They are called half-high blueberries. Highbush commercial plants, like those on the farms in New Jersey and Michigan that supply our supermarkets, were crossed with lowbush wild berries native to Minnesota. They would be about three feet tall when full grown, a nice picking height for someone five foot two like myself.

Blueberry bushes begin bearing in a couple years, according to Professor Jim Luby of the horticultural sciences department. It may take ten years for them to reach full size, he explains. Then, to the farmers' delight, they will keep bearing thirty-five or forty years.

North Sky and North Blue, those first winter-hardy blueberries, were followed in 1986 by North Country and in 1990 by St. Cloud. Two more blues, named Chippewa and Polaris, were introduced in 1996. Of two early berries, North Blue is a big berry, North Country, a smaller one.

It was North Blues that I picked at that same farm, renamed Berry Brook, in Brooklyn Center. The ripe berries grew in clusters and literally fell into my hands, they were so ripe. And the gentle breeze kept the mosquitoes away. However, owner Barbara Munoz warned this was the farm's last season. Suburban development was moving in, forcing out small family farms like theirs.

Back home, I spread the blueberries in single layers in shallow pans and froze them. With this method, you get individually frozen berries and can easily measure the amount needed. Once frozen, they went into freezer containers for use in the recipes that follow.

Check the *Minnesota Grown Directory,* a free publication of the Minnesota Department of Agriculture, to plan a summer berry-picking outing. The recent edition, available at public libraries, community centers, and on the Web, lists twenty-seven farms where blueberries can be found, along with many U-pick strawberry and raspberry farms.

Kay Sargent with an armful of the summer harvest.

True to my childhood, I can eat berries three times a day: on cereal for breakfast, stirred into orange or lemon yogurt at lunchtime, and on top of ice cream as a midevening dessert. It was hard to choose just four berry recipes.

BLUEBERRY MUFFINS

2 cups all-purpose
  unbleached flour
⅔ cup granulated sugar
1 teaspoon baking powder
1 teaspoon baking soda
6-ounce carton lemon yogurt
⅛ cup milk
¼ cup vegetable oil, such as
  canola
1 egg
2 cups fresh or frozen
  blueberries

The blueberry muffin was named Minnesota's state muffin in 1988. As a civics lesson third graders at South Terrace Elementary School in Carlton, Minnesota, followed a bill, their muffin bill, through the Legislature. Representative Mary Murphy of Hermantown introduced the bill. This recipe is my favorite.

Preheat oven to 400°F. Spray 12 muffin cups with nonstick vegetable oil spray.

Mix flour, sugar, baking powder, and soda in a large bowl. In a separate bowl, beat yogurt, milk, oil, and egg with fork or wire whisk. Pour the yogurt mixture into the flour mixture; stir just until flour is moistened—batter will be lumpy. Fold in blueberries—it's OK if they're frozen. Divide batter evenly among muffin cups.

Bake 20 to 25 minutes or until golden brown. Cool in pan 5 minutes, then remove to complete cooling.

BLUEBERRIES-AND-MORE PANCAKES

Fresh blueberries, washed and
  picked over
Halved ripe banana slices
Chopped pecans
Pancake batter—your choice
  of buttermilk, whole wheat,
  or sourdough pancakes
Plain yogurt mixed with
  additional blueberries,
  banana slices, and pecans
Vegetable oil as needed for
  frying pancakes

This recipe was inspired by the Kamikaze Pancakes served at The Egg and I restaurant on Lyndale Avenue in Minneapolis.

Fill bowls with berries, banana slices, and pecans; place bowls near the pancake griddle.

Prepare favorite pancake batter (I use Bisquick buttermilk baking mix following package directions).

Combine more fruit and nuts with plain yogurt in a large bowl to put on the table for pancake topping.

Heat griddle or skillet adding oil if necessary. Pour pancake batter by ¼ cupfuls onto hot griddle. Working quickly, sprinkle pancakes with berries, banana slices, and pecans. When edges of pancakes are dry, turn and cook on second side until golden. Serve immediately; each person tops pancake with fruit-yogurt mixture. No syrup needed.

Variation: Use sliced strawberries instead of pecans. Or use a mixture of berries and banana slices as topping omitting yogurt.

7 ½ cups fresh or frozen "dry
  pack" blueberries
1 tablespoon lemon juice
¾ cup granulated sugar
1 tablespoon cornstarch
1 teaspoon ground cinnamon
1 cup water

For dumplings:

1 cup all-purpose unbleached
  flour
2 tablespoons granulated
  sugar
1 teaspoon baking powder
½ teaspoon baking soda
pinch of salt
2 tablespoons butter, melted
½ cup buttermilk
Heavy whipping cream or ice
  cream for topping

MARJORIE'S BLUEBERRY GRUNT

MAKES 8 SERVINGS

An early American specialty from legendary B & B hostess Marjorie Bush. She served it as the breakfast dessert, first at Bluff Creek Inn near Chaska and later at Asa Parker House in Marine on St. Croix.

In a large bowl, toss berries with lemon juice. Add sugar, cornstarch, cinnamon, and water; stir well. Put berry mixture into a saucepan with cover. Bring mixture to a gentle boil.

In another large bowl, stir together flour, sugar, baking powder, soda, and salt. Stir in the melted butter. Next, stir in the buttermilk, using a little more as needed to make a soft dough. Drop spoonfuls of dough onto the blueberries. Cover pan tightly and simmer 15 minutes—do not lift lid or dumplings won't cook. Serve hot in individual serving bowls, topped with heavy cream or ice cream.

3 tablespoons (1 jigger) rum
3 tablespoons (1 jigger) fruit
  brandy (such as apricot
  brandy)
2 ½ cups frozen blueberries

BLUEBERRY MONDAY

MAKES 2 ½ CUPS, 6 TO 7 SERVINGS

My recipe card for this elegant sauce is stained with blueberry juice, left from the many times I've handled it over the years. The directions came from the late Irene D. Anderson, who directed the work in the test kitchens at Betty Crocker Kitchens during the years I was there.

Measure rum, brandy, and berries into a small saucepan. Heat and stir 2 to 3 minutes, until sauce forms. Serve warm over ice cream.

Variation: If fresh blueberries are used, use a dry pint (also about 2 ½ cups) and add ¼ cup granulated sugar.

12
THE BUTTER IS THE BEST

AT LAND O'LAKES

Butter is best. I've known that since I was a tiny child. I learned about butter at my mother's knee, as she read the delightful verses about the king's breakfast from A. A. Milne's *When We Were Very Young*. Here's how it goes:

> The King asked the Queen, and the Queen asked the Dairymaid:
> "Could we have some butter for the Royal slice of bread?"
> The Queen asked the Dairymaid, the Dairymaid said, "Certainly,
> I'll go and tell the cow now before she goes to bed."

But the cow refuses, saying, "You'd better tell His Majesty, that many people nowadays like marmalade instead." Eventually, in lilting rhyme, the cow relents, and the king—sketched in wig and crown, pj's and robe—gets a "bit of butter for his bread." I never tired of those lines, which Mother read to my brother and me often.

We liked butter on our bread, too. Living in Iowa's northeastern dairying area, we enjoyed our butter until World War II began. Butter was rationed and we got bags of funny white stuff called "ole" (short for oleomargarine) instead. Brother Bob and I took turns coloring the margarine, poking the yellow tablet of coloring, then working the bag back and forth. When colored, it looked like butter, but it didn't taste much like it.

Later, in the foods preparation lab at Iowa State, I learned the roles that butter plays in cooking. It is a desired flavoring in so many foods, and a structural element in cakes and desserts, combining readily with sugar and flour. And it adds satiety—a new word to me, meaning satisfaction—value.

Coming to the Twin Cities in 1955, I met women working with Minnesota's

This is the way Land O'Lakes trucks looked when the butter was delivered to the corner store in the mid-1920s.

Land O'Lakes butter through the Home Economists in Business group. But it wasn't until, on vacation, I saw Land O'Lakes butter prominently displayed in a fancy grocery store in New York City that I realized this was anything more than a popular Minnesota product.

Land O'Lakes had, in fact, been growing steadily since the Roaring Twenties. The dairy co-op, then called Minnesota Cooperative Creameries Association, was organized in 1921. It boasted some 320 local creameries working together to set standards of quality and to aggressively market their butter. The new co-op began making butter from sweet cream (sour cream was out) and selling it four sticks to the pound (no more tub butter).

By 1924, the butter-making businessmen heading the co-op wanted a new name. A contest was announced and $500 in gold (not incidentally the color of butter) offered as the prize. The winner: Land O'Lakes. Soon the association changed its name to match the butter and became Land O'Lakes Creameries in 1926. Come 1928, the now-famous Indian maiden was created to go on the butter box.

To boost sales, the fast-growing dairy co-op leapfrogged right over the middlemen selling to the grocery chains. "Butter doesn't keep well," says Steve Komula, a spokesman for Land O'Lakes. Sales direct from producer to retailer meant that cooks got fresher butter.

A butter carton from the early 1930s.

The 1920s were a time of rapid growth for the young organization. In 1925, according to Komula, Land O'Lakes marked its 39 millionth pound of butter sold; in 1930, they marked the 100 millionth pound of butter sold. In the early 1930s, they began selling their butter to a grocery chain that had 1,000 stores. From then on, Land O'Lakes has been the top selling butter in the nation. And, in 1927, the Little Falls Land O'Lakes creamery celebrated the transatlantic flight of native son Charles Lindbergh by airlifting forty pounds of butter to the flyer.

Decade by decade, Land O'Lakes consolidated its position as a dairy leader, marketing butter, cheese, and products made from butter's by-products: nonfat dry milk powder, casein, and buttermilk powder, all widely used in food manufacturing. And, bit by bit, it began to do business in other goods needed by farmers: feed, seed, plant food, and crop-protection products.

A butter substitute called, variously, oleomargarine, oleo, and, finally, margarine, was introduced in the United States in 1874. (It had been called "butterine" in Europe, where it was developed using hydrogenated vegetable oils.) Margarine's lower cost and, during the two world wars, its wider availability, brought it into many homes, though cooks decried its lack of flavor. The state of Minnesota did its best to help its butter producers, levying an oleo tax and requiring that consumers color the white product at home using a button of yellow color. Finally, in 1972, after much lab and market testing, Land O'Lakes introduced its own margarine. The advertising theme went something like this: "Who better to give you the best margarine than the makers of the best butter?" In 1982, a blend of butter and margarine, Country Morning Blend, was introduced to consumers.

From 1990 through 2001, Land O'Lakes butter sponsored a cooking and baking hot line called the Holiday Bakeline. Starting November 1 and running every day of the week through Christmas Eve, teams of home economists answered calls from cooks and sent them butter-rich recipes.

As one of the twenty-nine women working on the Bakeline, I learned that the most frequent question was: "What's the difference between salted and unsalted butter? The chefs on TV say there is." The difference is simple, we would reply: sweet, or unsalted, butter contains no salt, while salted butter contains salt, albeit a very small amount. Whichever butter the family uses for the table can also be used for cooking and baking—no need to keep both butters on hand. And, no, the salt amount in the recipe need not be changed, we added.

By 2002, Land O'Lakes had become the nation's top marketer of branded butter and deli cheese. It processes over ten billion pounds of milk every year and sells its 300-plus products in U.S. and world markets. It is owned by—and, at the same time, serves—over 7,000 farmers and about 1,300 local community co-ops. Members share in the company's profits, being paid according to their volume. In Minnesota and the other thirty-nine states plus two Canadian provinces that Land O'Lakes serves, these co-ops are the focus of many a rural community.

Fans of the delicate flavor of Land O'Lakes butter are legion. I spoke with hundreds of them when working on the Bakeline, women who always bought the butter for their holiday baking and had done so for thirty, thirty-five, forty years. I recently learned what a key role butter played in my own diet. My stomach had been upset and my doctor recommended a low-fat diet: no cheese, no chocolate, no butter. Sure, you can use jelly on toast at breakfast, but it doesn't go too well with soup at lunch. And, lemon juice and herbs are fine on hot vegetables, but somehow they're just not as satisfying that way. What a relief to learn that my tummy troubles were not caused by fat, but the reaction to a prescription drug. Happily, I returned to spreading Land O'Lakes butter on my bread—any time of day.

So many wonderful butter cookie recipes, so little time.

Employees displaying butter at the Land O'Lakes facility in Minneapolis in 1927.

For cookies:

1 cup Land O'Lakes butter, softened

⅔ cup granulated sugar

½ teaspoon almond extract

2 cups all-purpose flour

½ cup raspberry jam

For glaze:

1 cup powdered sugar

1 ½ teaspoons almond extract

2 to 3 teaspoons water

RASPBERRY ALMOND SHORTBREAD THUMBPRINTS

MAKES 3 ½ DOZEN COOKIES

One of the most popular recipes ever published by Land O'Lakes.

Combine butter, sugar, and almond extract in large mixer bowl. Beat at medium speed, scraping bowl often, until creamy (2 to 3 minutes). Reduce speed to low; add flour. Beat until well mixed (2 to 3 minutes). Cover; refrigerate at least 1 hour.

Preheat oven to 350°F. Shape dough into 1-inch balls. Place 2 inches apart on ungreased baking sheets. Make indentation in center of each with thumb (edges may crack slightly). Fill each indentation with about ¼ teaspoon jam.

Bake 14 to 18 minutes or until edges are lightly browned. Let stand 1 minute; remove from baking sheets. Cool completely.

Meanwhile, stir together all glaze ingredients in small bowl with wire whisk until smooth. Drizzle over cooled cookies crisscrossing in an attractive pattern.

For crust:

1 ⅓ cups all-purpose flour

¼ cup granulated sugar

½ cup Land O'Lakes butter or margarine, softened

For filling:

¾ cup sugar

2 eggs

2 tablespoons flour

¼ teaspoon baking powder

3 tablespoons lemon juice, fresh or fresh-frozen

Powdered sugar for top

LEMON-BUTTER BARS

MAKES 16 BARS

So tangy, so elegant. Now featured by many caterers and in bakeries.

Preheat oven to 350°F. Combine the 1 ⅓ cups flour, ¼ cup sugar, and butter in small bowl of electric mixer. Beat at low speed, scraping bowl often, until mixture is crumbly (2 to 3 minutes). Press mixture into bottom of 8-inch square ungreased baking pan. Bake 15 to 20 minutes or until edges are lightly browned.

Meanwhile, combine the ¾ cup sugar, eggs, 2 tablespoons flour, baking powder, and lemon juice in small mixer bowl. Beat at low speed, scraping bowl often, until well mixed. Pour filling over hot crust. Continue baking 18 to 20 minutes, or until filling is set. Sprinkle with powdered sugar; cool.

1 cup Land O'Lakes butter, softened
¾ cup firmly packed brown sugar
½ cup granulated sugar
2 eggs
1 tablespoon vanilla
2¼ cups all-purpose flour
2 teaspoons baking powder
½ teaspoon salt
1 (12-ounce) bag chocolate chips (2 cups)
¾ cup chopped pecans
⅔ cup English toffee chips

THE BIG ONE—A SUPERSIZE CHOCOLATE CHIP COOKIE

MAKES 20 SUPERSIZE COOKIES

A winner from the Land O'Lakes 1998 competition for family signature cookies. Chockful of chocolate chips, pecans, and toffee chips.

Preheat oven to 350°F. Combine butter, brown sugar, and granulated sugar in large mixer bowl. Beat at medium speed, scraping bowl often, until creamy (1 to 2 minutes). Add eggs and vanilla; continue beating until well mixed (1 to 2 minutes). Reduce speed to low; add flour, baking powder, and salt. Beat until well mixed (1 to 2 minutes). Stir in chocolate chips, pecans, and toffee chips by hand.

Drop dough by ¼ cupfuls 2 inches apart onto ungreased baking sheets. Bake 11 to 16 minutes or until edges are lightly browned. Cookies will look underbaked in center but will continue to brown while cooling. Let stand 2 minutes; remove from baking sheets.

3 cups all-purpose flour
½ teaspoon baking powder
½ teaspoon baking soda
½ teaspoon salt
1 cup Land O'Lakes butter, softened
2 eggs
1 cup granulated sugar
1 teaspoon vanilla
White or decorator sugar for topping

LOUISE'S SUGAR COOKIES

MAKES 4 DOZEN COOKIES

A tender cut-out cookie from Land O'Lakes American Heritage Cookbook *(1999), a collection of recipes from the company's dairy farmer members and its employees, which I edited.*

Combine flour, baking powder, baking soda, and salt in large bowl; cut in butter until crumbly. Set aside.

Place eggs in large mixer bowl. Beat at medium-high speed, gradually adding sugar and vanilla, until thick and lemon-colored (1 to 2 minutes). Reduce speed to low; add flour mixture. Beat until well mixed (1 to 2 minutes). Wrap dough in plastic food wrap. Refrigerate until firm (at least 1 hour).

Preheat oven to 350°F. Roll out dough on lightly floured surface, one third at a time (keeping remaining dough refrigerated), to ¼-inch thickness. Cut with assorted 2- to 2½-inch cookie cutters.

Place cookies 1 inch apart on greased cookie sheets. Sprinkle lightly with sugar. Bake 8 to 10 minutes or until lightly browned. Cool completely.

13 CABIN TIME
. . . AND THE COOKIN' IS EASY

When the weather warms and a reluctant spring begins, one starts hearing comments like these: "We have to go up and open the cabin." "We're going to the lake to see how the cabin came through the winter."

Years ago as a newcomer to Minnesota, I would ask, "Which lake?" Of course, the answer was always different. How could it not be with 10,000-plus named lakes? Eventually, I understood that thousands of lakes meant many thousands of places to have a cabin. And that didn't count the cabins that were on a river or just in a lovely piece of woods. It was a place to get away from it all. The weekend or summer retreat that city dwellers the world over seek.

On visits to the cabins of friends, I realized that the food one took to these hideaways was different from everyday at-home food. Cabin food was heartier, easier to prepare, fun to share.

"You want to make something easy at the cabin, so you'll have more time on the beach," says Margie Knoblauch of Excelsior. Or, more time to fish, walk through the pines, or play tag with the toddlers.

Margie knows whereof she speaks. She and her husband Joe have had a log cabin on Hines Lake near Park Rapids for forty-five years. When her three sons and three daughters were youngsters, she and the children would stay at the cabin all week, with Joe joining them whenever his work permitted.

"We found that folks had larger appetites up at the lake," Margie adds. Big appetites meant larger quantities of everything and she shopped accordingly. Institution management had been Margie's major in the University of Minnesota's School of Home Economics (now College of Human Ecology). Sometimes, during the years the six young Knoblauchs were growing up, she would say: "I'm managing an institution; right here." Husband Joe, a longtime school administrator in Hopkins, was a good cook too.

After the sun sets, there will still be time to gather 'round the fire, eat popcorn, drink cocoa, and tell stories.

Joe Knoblauch, an entrepreneur at heart, recognized that the food they served at their cabin was different: delicious and appealing yet quick and easy. "He's a good talker," Margie continues. "He went to Dorn [Bill Dorn, then head of Dorn Publications] and sold him the idea of a book of recipes for cabin cooking."

Margie enlisted the help of her good friend, Mary Brubacher of Hopkins. Mary and her husband Richard and their three daughters were "cabin people," too, with a place at Little Lake Hubert near Nisswa. Mary and Margie wrote letters to all their friends and relatives who had cabins. "Everybody responded. Some [of the recipes] were foods they made at home and brought along." Some of the recipes were that "something easy" to prepare at the cabin. The two women, with a little help from their friends, tested every recipe.

North Country Cabin Cooking, published in 1983, proved to be the first cookbook on the subject. The 218-page book was priced right: under ten dollars. Margie and Mary credited the 139 contributors in the back of the book.

"We got to pick the design on the cover (a woodsy photo)," continues

Margie. The logo (also on the chapter dividers) is a shoreline in silhouette with evergreens and a cabin, with a curl of smoke coming out the chimney. Just below the silhouette, is the line: "More than 300 quick 'n easy, sure-to-please recipes for your cabin kitchen."

"Readers have really loved the book," says Margie. They often send notes—very complimentary notes—when they order more books.

Dorn went out of business after the book was published, so the Knoblauchs began buying the books directly from the printer. They named their enterprise Garlic Press—the name Knoblauch means garlic. The coauthors market and distribute the books themselves.

"The cookbook just sells itself ," comments Margie. It has sold more than 100,000 copies. Cooks find it at gift shops all over Minnesota and at airports. They try the recipes, like them, and soon order copies to be sent far and wide.

Joe Knoblauch calls the cookbook an "evergreen," the rare book that just goes on forever.

Margie chose these typical "Cabin Cooking" recipes from the book.

---

6 cups rolled oats, quick or
  old-fashioned
1 cup chopped nuts
¾ cup wheat germ
½ cup brown sugar
½ cup flaked or shredded
  coconut
⅓ cup sesame seeds
½ cup vegetable oil
⅓ cup honey
1 ½ teaspoons vanilla
Raisins, optional

TOASTY NUT GRANOLA

MAKES 8 CUPS

"This is a popular, nutritious, and filling breakfast cereal for the late-rising college crowd. It tides them over until noon without messing up the kitchen!" wrote Mary and Margie.

Preheat oven to 350°F. Spread rolled oats in an ungreased 13 x 9-inch pan. Bake oats for 10 minutes. Mix nuts, wheat germ, brown sugar, coconut and sesame seeds into heated oats.

Combine oil, honey, and vanilla. Add to oats mixture, coating dry ingredients. Divide mixture into two equal parts, putting each in a 13 x 9-inch pan. Bake 20 minutes, stirring often to brown evenly. Cool. Store in tightly covered container. If you like raisins, add them to mixture after baking.

Serve granola with milk and, if desired, fresh fruit. It may also be used as a topping for ice cream.

4 (7 ½-ounce) cans
    refrigerated buttermilk
    biscuits
1 cup sugar
1 teaspoon ground cinnamon
1 cup brown sugar
¾ cup margarine or butter

MONKEY BREAD

This is one of those recipes where many hands (at least four) make light work. I love cinnamon and upped the cinnamon to two tablespoons mixed with the sugar.

Cut each biscuit into quarters (kitchens shears work well). Mix sugar and cinnamon. Dip biscuit pieces into sugar mixture or shake in a plastic bag. Put pieces in a well-greased Bundt or angel-food pan. Try to keep the overall depth of the circle of biscuit pieces relatively even as it builds up.

Preheat oven to 350°F. Melt brown sugar and margarine. Do not boil. Pour over pieces of biscuit in cake pan. Bake for about 30 minutes or until puffy and golden.

Cool about 10 minutes, then turn upside down on a plate. Tear off pieces of bread (source of the "monkey" name) or cut into slices.

2 whole chickens
1 cup butter, melted
2 cups Italian bread crumbs
1 cup grated Parmesan cheese
¼ teaspoon instant minced
    garlic
½ teaspoon salt or to taste
2 tablespoons parsley flakes

PARMESAN CHICKEN

Delicious hot or cold.

Preheat oven to 375°F. Skin chickens and cut each chicken into 8 pieces. Melt butter in 13 x 9-inch or 15 x 10-inch pan.

Combine bread crumbs, Parmesan cheese, garlic, salt, and parsley flakes. Dip chicken pieces into butter. Roll in crumb mixture. Arrange in pan.

Bake, uncovered, for 45 to 60 minutes, or until crumbs are browned and juices run clear when chicken thigh is pierced with a fork.

OLD-FASHIONED POTATO SALAD

MAKES 6 SERVINGS

2 ½ to 3 cups cooked, peeled, and cubed potatoes
1 teaspoon sugar
1 teaspoon vinegar
3 hard-cooked eggs, divided
½ cup sliced celery
⅓ cup finely chopped onion
1 teaspoon salt
¾ teaspoon celery seed
¾ cup mayonnaise
Parsley for garnish

Make it early in the day, suggests Margie, and have this part of the dinner finished.

While potatoes are still warm, sprinkle with sugar and vinegar. Toss with a fork. Set aside for an hour or so.

Chop two of the hard-cooked eggs; set third egg aside for garnish. Add chopped eggs and celery to potatoes. Mix onion and seasonings into mayonnaise. Add mayonnaise to potato mixture and toss to mix. Refrigerate to thoroughly chill.

At serving time, garnish with minced parsley and sliced hard-cooked egg.

MARBLE BARS

MAKES 48 SERVINGS

For marbling:
1 (8-ounce) package cream cheese, softened
⅓ cup granulated sugar
1 egg

For brownies:
½ cup margarine or butter
¾ cup water
1 ½ (1-ounce) squares unsweetened chocolate
2 cups all-purpose unbleached flour
2 cups granulated sugar
2 eggs
½ cup (4 ounces) sour cream
1 teaspoon baking soda
½ teaspoon salt

For topping:
1 cup (6 ounces) chocolate chips

These moist bars are a favorite of the three Knoblauch daughters for potluck at the cabin.

Grease and flour a 15 ½ x 10 ½-inch jelly roll pan. Preheat oven to 375°F.

Combine softened cream cheese and sugar, mixing until well blended. Blend in one egg. Set aside.

In a large pan, combine margarine, water, and chocolate. Bring to a boil. Remove from heat. Combine flour and sugar. Add to the chocolate mixture. Add eggs, sour cream, baking soda, and salt; mix well. Spread batter in prepared pan. Spoon cheese mixture over chocolate batter. Cut through batter with knife several times for marble effect. Sprinkle with chocolate chips.

Bake 25 to 30 minutes or until cream cheese marbling turns golden and toothpick comes out clean.

Cut into squares. Store covered in refrigerator.

14
BETTY CROCKER
TAKES THE CAKE: A VIEW FROM HER KITCHEN

"There's something new today," said the woman in the grocery store holding up a bag filled with what looked like flour. "It's a mix for making cake. The directions are on it," she continued, pointing to a note on the side of the bag.

My mother liked to try new things, so I added the bag to the groceries I was carrying home. Mother had telephoned the order to the store earlier. Adding an item was easy since the food was charged to my folks' account. In a town like Strawberry Point, Iowa, population 1200, everyone knew everyone else, and the man who published the weekly newspaper—my dad—could be trusted to pay his monthly bill.

The year was 1947—I was fourteen years old. Though I remember the bag and the fun of bringing something new home, I cannot remember whether the cake was good eating or, indeed, how easy it actually was to make. Little did I know that ten years later I would be working with cake mixes and all sorts of foods at Betty Crocker Kitchens at General Mills headquarters.

Thanks to a double major in journalism and home economics, I was assigned to the editorial department. As understudy to the longtime cookbook editor, I learned how to plan a book, select recipes, follow through on kitchen testing, edit copy, proofread—no mistakes allowed; even index.

Daily taste panels included all the recipes being tested that day whether for our upcoming cookbook, for an ad campaign for cake mix or Bisquick, or for a booklet promoting Wheaties, Cheerios, and the other popular cereals.

Picture a spacious kitchen, all gleaming stainless steel with plenty of space for two women to work without bumping into each other, then multiply that picture by four and you have an idea of the test kitchens in the then-new General Mills Building on Wayzata Boulevard in Golden Valley.

Four test-kitchen home economists keep the cakes coming in the Betty Crocker Kitchens in Golden Valley, 1961.

The taste panel was held each morning at 11:15 and each afternoon at 3:30. Recipes on the taste panel were rated "OK," "Drop," or "Try Again." I'll never forget then-director Janette Kelley, a blunt Montanan renowned in her field, asking: "What is that vanilla doing in there? Can you taste it? Do you need it? If you don't, take it out." Every ingredient was scrutinized, as was every step of the preparation. At this point—1960—long before worries about calories and fat grams, what mattered was eating quality, success (not just ease) of preparation, and suitability for its planned use.

Which brings me back to the cake mixes. Every year (I was there from 1956–1963) the home economist who was the "product girl" for cake mix did a presentation of possible ideas for the next year's national ads. Cakes had to be festive and showy, sure to bring "oohs" and "ahs" from family and friends. Sometimes an ad tie-in was planned, with everything including Baker's coconut or some brand of nuts. These were party cakes, and accessories such as flowers or gifts were used to enhance the party theme.

Six or eight new treatments would be developed and a "showing" set up for the General Mills advertising department and the creative people both from the local ad agency and the agency in New York. Everyone in the kitchen would pitch in to prepare the cakes, coming in at the crack of dawn to sculpt frosting, and put out cards showing the names of the desserts. Everything would be set up in the department's lovely dining room. The ad execs would circle the table, making notes, taking samples. As cookbook editor (I'd been promoted after my mentor retired), I was included in the group viewing the new offerings. Once, to my surprise, a suave New Yorker turned to me to ask, "Which would you like best if you were a woman?" Realizing that, though he said *woman,* he meant *homemaker,* I pointed to my favorite.

A mix for ginger cake was the first cake mix, introduced in 1947. Flour milling rival, Pillsbury, introduced white and chocolate-fudge cake mixes in 1948. Betty Crocker/General Mills introduced devil's food and party cake mixes in 1949. The company's yellow, white, and spice cake mixes followed in 1952. Through the ensuing years, new flavors were flirted with, an ill-fated black walnut cake for one. Other flavors, such as Sunkist Lemon, came and went as major food companies danced briefly with Betty Crocker, then went on to other partners.

From the beginning, the cake mix manufacturers knew that home cooks used the product as the basis for all sorts of cakes and desserts. New variations were constantly being tried. Additions included applesauce, pumpkin, crushed pineapple, and rhubarb sauce. Cakes were cut up, reshaped, and decorated as Valentine hearts, puppy dogs, and sailboats.

Cooks wanting denser, richer cakes began adding a package of pudding mix and some oil to the mixes, which already included a shortening. The popularity of these enhanced cakes led to the addition of the pudding mix to the cake mix formula. You'll see the words "pudding added" on the box of these cakes, now manufactured by General Mills and all the other national brands except Duncan Hines.

The practice of augmenting a basic cake mix with extra ingredients became widespread. So widespread that food writer Anne Byrn published the popular *The Cake Mix Doctor* (1999), then *Chocolate from the Cake Mix Doctor* (2001). And *Betty Crocker's Ultimate Cake Mix Book* (2002) takes cake mixes and turns them into all sorts of wonderful things.

Through the years, these cake mix variations have become favorites of mine.

PUMPKIN CAKE

MAKES 16 SERVINGS

The perfect choice for all sorts of fall entertaining.

1 package Betty Crocker
SuperMoist yellow cake mix
½ teaspoon baking soda
1 teaspoon ground cinnamon
½ teaspoon ground ginger
¼ teaspoon ground cloves
2 eggs
1 (15-ounce) can pumpkin
(not pumpkin pie mix)
½ cup Betty Crocker Rich &
Creamy or whipped cream
cheese ready-to-spread
frosting

Preheat oven to 350°F. Grease and flour a 12-cup Bundt cake pan.

Beat cake mix, soda, cinnamon, ginger, cloves, eggs, and pumpkin in large bowl on low speed 2 minutes 30 seconds, scraping bowl frequently. Pour batter into pan.

Bake 40 to 45 minutes or until toothpick inserted in center comes out clean.

Cool cake 10 minutes. Turn upside down onto heatproof serving plate; remove pan. Microwave frosting in microwavable bowl on 50 percent power 15 seconds. Spread over top of cake, allowing some to drizzle down side. Serve warm or cool. Store loosely covered.

PINEAPPLE UPSIDE-DOWN CAKE

MAKES 12 SERVINGS

An often-requested, often-featured recipe, according to the General Mills home economists. I adapted the cake to two round pans (below) because, to me, this old-time cake—originally baked in a skillet—just has to be round.

¼ cup butter or margarine
1 cup packed brown sugar
1 (20-ounce) can pineapple
slices in juice
1 (6-ounce) jar maraschino
cherries, stems removed
1 package Betty Crocker
SuperMoist yellow cake mix
⅓ cup vegetable oil
3 eggs

Preheat oven to 350°F. Melt butter in 13 x 9-inch cake pan in oven. Sprinkle brown sugar evenly over butter.

Drain pineapple slices and reserve juice. Arrange pineapple slices on brown sugar. Drain cherries. Place a cherry in center of each pineapple slice and arrange remaining cherries around slices; press fruit gently into brown sugar.

Add enough water to reserved pineapple juice to measure 1 ¼ cups. Make cake batter as directed on package, using oil, eggs, and pineapple juice mixture (omit water as directed on package). Pour batter over pineapple and cherries.

Bake 40 to 45 minutes or until toothpick inserted in center comes out clean. Immediately run knife around side of pan to loosen cake, and turn pan upside down onto heatproof serving plate; leave pan over cake 1 minute so brown sugar topping can drizzle over cake. Cool 30 minutes. Serve warm or cool. Store loosely covered.

Variation: Follow directions above— except use two 9-inch round cake pans instead of the oblong. Place 5 pineapple rings and half the cherries in each pan. Bake 30 to 35 minutes.

RHUBARB CREAM CAKE

MAKES 8 TO 10 SERVINGS

1 package Betty Crocker
   SuperMoist yellow cake mix
Eggs and oil as required to
   prepare cake batter
4 cups sliced rhubarb
1 cup sugar
1 cup heavy whipping cream

Rhubarb grows "free" in many Minnesota backyards. Every spring this dessert recipe makes the circuit, friend to neighbor to coworker. My friend Mickie Loegering of Burnsville worked out the low-fat variation below.

Preheat oven to 350°F. Grease or spray a 13 x 9-inch cake pan. Prepare cake batter according to package directions. Spread batter in prepared pan. Sprinkle with the rhubarb, then the sugar. Finally, slowly pour the cream over all. Last three ingredients will form a custard and sink through the cake. Bake for 40 to 45 minutes. To serve, scoop out portions with a large spoon (cake becomes like a rich cobbler).

Low-fat variation: Use 1 cup evaporated skim milk in place of whipping cream.

TRIPLE FUDGE CAKE

MAKES 12 SERVINGS

1 (4-ounce) package
   chocolate pudding mix (not
   instant)
2 cups milk or soy milk
1 package Betty Crocker
   devil's food cake mix
½ cup chocolate chips
½ cup chopped nuts

This dark, moist treat was featured in Betty Crocker's New Good and Easy Cookbook *(1962), which I edited. When retesting the cake for this book, I planned to share it with a friend who cannot eat dairy foods. So I made the chocolate pudding with soy milk and it worked just fine.*

Preheat oven to 350°F. Prepare pudding mix with milk as directed on package. Stir dry cake mix into hot pudding. Pour batter into greased and floured 13 x 9-inch pan. Sprinkle with chocolate chips and nuts.

Bake for 30 to 35 minutes or until toothpick inserted in center comes out clean. Serve warm or cold. Nice with whipped cream or topping.

15
SEEING RED
KEN DAVIS BAR-B-Q SAUCE

"Red is a power color," says Barbara Jo Davis, owner and president of Ken Davis Products, Inc., the company that produces her late husband's signature barbecue sauce. As she speaks, she gestures toward the reception area just outside her office in St. Louis Park. The walls are painted the same red that is used on the bottles of the sauce, a color just a touch darker than tomato red.

"I always wear red when I meet with my brokers," says Barbara Jo, resplendent in a well-cut red suit, her smile bracketed by large red and gold earrings.

She was referring to the food brokers who distribute Ken Davis Bar-B-Q Sauce to supermarkets throughout Minnesota, North and South Dakota, Wisconsin, Iowa, and Nebraska.

The story of the development of the sauce and the company revolve around Ken Davis, the man in shades shown on the barbecue sauce label. Barbara Jo loves to tell his story:

He was a great big bear of a man, imposing both in size and audacity. Wearing dark glasses and sporting a big cigar, he appeared on the Minnesota horizon in the mid-1960s. "Hey, baby," he'd say, grinning and extending his hand. "I'm Ken Davis." Ken opened a restaurant (Edina Chicken at Vernon Road and Highway 100) in the late 1960s. They served chicken, ribs, and pizza. And they served a *great* barbecue sauce.

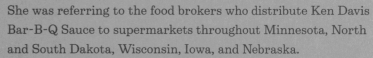

Barbara Jo Davis displays a bottle of the popular barbecue sauce her company sells in six Midwest states. The label depicts her late husband, Ken Davis, founder of the company that bears his name.

Sooner or later, mothers and grand-
mothers who regularly field calls
from family members for beloved
recipes decide to put together a
cookbook. Thanks to instant copying
services, the job is not nearly as
time-consuming as it used to be.
Some folks do a recipe box and
cards, but most compile a book,
large or small. One of the best I've
seen is called simply *The Hauke
Book,* the effort of an extended family
named Hauke. The sisters, sisters-in-
law, and cousins deciphered scrib-
bled notes, tested, and tasted. Best
of all, I thought, they wove family
history and anecdotes (including
each family members' favorite birthday foods) and snatches of favorite
songs into the pages. Such books are
most welcome gifts when a member
of the younger generation moves into
his or her own place.

But there was no recipe for the sauce, which his grandmother had taught him how to make. He just combined a little of this and a little of that until it tasted right. Finally, Ken hired home economist Barbara Jo Taylor to perfect the sauce and write it all down. (He later married her to keep the secret in the family.)

In 1970 Ken closed the restaurant, loaded his station wagon with barbecue sauce and, cigar in hand, started around to the local super-markets. Ignoring those who told him he couldn't go against the big national brands, he talked store managers into taking the sauce on con-signment. People found out about Ken Davis Bar-B-Q Sauce by word of mouth, in-store sampling, and by meeting and listening to Ken.

To his delight, his sauce became Minnesota's favorite, outselling even the national brands.

At one point in the expansion of his sales territory, Ken Davis had a huge recreational vehicle that he took to supermarkets for his weekend demo-festivals. This salesroom-on-wheels was fitted with a kitchen and carried barbecue gear for daylong tastings.

So proud was he of his sauce, Ken sometimes handed bottles to picnickers he'd spot on his way to and from his office. If folks were having a barbecue, Ken wanted them to have his sauce. He'd just pull over, offer the bottle, shake their hands, and drive off grinning.

After Ken turned the production of his sauce over to a commercial manu-facturer, he concentrated on developing new flavors and on sales and promo-tion. He headquartered his company in a suburban business complex where there was plenty of space for the staff of three *and* for a big beautiful kitchen for Barbara Jo, who had left Betty Crocker Kitchens after twenty years there. She calls her kitchen work "playing in the groceries."

The sauce line grew to five flavors: Original (which is sweet and smoky), Smooth 'n Spicy (Barbara's favorite, says the label) and Bold 'n Spicy, sold in supermarkets, plus Classic Deli, and Honey and Mustard, which, along with Original, are sold to food service outlets such as restaurants, schools, and hospitals.

Barbara Jo took the company reins after Ken's death in 1991, applying her considerable creativity to the business. She took voice training at the Guthrie Theatre so that she could record her own radio commercials. She began pub-lishing *Ken Davis News,* a tabloid packed with zippy recipes—every single one made with the sauce—and snappy copy. It includes Ken-isms like this: "If you're going to all the trouble to build a fire, you might as well cook a lot, wrap, and freeze it. Then, when you're hungry for barbecue, all you have to do is take it out and heat it up." She also launched a Web site that is loaded with her distinctive recipes.

Giving back to the community is important to Barbara Jo. She remains active in the National Coalition for Black Development in Home Economics after serving as the group's president in 2002. Her colleagues in Twin Cities Home Economists in Business named her Business Home Economist of the Year in 2002. She serves on the board of Stairstep Initiative, an African-American, community-building organization, and is a member of IACP (International Association of Culinary Professionals), NAACP, and the Global Women's Network. She speaks regularly on the importance of community service, putting the passion of a gospel minister into her exhortations on the value of helping others.

Besides their love of travel, of family, and, of course, of barbecue, Barbara Jo and Ken shared a love of jazz, Ken having played jazz bass as a young man. Barbara Jo uses a music metaphor when advising a young woman about starting a business. She says: "Running a business is like playing jazz: learn the basics, then improvise."

DON'T HAVE ENOUGH OF AN INGREDIENT? SUBSTITUTE

Despite a wonderful pantry closet that I keep chockfull, I often have to figure out a substitute for a needed ingredient missing from my stock. Sometimes I have a little of what I need, but not the stated amount. I use honey or white corn syrup in place of molasses or real maple syrup—they're all liquid sweeteners. I use plain yogurt in place of sour cream and vice versa. I've stretched vanilla yogurt by stirring in cottage cheese. One green vegetable can stand in for another. If I'm short of meat for a stew or stir-fry, I'll throw in a can of mushroom stems and pieces. You get the idea. No, you won't ruin the recipe.

Ribs are, of course, the ultimate barbecue food. Here's the Davis way.

KEN'S FAVORITE RIBS

Soak wood pieces (mesquite, hickory, or apple) in water at least 2 hours. Well-soaked wood will burn more slowly.

Choose about 1 pound pork spareribs or back ribs per person. Have the butcher trim off excess fat. Rinse and dry the ribs; place them in a roasting pan. Sprinkle ribs generously with salt-free Cajun Seasoning (or make your own rub using garlic and onion powder, cayenne, black pepper, and ground thyme). Cover and refrigerate at least 1 hour.

Fill a foil pan half full of kitty litter. Place the pan in the bottom of the grill, off to one side. Pour charcoal briquettes in the remaining half of the grill. Light the charcoal. When the coals are completely white, place the wet wood on top of the charcoal. Put the grill racks in place and oil them lightly.

Place ribs on the grill rack over the foil pan, bone side down. You could also use a special rib rack that holds ribs upright. Remember to keep the ribs on the side of the grill where there is no fire. *Let the heat, not the fire, do the cooking.* Cover the grill and cook 30 minutes.

Turn and rearrange ribs. Grills have hot spots so move the ribs around from time to time. Replace lid and cook ribs, turning frequently, until done, about 1 ½ hours. Ribs are done when you can wiggle the bones in the meat.

Cut racks of ribs into 4-bone portions or into individual bones. Place in foil pans or on large squares of heavy-duty foil. Slather ribs generously with Ken Davis Bar-B-Q Sauce. Cover tightly and return to grill. Cover and cook 15 minutes to heat through and caramelize sauce.

---

1 boneless pork shoulder or
   loin roast, about 3 pounds*
2 tablespoons vegetable oil
1 cup chicken broth, beer,
   apple juice, or water
1 (17-ounce) jar Ken Davis
   Bar-B-Q Sauce
Toasted, split hamburger buns
   or Kaiser rolls

*Don't be tempted to get a
  bone-in roast (as I did). It
  saves a little money but
  makes a lot of work.

BAR-B-Q PULLED PORK SANDWICHES

MAKES ABOUT 12 SERVINGS

Let this pork simmer while you pursue another activity, then shred it and add the sauce. Freeze in family-size portions. Thaw and reheat for satisfying sandwiches.

Brown pork on all sides in oil in a large Dutch oven over high heat. After browning, drain fat. Sprinkle roast with salt and pepper as desired. Add broth; heat to boiling. Reduce heat; cover and simmer until pork is very tender, about 3 hours.

Refrigerate pork in the broth until cool enough to handle. Holding the roast with your left hand and a fork in your right, pull the pork into long shreds. Return pork to pot. Pour sauce over pork; heat through. At this point, pork can be served on buns or frozen for later use.

GLAZED HAM AND SWEET POTATOES

MAKES 4 SERVINGS

1 ham steak (about 1 pound)

1 (23-ounce) can vacuum-packed sweet potatoes

½ cup Ken Davis Bar-B-Q Sauce

½ cup orange marmalade

2 teaspoons prepared mustard

¼ teaspoon ground cloves

This is a quick, easy dinner. Add a spinach salad and rolls.

Preheat oven to 350°F. Cut ham into 4 equal serving portions. Arrange ham and potatoes in baking dish. Stir together the sauce, marmalade, mustard, and cloves in a small bowl; pour over ham and potatoes.

Bake uncovered for 30 minutes, basting occasionally.

Note: Any leftovers freeze and reheat well.

MINNESOTA JAMBALAYA

MAKES 8 SERVINGS

1 cup Ken Davis Bar-B-Q Sauce, preferably Bold 'n Spicy

1 pound raw shrimp, shelled and deveined

1 pound spicy smoked sausage, such as kielbasa or andouille

2 tablespoons butter or margarine

1 large onion, chopped

1 large green pepper, seeded and chopped

1 large red pepper, seeded and chopped

1 tablespoon vinegar

¼ teaspoon cayenne pepper, optional

2 large tomatoes, chopped

1 cup uncooked long-grain rice

1 cup coarsely chopped smoked ham

1 (14.5-ounce) can chicken broth

It's only natural that jazz lovers like Ken and Barbara Jo would want to adapt a New Orleans favorite using their product.

Measure 2 tablespoons Bar-B-Q Sauce; set aside. Place shrimp in a 1-gallon sealable plastic bag; pour the remaining sauce over the shrimp. Seal and refrigerate 30 minutes.

Meanwhile, brown the sausages in a Dutch oven over medium heat. Remove the sausages and melt the butter in the same pan. Stir-fry the onions and peppers in the butter until onions are translucent and tender, 4 minutes. Stir in the tomatoes, reserved Bar-B-Q Sauce, vinegar, and, if using, cayenne pepper. Cover and simmer 15 minutes.

Slice the sausage and add to the pot along with the rice and ham. Stir in the chicken broth. Heat to boiling; reduce heat and simmer covered about 20 minutes, until rice is nearly done. Stir in the shrimp, including the marinade, and cook, stirring frequently, until the shrimp is pink, 3 to 5 minutes longer.

3 slices bacon, cut into 1-inch
  pieces
1 small red bell pepper,
  seeded and chopped
1 small green bell pepper,
  seeded and chopped
4 green onions, thinly sliced
2 cups whole kernel corn
½ teaspoon salt
¼ teaspoon pepper
⅓ cup Ken Davis Bar-B-Q
  Sauce

FRIED CORN

For a taste of summer midwinter, prepare this yummy side dish with frozen or canned corn.

In large skillet, cook bacon until crisp. Pour off all but about 2 tablespoons bacon fat (you can eyeball that amount). Stir in peppers and onion; stir-fry until tender. Stir in corn (drained, if canned), salt, pepper, and sauce. Cover and cook over low heat.

16 WILD FRUIT

TO SPREAD, POUR, AND SIP

Picking wild fruit is real work. Making jellies, syrups, and wines from that fruit is real work, too. Folks who love plum jelly and chokecherry syrup made from wild fruit don't have to do that work anymore. Instead, they can look for the Minnestalgia label at the grocery. These north woods treats come from a young company called Minnesota Specialty Crops based in McGregor.

Lori Gordon and Jay Erkenbrack launched their business in 1990, after attending a fancy food show featuring lots of food items made with wild ingredients. They became partners in producing a line of fruit jellies and set up shop in a McGregor plant for which Jay was already marketing wild rice. Aiming to capitalize on the growing popularity of wild fruit products, Lori and Jay began planning their new business. While Jay began alerting skilled fruit pickers around northern Minnesota, Lori got started with the marketing plan. Their line, first named Minnesota Wild, is now Minnestalgia—short for Minnesota nostalgia.

Their jellies are distinctive in flavor, jewel-like in color, ranging from the near-purple of the wild grape and plum through the red-orange of chokecherry to the soft pink of crab apple and rose hip. A line of syrups—again with the tangy, true ripened-in-the-woods flavor—soon followed the jellies. I first bought the jellies at my local co-op and was impressed with their unusual flavors and unique colors. And, they were so uniquely Minnesotan, evoking the wooded northland and fruits that thrive here.

Berry picking is best in the cool of the morning, according to Lori. Often entire families go picking together with the grandparents showing children, some only four or five, how to spot the fruit and gather it carefully by hand. Blueberries and raspberries make a good snack while picking, but many of the other fruits are not sweet enough to eat out of hand.

The Savannah State Forest near McGregor is a good source for wild fruit. Here berry corridors some two hundred feet wide have developed, Jay explains. Foresters clear the forest's underbrush with heavy machinery. Wild blueberries and raspberries spring up in the cleared space. Later chokecherries and pin cherries follow the berries. The price Jay pays for the fruit depends on the difficulty of picking and the demand for the fruit. Pin cherries and highbush cranberries usually bring the highest prices.

As demand for their products grew, Minnestalgia began purchasing commercial berries to augment the native fruit supply. Blackberries, blueberries, black currants, and raspberries are the fruits they may buy commercially. Lori reports that the company is working through programs of the Department of Transportation and Department of Natural Resources to promote the use of fruit bushes and trees as windbreaks and to prevent soil erosion. "Hopefully, this will give farmers and landowners a chance to harvest the fruit or, at the very least, birds and wildlife will have an extra source of food and shelter," she says.

Each of the wild fruits used in Minnestalgia products has its own unique color and flavor.

Chokecherries, with their brilliant red color and strong flavor, are the banner fruit for the company. Jay feels that it is nostalgia that sells chokecherry products. Customers remember the chokecherry jelly or wine made by their grandmother or their parents and they associate that chokecherry flavor with an earlier, happier time. He's no longer surprised when someone wants to buy the entire case of chokecherry jelly that he's delivering to a market. Lori reports getting a letter from a woman wanting to buy the chokecherry jelly without the labels so that she could give it as her own homemade jelly.

Wild plums are the parents of today's orchard plums. The riper the plum, the sweeter the juice for jelly, syrup, or wine. Their natural color ranges from light pink to light red. The company makes both a wild plum wine and a wild plum honeywine, which combines the fruit juice with honey-sweetened white wine.

Highbush cranberries, though not a relative—botanically—of the well-known bog cranberries, are similar in their tart flavor and red color. And how high is highbush? Twelve to fifteen feet. The winemaker at Minnestalgia uses the berry in a honeywine combination that he suggests serving with meats.

Wild grapes, those vines that send tendrils far and wide, are used by the company for both jelly and one of its honeywines. Tangy is the word for both these products.

Black currants are popular in Europe, where they go into a syrup for making fruit drinks and the famed crème de cassis liqueur. At Minnestalgia, they go into a dark, glossy syrup and a robust semidry honeywine.

The tiny pin cherry, so good for jelly, has become a delicacy because it's hard to find.

The rose hip, the fruit of the rose that swells after the petals have fallen, makes unusual pink-orange jelly that's high in vitamin C.

Hawthorn, or thorn apple, tastes like a mating of crab apple and plum, but looks like an old wrinkled crab apple.

These jellies are a rarity to taste and perfect offered with hot, buttered scones or biscuits and a restoring cup of tea. Lori suggests the fruit syrups, with their rosy hues, as toppings not only for pancakes and waffles but also for ice cream and fruit sherbet. (I like to stir them into plain yogurt too.) The fruit wines also make a quick, elegant ice cream sauce.

Left. The wine press at Minnesota Specialty Crops in McGregor presses the juice from a batch of wild plums.

Middle. Out of the vat and into the bottles goes the new wine.

Right. "The hardest part of making wine," says Jay Erkenbrack, right, "is running the corker." Partner Lori Gordon looks on.

New products have been added to the company's roster regularly since the label was launched. The Winery, which was started with fifteen wines in 1995, is said by Lori to be the most fun part of the business. There are plans to introduce elderberry, lingonberry, and strawberry wines. The company also markets wild rice (both hand-harvested lake rice and cultivated rice), maple syrup, and flavored honeys. Not to be outdone by regional entrepreneurs in the southwest and California, Jay and Lori have started making berry salsas and berry salad dressings too. There's also a line of prepared mixes, including one for bannock, the old-time griddle bread.

Minnestalgia products can be found throughout the state in supermarkets, food co-ops, and gift shops, at the Mall of America and the Minneapolis-St. Paul International Airport. Travelers in the McGregor area can visit the Minnestalgia store and buy products direct. Their gift boxes are an ideal Minnesota-pride gift, particularly when the recipient is a former resident.

Our state is filled with wild things! Just as wild rice is the state grain, so morels are the state mushroom. May is the time to find them. A woods that contains dead elm trees is the place to find them. But you have to be very careful, and know just how and where to look to find the tree-shaped fungi, which have been described as "sponge on a stalk." I know of a St. Peter husband and wife who hunt together in the woods on the their farm; he sees nary a morel, she fills a basket with them. They're delectable washed, dried, halved, and cooked in butter. For information, go to www.morels.com.

These recipes are from my home test kitchen and show off the unique flavors of the jellies, syrups, and wines.

3 ounces cream cheese, softened, *or* 4 ounces (½ of an 8-ounce container) whipped cream cheese

1 to 2 tablespoons Minnestalgia berry jelly (your choice of the seven flavors)

WILD FRUIT BAGEL SPREAD

A smart way to use up the last jelly in the bottom of the jar. I made the spread with wild plum jelly and it was a pretty pink color with intriguing flavor. This spread also works as a filling for sandwich cookies made of vanilla wafers or gingersnaps.

Place cream cheese in a small bowl. Put the jelly into a custard cup and heat in the microwave oven until melted. Pour the jelly into the cream cheese and whip together with a wire whisk. Serve as a spread for toasted bagels for breakfast or brunch. Cover and refrigerate any remaining spread.

Vanilla ice cream or ice milk
or vanilla frozen yogurt
Fresh berries in season,
washed and picked over
Minnestalgia berry syrup of
your choice

DOUBLE BERRY SUNDAES

The variations of this idea are limited only by your imagination. I plan to try orange sherbet or orange sorbet with blueberries and one of the syrups next.

Place small scoops of ice cream in pretty glass dessert dishes, so that you can enjoy the colors of the fruit and syrup. Cover ice cream with a generous portion of fresh berries—if using large strawberries, cut them up. Carefully pour syrup over fruit and ice cream.

Fresh raspberries with black currant syrup is a good combination, so is fresh blueberries with chokecherry syrup. And when fresh peaches are available, the combination of diced peaches atop the ice cream with blueberry syrup is unbeatable.

---

1 tablespoon butter
⅓ cup Minnestalgia berry jelly
Juice of ½ lemon
Dash of cayenne pepper
½ cup water
3 whole cloves
½ teaspoon salt
½ cup Minnestalgia wine

WILD FRUIT WINE SAUCE
FOR WILD GAME
MAKES 1 ¼ CUPS, ABOUT 5 SERVINGS

Adapted from a basic recipe in a favorite reference, The Culinary Arts Institute Encyclopedic Cookbook.

Simmer butter, jelly, lemon juice, pepper, water, cloves, and salt together 5 minutes. Strain through a fine sieve to remove the

cloves. Stir in wine. Keep warm over very low heat. Serve with roast venison or roast wild duck.

Ice
Minnestalgia chilled berry
wine or honeywine
Slices of fresh ripe limes

SUMMERTIME WINE COOLER

A simple, and simply delicious, drink. Made with Minnestalgia fruit blush wine, it reminded me of Spanish sangria.

Fill wine glasses with ice. Pour wine to cover ice. Float a couple of lime slices in the drink, adding a subtle lime flavor to the wine.

Variation: Fill glasses only half full of ice. Pour wine over ice to half-fill glass. Finish filling glass with chilled sparkling water.

17 SCHWAN'S ICE CREAM

A SWEET STORY

"Schwan's? Why, it's the best ice cream in the world!" This from my neighbor Beth, who grew up on a farm near Dawson, Minnesota. Her mother always kept Schwan's ice cream on hand for drop-in visits from friends and family.

"Schwan's? Oh, yes, Schwan's was a standby at our house," says Geri, a friend who grew up in North Dakota. "Mom had seven kids to feed, and Schwan's products saved her many a trip to town."

"Schwan's? The Schwan's man came to our rescue one time when my son and I went to visit my mother," says Carolyn, another neighbor. "We got to my mother's in Plato about five o'clock. Would you believe, the Schwan's truck pulled up and everybody in her apartment complex came out to get their favorites? We got chicken breasts, vegetables, and, of course, ice cream. It worked out so well."

The Schwan Food Company, headquartered in Marshall, is a true Minnesota success story. The man behind that success is the late Marvin Schwan. (His father, Paul Schwan, was a German immigrant, who, in earlier

The late Marvin Schwan, founder of the Marshall-based food empire, in 1954.

years, had taken milk door-to-door in a horse-drawn wagon.) March 18, 1952, Marvin loaded his 1946 Dodge panel van with fourteen gallons of ice cream and headed out to the country. The ice cream sold to farm families in short order, and he knew he had a good idea.

Schwan's Home Service started small with one truck selling cartons of Schwan's "Delicious Ice Cream" in southwestern Minnesota. That number had grown to over 2,000 vehicles selling all over the United States at the time of Marvin's death in 1993, and today more than 6,000 of the company's distinctive yellow trucks carry the company's name to approximately 5 million homes across America.

By 1962, Schwan's salespeople were also offering frozen fish. Vita-Sun drink concentrates were added in 1965. The buy-at-home concept snowballed. Despite a flood in Marshall in 1957 and a devastating fire in their plant in 1974, Schwan's kept building and growing. By 2002, the company was marketing over 300 frozen food items including pizza, soups, ice cream novelties, meats, and Asian and Mexican specialties.

With Schwan's Home Service offering so many frozen items, it was only natural that customers would start putting them together in creative dishes. In 1994, the company launched Schwan's Great Recipe Roundup, a contest for recipes using their products as part of the ingredients. Attractive cash prizes—$1,000 for runners-up and $5,000 for top prizes—were offered.

Alfred Schwan (Marvin's brother), then the company's chairman and CEO, called the response to the contest "overwhelming." Recipes poured in from all over the country. After much testing and tasting, winners were chosen and two recipes were picked to be featured in a hardcover cookbook called *Schwan's Family Favorites—The Best of the Roundup* in 1995. It includes company history and winners' photos and comments along with the recipes.

When this ad appeared back in 1958, Schwan's ice cream offerings included old-time flavors such as plum and grape.

But the ice cream trucks that became frozen food stores on wheels are only half of Schwan's story. By the mid-1960s, Marvin Schwan was ready to branch out. In 1966, the company sold its first frozen pizza, and soon Marvin placed a small ad in the *Wall Street Journal:* "Wanted—One pizza plant." The company found such a plant in Salina, Kansas. As my neighbor Beth says, "Ice cream is the perfect dessert after pizza."

Ours is a nation of pizza lovers, and the huge potential prompted the company to enter the retail market. First came Tony's Pizza (1970), then Red Baron and, more recently, Freschetta. Today, the Salina plant is the world's largest pizza manufacturing facility and has been joined by Schwan pizza factories in Florence, Kentucky; Leyland, England; and Magdeburg, Germany.

The Red Baron pizza brand and its fleet of graceful World War II-era biplanes generate good press for the company. The Red Baron Squadron flies both two-ship and four-ship shows as America's most popular civilian airshow act. A daylong air show featuring famous planes and aerobatic maneuvers was one feature of the ten-day Schwan's Fiftieth Anniversary Festival held in Marshall during July 2002. Other festivities included a 200-unit parade, big-name entertainment every night, art shows, and an ice cream-sandwich-eating contest and free cake and ice cream downtown on the day of the parade. Folks in town for the anniversary also toured the new Schwan Museum.

Farm and city kids alike raced home when they saw the Schwan's truck delivering their favorite—ice cream!

Here is just a sampling of the quick and easy customer recipes featured in *Schwan's Family Favorites*.

EASY ELEGANCE ORANGE CREAM PIE

MAKES 6 TO 8 SERVINGS

4 cups Schwan's premium
   vanilla ice cream
6 ounces (from 8-ounce
   carton) Schwan's orange
   juice concentrate
3 tablespoons orange liqueur,
   such as Grand Marnier or
   Triple Sec
1 (8-ounce) prepared pie crust
   or graham cracker crust
Chocolate syrup
Fresh mint sprigs

This recipe won an Oregon customer $5,000 in Schwan's Great Recipe Roundup. Rather than buy a little packet of mint sprigs at the supermarket, I purchased a live mint plant for my windowsill so that I could have mint leaves handy for garnishes all year long.

Slightly soften ice cream. In food processor or with mixer, combine ice cream and orange juice concentrate; add liqueur. Spoon mixture onto crust. Drizzle chocolate syrup over pie before freezing or wait and drizzle syrup over wedges of pie before serving. Freeze 2 hours, or until firm. Let stand 5 to 10 minutes before cutting. Garnish with mint sprigs. Freeze leftovers.

AMBER'S DELIGHT

MAKES 12 TO 15 SERVINGS

1 (20-ounce) can crushed
   pineapple, drained
1 (16-ounce) can whole
   cranberry sauce
1 (14-ounce) can sweetened
   condensed milk
½ cup chopped walnuts or
   pecans
¼ cup bottled lemon juice
2 cups Schwan's premium
   vanilla ice cream, softened
1 (8-ounce) carton whipped
   topping, thawed

One taster describes this do-ahead treat as "scrumptious." A South Dakota cook entered this pink-and-pretty dessert in Schwan's contest. Rather than using one big oblong pan, I divided the mixture into four freezer containers so that I could share the cool treat with three friends.

In medium bowl, mix together pineapple, cranberry sauce, condensed milk, nuts, and lemon juice. Stir until well mixed; set aside.

In large bowl, combine ice cream and whipped topping. Gently fold fruit mixture into ice cream mixture. Pour into 13 x 9-inch pan. Freeze 2 hours or until firm. Remove from freezer 5 minutes before serving. Freeze leftovers.

1 pound Blue Hake prime cut
  loins
½ cup sour cream
1 tablespoon lemon juice
1 tablespoon milk
¾ cup finely crushed corn
  chips
2 tablespoons butter or
  margarine, melted
Shredded cheese
Shredded lettuce
Salsa, if desired

SOUTH OF THE BORDER
FISH BAKE

MAKES 3 TO 4 SERVINGS

Minnesota's Ardelle Peka received $1,000 in the Recipe Roundup with this colorful main dish.

Preheat oven to 400°F. Place foil in 13 x 9-inch baking pan; grease foil, set aside.

Cut frozen fish into serving-size pieces. Combine sour cream, lemon juice, and milk in a shallow dish; put crushed corn chips in another. Dip fish in sour cream mixture and then into chips; place in prepared pan. Drizzle with melted butter.

Bake for 15 to 20 minutes or until fish flakes easily with a fork. Serve topped with cheese and lettuce, and, if desired, salsa.

2 cups (12 ounces) Schwan's
  diced chicken meat, thawed
1 garlic clove, minced
2 tablespoons lemon juice
1 ½ teaspoons chili powder
½ teaspoon salt
1 large ripe avocado, peeled,
  pitted, and chopped
½ pint (about 10) cherry
  tomatoes, cut in half
¼ cup chopped red onion
½ cup sour cream
Shredded lettuce

CHILI-CHICKEN SALAD

MAKES 4 (1-CUP) SERVINGS

A $1,000 winner by an Iowa cook. Schwan's provides the cooked and diced chicken, you add seasonings, vegetables, and sour cream, then toss.

In large bowl, combine thawed chicken, minced garlic, lemon juice, chili powder, salt, cut-up avocado, cherry tomato halves, chopped onion, and sour cream; toss gently. Serve on plates over lettuce.

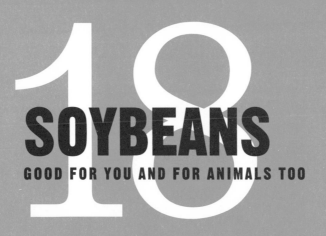

18 SOYBEANS
GOOD FOR YOU AND FOR ANIMALS TOO

Soybeans can be beautiful. Soybean plants, with their deep green leaves, are covered with small flowers. "Yes, they're beautiful," says Barb Overlie, partner with husband Don in a 220-acre bean-and-corn farm in Blue Earth County near Lake Crystal.

The clear, golden oil pressed from soybeans is beautiful too. I had the good fortune to see it come whirling out of the crusher at a soybean plant in Dawson, Minnesota, during my *Star Tribune* days.

The Midwest, with its rich soil and reliable rains, is ideal for growing the little beans. Iowa is the leading soy-producing state with Illinois running second and Minnesota third. Farmers like the Overlies produced a U.S. average of 283 million-plus bushels of soybeans during the 1999–2001 crop years. At sixty pounds of beans per bushel that's a mountain of beans.

"We plant 50–50 beans and corn," says Don Overlie. "Started planting soybeans in the late 1940s. They were a new crop then. Beans are cheaper to plant than corn, and they're less costly to harvest too." He rotates the two high-demand crops for continued fertility of his land.

The couple work together during the harvest of the beans with Barb, a former teacher, driving the grain truck. "The whole vine goes into the combine," she explains. "The machine saves the beans and returns the stems and leaves all chopped, ready to use as mulch. A beautiful mulch."

The Overlies' beans go to the Lake Crystal elevator, then to the Honeymead plant in Mankato to be processed. There the beans are crushed to produce soy meal and soy oil. The high-protein soy meal is typically used as feed for hogs and turkeys. "They say there are more hogs than people in Martin County (the county adjacent to Blue Earth) and those hogs eat a lot of soy meal," says Don.

This huge combine crosses a Minnesota field cutting the dried soybean plants, separating the nutrient-rich beans, and pouring them into the waiting truck.

Thanks to the nutrient density of the soybean and to extensive research of its properties, the little beans are widely used and the demand for them continues to grow. Farmers like the Overlies pay a one-half percent checkoff to the Minnesota Soybean Research and Promotion Council. Soybean oil (the bean is 17 percent fat) is used in many commercial salad dressings and sold bottled as vegetable oil. "I think they use soybean oil for those dressings because it's cheaper than those other oils," says Don. The fact that the oil contains no cholesterol and is unsaturated are selling points too. Soy oil is so mild it doesn't compete with other flavors—such as garlic or blue cheese—in a dressing. "And soy oil works well for frying," adds Barb.

Barb knows whereof she speaks. She works with soy foods as a volunteer with the Minnesota Soybean Growers Association, a group headquartered in Mankato. When she presents programs on soy foods in grade schools, Barb often opens the hour by asking, "How many of you like chocolate?" When hands are waving, she explains, "Did you know lots of chocolate is made with a soy product called lecithin? It makes the chocolate smooth; it's called an emulsifier." She shows the children a bottle of the clear, liquid lecithin and tells them that soy lecithin is also used in nonstick vegetable sprays. "Lecithin makes it slick," she explains. She also talks about soy sauce, soy nuts (roasted soybeans), tofu (soybean cake), and other edible forms of the little bean.

"I figure I talk to about one thousand kids a year," says Barb, who thinks nothing of presenting five 45-minute classes in a row. To bring the bean fields into the inner city schools, she made a fifteen-minute video of Don at work in the bean field, planting and harvesting. "That way, kids who have never been on a farm can see the beans growing and see the equipment—a huge combine—we use."

With adult audiences, she stresses the health benefits of soy. For example, soy is widely used as an inexpensive protein source (the beans are 34 percent protein) in commercial drink mixes, such as Ensure. When Barb demonstrates soy recipes to groups of homemakers or seniors, she recommends selecting a soy food, such as tofu, and adding it to family favorites.

Her wide knowledge of tofu led to Barb's role as a soy spokesperson. She had taught in Japan and was familiar with tofu when it was introduced in this country in the 1980s. "The Japanese eat it at every meal," she says. Here in Minnesota, she fried tofu and offered samples at an "Ag Day," an annual one-day gathering of farmers for education and camaraderie. Soon she was dubbed "The Food Lady," and became a regular presenter at the meetings of soybean growers, demonstrating and answering questions about soy foods. Now her cupboards bulge with soy products and her notebooks bulge with notes on how to get more soy into the American diet.

The couple got a sneak preview of a new soy milk being introduced by General Mills, thanks to a niece who works at the company. It's called Eighth Continent Soy Milk, and Barb rates the flavor excellent. She thinks the vanilla flavor of this new milk will work well in cooked and instant puddings.

When we met, Barb Overlie was packing her bags for a trip to St. Petersburg, Russia, via Istanbul, Turkey. She was accompanying Honeymead's representative on the trip. In Turkey they were to visit the plant producing a new flaked soy product, which will add needed protein to all sorts of foods. Then on to St. Petersburg for an international meeting on soy flour. Yes, Minnesota-grown beans have become part of a global soy market.

Here are but two of Barb Overlie's many recipes using soy foods, along with a variety of ideas for serving them.

Soybean pods, heavy with two or three beans each, cling to the drying stalk awaiting harvest.

TACO SALAD

1 cup textured vegetable protein (TVP)

1 ½ cups water, divided

1 ½ tablespoons Kitchen Bouquet

½ lb. regular ground beef

1 package taco seasoning mix

1 ¾ cups drained kidney beans (15-ounce can), optional

2 medium tomatoes, coarsely chopped

½ cup seeded, chopped green pepper

1 head lettuce, torn into bite-size pieces

1 cup (4 ounces) shredded cheddar cheese

1 (7 ½-ounce) package corn or tortilla chips, crushed

1 cup sour cream

This is ideal for a supper when you need to keep mealtime flexible. Make the beef-soy mixture, then chill ready to reheat; have all the accompaniments (lettuce, cheese, etc.) at hand so you can put the salad together quickly. I bought the TVP for this recipe at my local food coop.

Stir together textured vegetable protein (TVP), ¾ cup of the water, and Kitchen Bouquet. Set aside while TVP absorbs the water, about 15 minutes.

Meanwhile, brown the ground beef in a 10-inch skillet. Drain off excess fat. Stir taco seasoning and remaining water into beef in skillet. Cook 5 minutes. Add TVP mixture. Cook and stir another 5 minutes. If using kidney beans, stir them into hot meat mixture at this point. Remove from heat. Set aside.

To serve: Use large salad bowl, layering first lettuce, then heated beef mixture, then tomatoes; top with cheese. Arrange crushed chips all around the edge of the bowl. Guests scoop out portions of all ingredients, then garnish it with a dollop of sour cream.

Alternate serving plan: Set out lettuce, meat mixture, tomatoes, cheese, and chips in serving bowls so that diners can serve themselves.

PARTY-PERFECT STUFFED SHELLS

12-ounce package jumbo shell pasta

1 (10.5-ounce) package silken soft tofu, drained

3 cups shredded mozzarella cheese, divided

½ cup shredded Parmesan cheese

2 eggs

1 teaspoon dried parsley or 1 tablespoon snipped fresh parsley

½ teaspoon seasoned salt

½ teaspoon garlic powder

½ teaspoon ground black pepper

3 ¼ cups spaghetti sauce, homemade or commercial (26-ounce jar), preferably meatless

8-ounce can tomato sauce

3 teaspoons fennel seed

After baking for almost an hour, these delicious shells will stay hot for another hour, so they're ideal for a buffet or a potluck.

Preheat oven to 350°F. Cook the pasta just half the time directed on the package. Drain and set aside.

Prepare stuffing: Mash the tofu and combine it with 2 cups of the mozzarella cheese, egg, parsley, seasoned salt, garlic powder, and pepper. Mix thoroughly.

Stir together spaghetti sauce, tomato sauce, and 2 teaspoons of the fennel seed in saucepan. Heat through.

Spread 1 cup spaghetti sauce evenly in a 13 x 9-inch pan. Stuff the pasta shells with the tofu-cheese mixture using about 1 heaping tablespoon of filling in each shell. Arrange stuffed pasta in single layer in prepared pan—the pan will be chockfull. Cover with the rest of the sauce. Sprinkle with remaining cheese and fennel seed.

Bake for 45 to 60 minutes or until bubbling.

SOY ADD-INS FOR FAVORITE FOODS

SOY NUTS

- Substitute for peanuts in sweet treats such as microwave-made peanut brittle.
- Open a tube of refrigerated chocolate chip or oatmeal raisin cookie dough into a bowl and work in soy nuts, as many as you think the dough can hold. Bake as directed.
- Toss into homemade or commercial snack mixes such as Chex Mix.

SOY FLOUR

- Replace 1 tablespoon per cup of all-purpose or bread flour with 1 tablespoon soy flour when making yeast bread by hand or in the bread machine.

TOFU

- Substitute for ricotta cheese in homemade lasagna.
- Substitute for cream cheese or sour cream in making dips.
- Freeze the block, then cube the frozen tofu and squeeze out excess water, then flavor with soy sauce and add to stir-fries in place of meat.

TEXTURED VEGETABLE PROTEIN

- Soak in water, then mix 50–50 with ground beef when making meat loaf or spaghetti sauce; add Kitchen Bouquet for beefy color.

SWEET SOYBEANS (may be labeled edamane)

- Thaw and stir-fry with cut-up vegetables such as broccoli, bok choy, carrots and mushrooms for a filling lunch.
- Add to pasta salad (from the deli or a package mix).

19

SPAM

NOTHING SHORT OF A PHENOMENON

SPAM luncheon meat, produced by Hormel Foods in Austin, Minnesota, is sold in thirty-five countries and known all over the world. It's manufactured all over the world, too, in five plants in four countries. Total sales of those familiar oblong cans with the rounded ends topped $6 billion in July 2002.

Two uniformed women check cans of SPAM Luncheon Meat coming off the production line in the late 1930s.

The famous pink meat is featured in a slick museum, a stack of cookbooks, and a busy Web site, plus a book of poetry. Not bad for a product created in 1937 to use up leftovers—an oversupply of pork shoulder meat. Jay Hormel, son and heir of company founder George Hormel, put together the mixture of chopped pork, ham, and spices. Its catchy name, dreamed up by the actor brother of a Hormel executive, helped make it an immediate hit. Its reasonable price and infinite shelf life were added attractions.

Early advertisements touted the pink meat for breakfast, lunch, dinner, and snacks. Cooks were told "Slice It, Dice It, Fry It, Bake It." They did all that and more. They sauced it (with cheese), tossed it (with salads), even kabobed it (with pineapple).

World War II made SPAM a household word. On the home front, where the demand for SPAM sometimes exceeded the supply, cooks stretched it by chopping it for casseroles and sandwich fillings. It became a lend-lease staple because it was filling, nutritious, and would keep without refrigeration. Much food was among the $50 billion worth of goods the United States supplied to nations whose defense was vital to us. Uncle Sam sent 100 million pounds of SPAM to feed American, European, and Russian troops. Back home after the war, some G.I.'s would never look at the stuff again.

One Brit who remembers SPAM is Margaret Thatcher, former British Prime Minister. The time was Christmas 1943 and Margaret, then 18, and her

Welcome to SPAMVILLE, established Dec. 8, 1942, by the U.S. Air Force, population 225. SPAM, which needed no refrigeration, nourished millions of soldiers, airmen, and seamen.

family lived in their grocery store. Wartime austerity and rationing meant a limited diet. But on Boxing Day (the day after Christmas), her family had friends in and served SPAM and salad.

In 1966, former president Dwight D. Eisenhower, then retired to Gettysburg, wrote Hormel a congratulatory letter when the company turned seventy-five. "During World War II, of course, I ate my share of SPAM along with millions of other soldiers . . . As former Commander in Chief, I believe I can still officially forgive you your only sin: sending us so much of it."

From the day it was created, SPAM has been marketed constantly and cleverly. Early magazine ads depicted real-life situations; for example, a mother wonders what to cook and her family asks for SPAM Bake (the loaf straight from the can is baked in the oven). Hormel's colorful ads usually included easy recipes, dishes you could make quickly if you had that all-important can in the cupboard. You can now buy it in over 99 percent of U.S. grocery stores. In 1962, a 7-ounce can, for singles and small families, joined the original 12-ounce can on the shelf.

Hawaiians love SPAM, using it in traditional Polynesian foods. Honolulu tops U.S. cities in SPAM consumption. Four cities of the South follow on the

Here's an early SPAM ad from Hormel's "Cold or Hot, SPAM Hits the Spot!" campaign.

SPAM consumption chart: #2: Little Rock; #3: Memphis; #4: Birmingham; and #5: Charlotte.

SPAM special events and celebrity moments abound. SPAM recipe contests, held annually at many state fairs, yield sheaves of original (sometimes far-out) recipes. One cook turned it into "cupcakes"—this idea, a SPAM recipe contest winner, was savory, not sweet, I should add. The Maui mall holds an annual SPAM Cook-Off; then there's the SPAM-orama barbecue contest in Austin, Texas. When Seattle held a SPAM carving contest in 1990, SPAM-henge, a replica of Stonehenge, won the prize.

SPAM fan T. Graham Brown, a country western singer, has been known to wear a SPAM key on a chain around his neck when he performs. Senator Robert Byrd of West Virginia is said to order, "SPAM on white" for lunch three times a week.

Making fun of SPAM, begun in World War II, never stops. Telling stories about the luncheon meat *is* the program at meetings of SPAM fan clubs. And now the clubs have their mecca, the SPAM museum in Austin, Minnesota, where the self-guided tour starts at the Wall of SPAM: nearly 3,500 cans row on row, two stories high in the entry hall. As you tour, you follow the luncheon meat's success via film clips, interactive displays, and old ads. At the Chez SPAM exhibit, there are exotic recipes from famous chefs. The museum, which opened quietly in fall 2001, opened officially in June 2002. Marion Ross of *Happy Days* and other famous moms were on hand. The museum is a popular site for bus tours.

Fans meet online, too, using the countless SPAM Web sites, some unofficial. John Nagamichi Cho, set up a SPAM haiku archive on the Web, inviting fans to submit poems written in the seventeen-syllable haiku form: five syllables in the first line, seven in the second, five more in the third. Long used by the Japanese, haiku proved a great way to talk SPAM. Cho published a selection of the poems titled *SPAM-KU, Tranquil Reflections on Luncheon Loaf* in 1998. It was *the* trendy holiday gift that year.

Variants of the luncheon meat come and go. SPAM Lite (part chicken for fewer calories) seems to sell well. So does SPAM Smoke Flavored, a substitute for sausage that won't spoil. After Hormel acquired Jennie-O Turkey Store's massive turkey operation, it came out with SPAM Oven Roasted Turkey. I always have a can of SPAM in my storm-ready "blizzard box," right next to a package of pasta and a can of cream-of-something soup—so I can put together a comforting casserole amid a storm.

SPAM

C H R O N O L O G Y

SPANS THE DECADES

1937	SPAM luncheon meat born in Austin, Minnesota. Named by Kenneth Daigneau, who won $100 for his effort. Combination of chopped pork shoulder and ham. Originally called Hormel Spiced Ham. Developed by Jay C. Hormel, son of George A. Hormel, who had founded the company in 1891.
1940	Spammy the pig, SPAM's mascot, appears with George Burns and Gracie Allen on their hit radio show. Hormel airs the first singing commercial: Spammy lyrics sung to the tune of "Bring Back My Bonnie to Me."
1941–45	SPAM feeds Allied troops, winning many fans.
1950	60-member Hormel Girls troupe, formed in the late 1940s, performs around the country, distributing samples of products and doing a Sunday night radio show.
1957	Agreements made to sell SPAM in Ireland, Canada, England and Venezuela. By 2001 SPAM trademark is registered in 93 countries.
1959	One billionth can of SPAM produced.
1964	New hydrostatic cooker allows one operator to produce 350 cans of SPAM per minute.
1970	Second billionth can produced. SPAM debuts on television with a Monty Python Flying Circus sketch in which the Green Midget Café serves the luncheon meat with eggs all sorts of ways.
1971	Smoke-flavored SPAM introduced.
1980	SPAM reaches 4 billion mark, just six years after the 3 billionth can. SPAM Less Sodium put on the market.
1987	50 years old and going strong.
1992	SPAM Lite hits supermarket shelves.
1994	5 billionth can produced.
1998	New SPAM look: a gold can, a new label. New SPAM book: *SPAM-KU* by John Nagamichi Cho.
2001	SPAM Museum opens in Austin.
2002	6 billionth can shipped.

Try these good and easy ways to serve the world-famous luncheon meat.

SPAMBURGERS

MAKES 6 SERVINGS

1 (12-ounce) can SPAM
  Luncheon Meat
6 hamburger buns, split
3 tablespoons mayonnaise
6 lettuce leaves
6 (⅔- or ¾-ounce) slices
  American cheese
2 tomatoes, sliced

A standard for Super Bowl buffets. Especially good with toasted buns.

Slice SPAM lengthwise into 6 equal slices. In a large skillet, fry SPAM until lightly browned. Spread mayonnaise equally on buns. Layer ingredients on bun bottoms as follows: lettuce, SPAM, cheese, tomato. Cover with bun tops.

ROBERT MOULTON'S SPAM 'N KRAUT SOUP

MAKES 8 GENEROUS SERVINGS

2 slices Hormel bacon
1 (12-ounce) can SPAM or
  SPAM Lite Luncheon Meat
1 cup diced onions
1 cup chopped celery
1 cup coarsely grated carrots
1 (16-ounce) can sauerkraut
1 large clove garlic
8 cups chicken broth (8 cups
  water plus 8 teaspoons
  chicken bouillon granules)
2 tablespoons tomato paste
2 teaspoons caraway seeds
½ teaspoon dried oregano
1 bay leaf
6 peppercorns
1 cup plain yogurt
2 tablespoons chopped
  parsley

The $50 second place winner in the 1992 SPAM recipe contest at the Minnesota State Fair. A wonderful old-fashioned soup to brew on a cold or rainy evening.

In large heavy frying pan, cook bacon until crisp. Remove from pan and blot on paper towels.

Slice SPAM; brown in the bacon drippings. Remove from pan. Cut into bite-size pieces; set aside with bacon.

Add onions and celery to remaining drippings and brown 5 minutes over medium heat. Add carrots, kraut, and garlic; cook 5 minutes.

Heat broth in soup kettle. Add tomato paste, caraway seeds, oregano, bay leaf, and peppercorns. Add vegetable mixture and crumbled bacon. Cook over low heat 30 minutes. Add SPAM and cook 15 minutes more. At this point, soup may be refrigerated up to two days or frozen and then reheated.

Serve hot in bowl with a dollop of the mixed yogurt and parsley.

SPAM-FILLED BUNS

1 (12-ounce) can SPAM Luncheon Meat, cubed

1 cup cubed pasteurized process cheese food, such as Velveeta

3 to 4 hard-cooked eggs, shelled and chopped

1 tablespoon chopped sweet pickle

2 tablespoons chopped onion, optional

2 tablespoons chopped green pepper, optional

½ to 1 cup mayonnaise

8 hamburger or hot dog buns

When my Star Tribune *colleague Mary Hart (a.k.a. Mary Engelhart Sorenson) requested a SPAM-n-cheese-filled sandwich in her popular "Ask Mary" column, she got nearly one hundred replies. Among the fun names for individual versions of the recipe were Bumsteads, Silver Dogs, Powwow Buns, Night Owls. Amounts of ingredients varied but the basic idea was pretty much the same.*

Preheat oven to 350°F. Mix meat, cheese, eggs, pickles, onion, green pepper, and mayonnaise together. Spoon into buns. Wrap in foil. Bake for 12 to 15 minutes, or until hot and melty. Serve at once with ice-cold milk. Note: Wrapped filled sandwiches can be made ahead of time and chilled until ready to bake and serve.

MARION ROSS'S CHEESY MACARONI BAKE WITH SPAM

2 cups elbow macaroni

1 (12-ounce) can SPAM Luncheon Meat, diced

2 tablespoons butter or margarine, divided

1 tablespoon flour

¼ teaspoon salt

¼ teaspoon dry mustard

Pepper to taste

Dash of cayenne pepper

2 cups milk

½ pound pasteurized process American cheese food, diced

½ cup bread crumbs

⅛ teaspoon paprika

This recipe from the TV mom of Happy Days *fame was featured on the SPAM Web site when she appeared at the opening of the SPAM museum.*

Preheat oven to 400°F. Cook macaroni according to package directions; drain.

Combine SPAM with macaroni in greased 2-quart casserole. In medium saucepan, melt 1 tablespoon butter; blend in flour, salt, mustard, pepper, and cayenne until smooth. Stir in milk; cook over medium heat, stirring frequently until mixture thickens and boils. Add cheese; cook, stirring until cheese melts. Pour over SPAM mixture, mix well. Melt remaining butter, combine with bread crumbs and paprika; sprinkle over top.

Bake for 15 to 20 minutes, or until mixture is bubbling and crumb topping is golden.

20
GOBBLE, GOBBLE, GOBBLE
THE WHOLE WORLD EATS MINNESOTA TURKEY

Let's talk turkey. Minnesota turkey, of course. Let's start with turkey numbers. Minnesota is the number one turkey producer in the United States. In 2000, Minnesota raised 43.5 million turkeys. From those turkeys came approximately 971 million pounds of turkey meat. There are some 600 turkey farms in Minnesota. The top five turkey-producing counties are Kandiyohi, Morrison, Stearns, Becker, and Otter Tail. A typical Minnesota turkey farm raises 165,000 turkeys a year.

Minnesota is also home to the world's—yes, I said world's—largest turkey company: Jennie-O Turkey Store. The company, headquartered in Willmar, processes more than one billion pounds of turkey every year. Their turkey products are distributed throughout the United States and twenty-six other countries.

More than $223 million worth of turkey products were exported by the U.S. turkey industry in 2000, according to industry estimates. The top export market was Mexico, which imported nearly 224 million pounds of turkey. Russia, Hong Kong, Poland, and Canada followed Mexico in import volume.

Second, let's talk turkey growing. "We get our toms [male turkeys] from the hatchery when they are a few hours old," explains Dave Burkel, Jr., of Frazee, a fourth-generation turkey grower whom I met at a Minnesota Turkey Growers meeting. "We sell them when they are 22 weeks old and weigh about 40 pounds." Thus, this turkey farmer's life goes in 22-week cycles.

Turkeys are very curious birds, says Eric Jenkins, an English turkey expert also attending the growers' meeting.

Mrs. S. A. Topness of Fillmore County feeds one of her birds and its chicks in 1903, the early days of the state's flourishing turkey industry.

"They love to sunbathe by a window and they love to dust bathe." It's important to keep the barn regulated; they like it cooler rather than hotter. Raising turkeys is round-the-clock work. "We want to keep the birds comfortable. They're our livelihood," observes Paul Hanowski, a Swanville turkey farmer.

Turkeys are big eaters: to produce a 45-pound bird requires 2.4 to 3 pounds of feed per pound of finished meat. Their grain diet is two-thirds corn, one-third soy meal. No, turkeys don't eat constantly. Periods of rest follow periods of eating, says Paul.

A turkey by-product, the manure, is a cheap source of energy. In fact, turkey manure is running three power plants in England. In 2003, a similar plant is opening in Benson, the first of its kind in this country. It is expected to provide electricity to 55,000 homes, according to Eric Jenkins, who brought his expertise from England to Minnesota.

Third, let's talk turkey processing and marketing. Through the 1970s, turkey was considered a holiday entrée. Period. "Now, turkey parts, including ground turkey, and value-added products, such as marinated turkey tenderloin, are on the consumer's table every day, not just Thanksgiving and Christmas," says Jerry Jerome, CEO of the giant processor, Jennie-O Turkey Store. The Jerome family, led by his father Wally, who had been raising turkeys since 1922, was a major player in the turkey game, with headquarters in Barron, Wisconsin. Minnesota's major player was Willmar-based Jennie-O, run by Earl Olson, a legendary figure in the turkey world. The two companies were merged in 2002, by the Austin, Minnesota, parent company, Hormel Inc.

"We [Jerome Foods] decided to integrate the process, putting the raising of the birds, the processing, and the marketing into a continuum." This approach and the umbrella name they chose, Turkey Store, worked brilliantly. In the mid-80s, Turkey Store began offering fifteen to twenty value-added turkey products. They went into the marketplace with ground turkey, turkey slices, turkey breasts, and other parts, plus turkey sausages. The products took hold and sales have been growing ever since.

Health concerns about red meat and its marbling of fat were a factor in the quick consumer acceptance of low-fat turkey products. Ground turkey proved a healthful substitute for ground beef in the Midwest's beloved hot dishes. And the turkey breast, weighing 2 to 6 pounds, won popularity as an easily prepared stand-in for the whole bird. Thanks to other processed turkey items, including turkey ham and turkey pastrami, American annual turkey consumption jumped from 10 pounds per person in 1980 to 18 pounds in 1990. "We would love it see it go up another 10 pounds," says Jerry.

FOOD CAN COMFORT US

We all seek the solace of comfort foods. Foods that, according to one writer, bring "the satisfaction of a culinary hug." For some of us, comfort foods are what the British call "nursery foods." Things like mashed potatoes with lots of butter, rice pudding, even milk toast (hot milk poured over buttered toast). For others, it's foods that satisfy us for a long time (thanks to their fat content), such as crème brulée, blintzes topped with sour cream, or a hot beef sandwich.

Some of the comfort foods you'll find recipes for within these pages are Grandma Schumacher's Hash Browns (page 168), Beth Dooley's Chicken Pot Pie (page 187), Lynne Rosetto Kasper's Panna Cotta (page 214), and the Sweet Potato Pie included in "Rondo Days" (page 42).

Jennie-O Turkey Store has a corps of food scientists working on new products. These days they are focusing on food-service products. "Retail products are cooked at home, but home cooking is on the decline while food service is on the rise," says Jerry Jerome. "Nationally, it's about 50–50, with half the meats eaten out, and half cooked and eaten at home."

Marketplace Sandwiches offered at Arby's Restaurants nationwide are a recent success story for Jennie-O Turkey Store. "We worked closely with Arby's in developing those sandwiches, and they've been very successful," Jerry adds. In the works is the "two-bib rib." It's made of bone-in turkey thighs, which are trimmed to look like a pork rib, then precooked and barbecued. All the vendor would have to do is reheat it and hand out the bibs.

These recipes are from Marilyn McAlpine, Stillwater, longtime home economist with the Minnesota Turkey Research and Promotion Council.

ROAST TURKEY

You only need these directions once or twice a year—but then you really need them.

ROASTING TIMES

8 to 12 pounds	2¾ to 3 hours
12 to 14 pounds	3 to 3¾ hours
14 to 18 pounds	3¾ to 4¼ hours
18 to 20 pounds	4¼ to 4½ hours
20 to 24 pounds	4½ to 5 hours

Purchase 1 pound of uncooked turkey per person. If you like leftover turkey for sandwiches and casseroles, increase the total.

If it is a frozen turkey—and it probably is—thaw it in the refrigerator. Figure 24 hours thawing time for every 5 pounds of the whole turkey. If you learn about the 5-pounds-per-day rule too close to the cooking day (i.e. Thanksgiving), you can thaw the bird (still in its wrapping) in cold water at the rate of about 30 minutes per pound. You must change the cold water every 30 minutes.

Preheat oven to 325°F. Remove neck and giblets. Place the turkey breast-side-up on a rack in a shallow roasting pan. For best results, cook the stuffing outside the bird.

Be sure to wash hands, utensils, sink and anything else that has been in contact with the raw turkey with hot, soapy water.

Roast the unstuffed turkey, planning time according to the size of the bird.

Continue roasting until the meat thermometer, placed in the turkey thigh, reaches 180°F. The juices of the bird should be clear when the bird is pierced with a kitchen fork.

Let the turkey stand 20 minutes before carving. If desired, place a tent of aluminum foil over the bird to keep it warm during this standing time.

After carving and serving, within two hours of cooking, cut the turkey meat off the bone and refrigerate all leftovers in shallow containers. Use leftover turkey within 3 to 4 days, gravy within 1 to 2 days, or freeze for later use. To serve leftovers: reheat thoroughly to a temperature of 165°F, or until hot and steaming.

MINNESOTA WILD RICE STUFFING

⅔ cup uncooked wild rice (4 ounces)
½ pound turkey breakfast sausage
4 slices turkey bacon, cut into 1-inch pieces
1 cup chopped onion
1 cup chopped celery
½ pound fresh mushrooms, sliced
2 cups bread crumbs
1 teaspoon dried oregano
½ teaspoon dried sage
Salt and pepper, optional

Ahead of time: cook wild rice according to directions on page 125. Brown turkey sausage, breaking up chunks with a spoon.

Preheat oven to 325°F. In medium-size skillet over medium heat, fry bacon until almost crisp. Add onion, celery, and mushrooms; continue cooking until vegetables are tender. In large bowl combine the bacon mixture, wild rice, bread crumbs, sausage, oregano, and sage. Season to taste with salt and pepper. Spoon dressing into lightly greased 2-quart baking dish. Bake covered for 35 to 40 minutes, or until steaming hot.

BASIC TURKEY BURGERS

2 pounds ground turkey
1 (1-ounce) package dried onion soup mix
½ cup ketchup or tomato juice
2 teaspoons dry or prepared mustard
½ teaspoon ground pepper

Burgers made of turkey require a light touch. When forming into patties, don't make the burger too dense or compact. And don't press down on the meat while the burger is cooking. Take your pick of three cooking methods.

In a large bowl, combine turkey, soup mix, ketchup or tomato juice, mustard, and pepper. Shape into 8 patties about 4 inches in diameter. Cook as desired until internal temperature reaches 160 to 165°F and juices run clear. If possible, use a meat thermometer.

To grill: Remove grate from grill and coat with nonstick cooking spray; set aside. Prepare coals to medium-hot heat. Replace grate; place burgers on grate over hot coals. Grill about 5 to 6 minutes per side.

To cook on stove top: Coat a large nonstick skillet with cooking spray. Cook burgers over medium-high heat 6 to 7 minutes per side.

To broil: Preheat broiler. Broil burgers on a rack of a two-part broiler pan 4 inches from heat for 5 to 6 minutes per side.

½ cup plain yogurt

1 tablespoon Dijon-style or brown mustard

2 teaspoons curry powder

¼ teaspoon salt

¼ teaspoon coarse ground pepper

1 pound smoked turkey breast, finely chopped

1 cup tart dried cherries

½ cup (4 ounces) carrots, shredded

½ cup finely chopped and seeded cucumber

¼ cup sliced green onion

TURKEY 'N FRUIT SANDWICH FILLING

ENOUGH FOR 4 SANDWICHES

I suggest using the popular dried cranberries (also called craisins) in this delicious salad sandwich, rather than the more expensive cherries.

Stir together yogurt, mustard, curry powder, salt, and pepper in a medium-size bowl. Gently stir in turkey, cherries, cucumber, and green onions. Use as a filling for pita bread halves or roll up in a flavored flour tortilla for a wrap sandwich. Or, revert to the ordinary, and make the sandwich of sliced bread, mayo, and lettuce.

2 egg whites

1 tablespoon water

½ cup seasoned bread crumbs

2 tablespoons grated Parmesan cheese

1 pound turkey breast slices or cutlet, ¼-inch thick

1 cup (15-ounce can) Italian tomato sauce*

1 cup (4 ounces) shredded mozzarella cheese

*Regular canned tomato sauce may be used; add 2 teaspoons bottled Italian seasoning.

TURKEY PARMIGIANA

MAKES 4 SERVINGS

This is an adaptation of the classic veal parmigiana.

Preheat oven to 400°F. Spray or grease a 15 x 10-inch jelly roll pan. Place egg whites and water in a shallow bowl and beat until frothy. Combine crumbs and Parmesan cheese in another shallow bowl. Dip turkey slices or cutlets into egg mixture, then into crumb mixture. Arrange coated pieces on greased pan. Bake 4 to 5 minutes.

Pour Italian tomato sauce evenly over turkey and top with mozzarella cheese. Bake 4 to 5 minutes or until sauce is heated and cheese is melted. Delicious served with spinach fettuccini or egg noodles.

21
WATKINS VANILLA
A FAVORITE FLAVOR, A FASHIONABLE SCENT

It was the Aztecs of Mexico who discovered the flavor we now call vanilla. They learned that the seedpods of a beautiful wild orchid could be processed to release a distinctive flavor. They used the seedpods as an aphrodisiac, an herbal medicine, and a sort of money. Then, in a stroke of genius, they added it to powdered cocoa beans, which had been thickened with corn and sweetened with honey. The result: *xocoatl,* the prized confection, chocolate. Their Spanish conquerors, who learned the process from the Aztecs about 1528, called the pods "*vaina.*"

News of this exotic flavoring spread across Europe. In 1602, the apothecary to Queen Elizabeth of England recommended that vanilla be used as a flavoring by itself (apart from the cocoa powder). Legend has it that good Queen Bess ate only foods flavored with vanilla during the last years of her life. Because growing the orchids and processing the pods was painstaking work, vanilla was costly.

Thomas Jefferson, having tasted vanilla in Paris while serving as U.S. minister to France from 1785 through 1789, requested the French begin shipping it to Virginia. Then, in 1841, a one-time slave named Edmund Albius, living on the French island of Reunion, devised a way of hand-pollinating the orchid that bore the vanilla bean. His skill meant that, for the first time, the valuable plants could be grown outside Mexico. Eventually vanilla plantations were started in other tropical places, among them Madagascar, Mauritius, Ceylon (now Sri Lanka), the Seychelles, French Indonesia (now Southeast Asia, including Vietnam and Laos), and parts of mainland Africa. With more of the orchids being grown, the price of the beans and the vanilla made from them gradually came within the budget of common folks.

Watkins handsome home office building was designed by noted Prairie School Architect George Washington Maher and opened in 1912.

In 1895, J. R. Watkins, a businessman in the river city of Winona, Minnesota, and founder of the J. R. Watkins Medical Company, sat down to choose some new products for his peddlers. They were selling his medical products, items from faraway places purchased through his brokers around the world—things like Hindu Pain Oil and Oriental Nerve Tonic. It is easy to picture Watkins, in a black frock coat, stroking his walrus mustache as he pondered what he might add to his peddlers' packs. Finally, he chose vanilla from Madagascar, cinnamon from Southeast Asia, and black pepper from India. They became the flavor trinity that helped make the "the Watkins man" a legend.

Unfortunately, J. R. Watkins died in 1911 and did not see his company become the largest direct-selling company in the world in 1915. Nor did he see his trinity of flavorings awarded the Grand Prix with Gold Medal at the International Exposition in Paris in 1928.

Touring his assigned territory by wagon (and later by car), the Watkins man, one of a fleet of direct-to-consumer salesmen for the company, brought neighborhood news right along with quality household products. Edibles like the popular "nectars" for making fruit-flavored drinks vied with medicinals—salves, ointments, and creams—for customer interest. As early as 1914 the Watkins

Employee Curt Heyer tends a machine carrying cinnamon tins on their way to being filled at the Watkins plant in Winona.

Company was operating training centers for the dealers. At one, the awning bore the motto: "The Welcome Visitor Brings the Store to Your Door."

Watkins had put his vanilla into the same bottle that was such a success with his red liniment, the company's first product. The tall, narrow, squared-off bottle had the word "Watkins" down the center and a line with the words "Trial Mark" across the bottle one-third of the way down. Customers could use the vanilla (or the liniment) down to this line and, if not satisfied, would get the full price back when the Watkins man returned. Introduced in the early days of the company, this was the first documented money-back guarantee. Watkins put his signature or his picture or both on all his products.

J. R. Watkins built a business empire, based in a magnificent building in Winona, and made his name a household word. At the time of his death, 2,500 dealers nationwide were selling the products.

The big three: Watkins vanilla, pepper, and cinnamon. The trio won gold medal honors at the 1928 International Exposition in Paris.

"Vanilla is the number one selling Watkins product," says Clem Birch, of Navarre. He and his wife Barb are Gold Executives—the top echelon—in the Watkins sales organization. Barb Birch and legions of other hard-working women have changed the job name from Watkins man to Watkins associate. The Birches sell the products but they also provide counsel to other sales associates whom they have recruited. Watkins dealers no longer have territories but sell to any and all, according to Birch.

Since the introduction of vanilla in 1895 through 2000, Watkins associates have sold 13.5 million gallons of vanilla, according to Clem. That's enough to fill 17 Olympic swimming pools or 213,000 bathtubs. (Wouldn't the bathroom smell yummy?) A month's supply of vanilla extract is made at one time at the Watkins headquarters in Winona, he says.

"There was a great hue and cry in the late 1990s when the company switched from glass bottles for the vanilla to plastic bottles," Clem continues. The weight and the breakability of the glass were the problem. Savings in shipping and breakage are huge, according to Clem. The new, lighter plastic bottle looks identical, of course. (Loyal users have been known to save the glass bottle and simply pour the contents of each new plastic bottle into the beloved old bottle.)

"Watkins always has two booths at the Minnesota State Fair," says Barb. "We know that from 220 to 250 bottles of vanilla will walk out the door each of the three days we sell at the Fair. Getting a bottle of Watkins vanilla at the Fair is a tradition in many families."

Though Watkins makes three vanillas, I buy the Double-Strength because it is both bake-proof and freeze-proof (that means the flavor stays through the baking and/or freezing of the recipe in which it is used). Clem and Barb Birch assert that no one ever goes back to supermarket vanilla after using Watkins, and that's true for me. The other Watkins vanillas are Pure Vanilla Extract, which by law contains 35 percent extract, and White Vanilla Flavor, the choice of professional bakers because it does not discolor foods such as wedding cakes.

Since 1978, Watkins has been owned by Irwin Jacobs, a well-known

Minnesota entrepreneur who bought the company out of bankruptcy. "I understand Jacobs had always wanted a family business," Clem says. "And he invested a lot in the company." Watkins now holds national conventions at which associates are introduced to new items, from Inferno Sauce (a spicy condiment used often for meats) to Invigorating Peppermint Foot Scrub. Mark Jacobs, Irwin's son, took over as Watkins president in 1996. The Birches have found Mark to be bright and a good listener, a man who empowers his representatives.

The Watkins catalog describes the 400-plus products available. The four product categories are gourmet specialty foods, health and nutrition, personal care, and earth-friendly care products (including detergents and disinfectants). At the Birches's cozy home, I got a look at the office, which also functions as their mini Watkins storeroom. The shelves are packed with their most popular items, the ones that customers call for in a panic or that are sent quickly upon request from a far-off associate.

The 2002 Watkins catalog devotes an entire page to vanilla personal care products. "Deliciously Enticing," is the headline. The introduction says: "Vanilla is one of the most fashionable scents on the market today." There's cologne, bubble bath, body lotion, and lip balm, all formulated with the famous Watkins vanilla.

I chuckled when I spotted, on the final page of the catalog, under the headline, "Pets are people, too" a product I'd never dreamt of: Vanilla Dog Bone (a twist of rawhide basted with the extract).

In 1994, Watkins published centennial cookbooks for each of its award-winning flavor trio: *Vanilla*, *Cinnamon*, and *Pepper*. The macaroons and salad are from the *Vanilla* volume. The others are from my own recipe collection.

MACAROONS

4 egg whites
⅔ cup granulated sugar
¼ cup all-purpose flour
Dash of salt
1 tablespoon Watkins Double-Strength Vanilla
2 cups shredded coconut
¼ teaspoon dried orange peel

Preheat oven to 325°F. Grease and flour two large baking sheets. If preferred, cover baking sheets with kitchen parchment paper.

In medium bowl, beat egg whites lightly. Add sugar, flour, salt, and vanilla. Stir in coconut and orange peel.

Drop dough by tablespoonfuls 2 inches apart onto prepared baking sheets. Place both baking sheets in preheated oven at the same time, using top and lower racks. Bake 13 to 17 minutes rotating sheets of cookies after 6 minutes. Bake until cookies are set and lightly browned. Remove cookies to wire rack to cool immediately.

BLANC MANGE

MAKES 4 SERVINGS

⅓ cup granulated sugar
3 tablespoons cornstarch
¼ teaspoon salt
2 ¼ cups milk
1 ½ teaspoons Watkins Double-Strength Vanilla

The name of this inexpensive dessert means "white food" in French and is pronounced "bla mahnge." Toddlers love it.

Mix the sugar, cornstarch, and salt in saucepan. Gradually stir in the milk. Cook over medium heat, stirring constantly, until mixture boils. Boil 1 minute. Remove from heat. Blend in the vanilla. Pour into small bowl, cover, and refrigerate. Serve it alone or topped with fresh fruit or whipped cream.

SEAFOOD SALAD WITH VANILLA MAYONNAISE

MAKES 6 SERVINGS

¾ pound medium-size shrimp, peeled and cooked
¾ pound imitation crabmeat, broken into bite-size pieces
1 cup cherry tomatoes, halved, or sweet grape tomatoes
½ cup sliced green onion
½ cup sliced celery
½ cup pecan halves
½ cup real mayonnaise
1 tsp. Watkins Parisienne or a Dijon-style mustard
2 tsp. Watkins Vanilla Extract
Salad greens

In a large bowl, combine shrimp, crabmeat, tomatoes, green onion, celery, and pecan halves. Toss seafood, vegetables, and pecans together. In small bowl, mix the mayonnaise, mustard, and vanilla. Pour over shrimp mixture; toss again. To serve, place greens on serving plates and top with salad.

1 cup granulated sugar
½ cup butter
½ cup half-and-half
1 teaspoon Watkins Vanilla
  Extract

VANILLA SAUCE

MAKES 1 ½ CUPS, ENOUGH FOR
4 TO 6 SERVINGS OF CAKE/DESSERT

Highly recommended over any cake or dessert; a great way to dress up cake that is a day or two old. Just reheat cake and top with sauce.

Combine sugar, butter, half-and-half, and vanilla in saucepan. Bring to a boil over medium heat, stirring constantly. Boil 4 minutes. Serve warm.

3 egg yolks
¼ cup granulated sugar
1 ¼ cups milk (part half-and-
  half is recommended)
2 teaspoons Watkins Vanilla
  Extract
1 tablespoon butter, optional

FRENCH-STYLE CUSTARD SAUCE

MAKES 1 ¼ CUPS, ABOUT 5 SERVINGS

Pretend you're a restaurant chef and use this to paint (drizzle back and forth across) a dessert plate, serving it under anything from warm gingerbread to an apple dumpling. Pass the rest in a pitcher so guests can use it to top their portions.

In small bowl, beat the eggs until thick—use your choice of rotary beater or electric mixer. Beat in the sugar. Heat the milk—the microwave oven works well for this. Transfer the egg mixture to a small heavy saucepan. While continuing to beat the mixture, pour the hot milk, a little at a time, into the egg mixture, continuing until well mixed. Place pan over medium-low heat. Cook, stirring constantly, until sauce coats the spoon. Remove pan from heat and stir in vanilla and, if using, butter. Serve warm or cold. May be made up to two days ahead and chilled, covered.

22 WILD RICE
MINNESOTA'S GRAIN OF CHOICE

People like wild rice. And so do deer. That fact became clear as we watch a red deer glide down a path and into the water on the shore of Lake Itasca in northern Minnesota. A state park naturalist points out the deer as we travel the lake in a tour boat. "It's found the perfect way to cool off on a warm day," she says. It's hot and muggy. "Look, it's eating some of the wild rice there at the shore." The tall grass with the grain heads at the top is thick along the shore. Enough stalks for a herd of deer.

This is the rice that the Ojibwe call *manoomin,* the grain they harvested for centuries before white people arrived, and they continue to harvest it today. In their calendar, the wild rice moon (August) comes right after the blueberry moon (July), which follows the strawberry moon (June).

The Ojibwe (also called Chippewa) people harvest the wild rice from Minnesota lakes and streams. After offering thanks to the gods, they bend the tall stalks over the side of the canoe and tap the grain heads with cedar sticks. The ripe grain falls into the canoe. Later the grain is placed in wide metal kettles and parched over the fire to crack the hulls. Next the grain goes into a depression in the ground where it is tramped to knock off the hulls. Finally, trays filled with rice are tossed up and down so that the hulls blow away. Another method, called winnowing, calls for holding a birch bark basket of rice high and pouring it into another basket, so that the chaff is blown away by the breeze.

The bags of rice were wrapped in skins and buried in the cool earth for

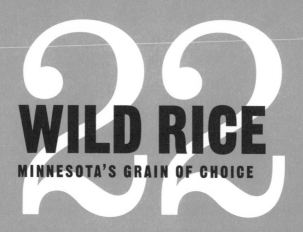

Wild rice was growing here—this is Tamarac Lake in Becker County, 1926—centuries before the area became Minnesota.

winter, reports Beth Anderson (now Erickson) in her *Wild Rice for All Seasons Cookbook*. (The book, with 150 recipes, has helped promote wild rice nationwide.)

Voyageurs and fur traders working in the area that is now Minnesota tasted the grain that the Indians had long enjoyed as part of their diet, which also included fish, game, and berries. These new immigrants liked the chewy texture and nutty flavor. And the rest, as they say, is history. Wild rice, though expensive to harvest, developed prestige. After World War II, it began to be served in upscale restaurants and in the homes of well-to-do gourmets. I remember paying $9 a pound for wild rice in the early 1950s, a time when a pound of ground beef cost about 45 cents. No wonder wild rice was often mixed with white or brown rice. And when a few grains spilled on the counter as I measured the wild rice while cooking in my own kitchen, I picked up every precious grain.

Also in the early 1950s, agricultural experts and wild rice marketers teamed up to launch wild rice cultivation in Minnesota. It required turning fields into paddies much like paddies used for growing white rice. It also required an investment in dikes and water systems plus modifying combines to harvest the rice.

This canoe is fitted with "knockers," sticks used to knock the wild rice from its stalks after bending them over the side of the boat.

The paddy plan succeeded. The unique grass flourished; the number of farms grew. Thanks to the increased production, wild rice prices fell, making it affordable for most consumers. Food writers touted the rice, not only for its distinctive texture and flavor, but also for its high fiber and complex carbohydrates. Manufacturers began adding a little of the grain to new convenience foods. The words "wild rice" in a product's name gave it gourmet cachet.

Though farmers in California are also producing paddy wild rice, the Minnesota industry is strong. In 2002, there were forty paddy rice farms in the state, according to Beth Nelson, president of the Minnesota Cultivated Wild Rice Council, based in St. Paul. The year 1999 proved a peak year, with 20,000 acres planted with wild rice producing 6.25 million pounds of finished rice. In 2000, 5.5 million pounds of rice were produced on 17,000 acres. Bad weather took its toll in 2001 when 17,500 acres yielded 4.4 million pounds. In contrast, the annual yield of hand-harvested rice, often called lake rice, is no more than 500,000 pounds.

Most people cannot distinguish hand-harvested rice from cultivated rice after both have been cooked. It's the processing methods that make the difference. Thus, wild rice grown in paddies will cook up the same as wild rice

- 1 cup uncooked wild rice = 3 to 4 cups cooked wild rice
- 1 pound wild rice measures about 2¾ cups
- Uncooked wild rice will keep up to ten years in an airtight container
- Cooked wild rice (plain) will keep six months in the freezer

Take your pick of these four easy methods for turning grains into chewy kernels.

On the Range Top: Bring 4 cups water or chicken broth to boiling in a heavy saucepan; stir in 1 cup wild rice. Simmer, covered, about 45 minutes or until tender but not mushy. Uncover; fluff with fork. Simmer 5 minutes. Drain if necessary.

In the Conventional Oven: Add 1 cup wild rice to 4 cups hot water or chicken broth in a casserole with lid. Bake, covered, at 350° for 1 hour. Check rice and add more water, if needed. Fluff with fork and bake another 20 minutes. Cooked rice should be moist.

In the Microwave Oven: Stir 1 cup wild rice into 4 cups hot water or chicken broth in a 4-quart baking dish; cover. Microwave on high setting 30 to 35 minutes, stirring every 10 minutes. Cook until rice is tender and grains have opened; let rice stand, covered, 15 minutes.

The Soaking Method: Add rice to 3 cups boiling water in saucepan. Parboil 5 minutes only. Remove from heat and let stand, covered, 1 hour or longer; drain. Complete cooking by boiling in salted water to cover 30 minutes, or until tender.

grown in lakes and rivers, providing both have been processed the same way. The grain will curl when it opens during cooking, and there's an aroma much like brewing tea. The opening process has also been called "blossoming" because the white interior blossoms from within the dark exterior. For consistent results, savvy cooks stick with the same cooking method and the same brand of wild rice, even if it means ordering the grain by mail. A fortunate few Minnesota families seek out hand-harvested rice as a way of preserving traditional Native American practices.

Wild rice is Minnesota's official state grain. By state law, wild rice that has been grown in paddies must be labeled "paddy" or "cultivated." Long popular in stuffings and casseroles and as an accompaniment to fish and game, wild rice is now equally popular in salads, stir-fries, and breads.

Many still practice traditional winnowing (as done by Jim Drift here in 1946).

BYERLY'S WILD RICE SOUP

6 tablespoons butter

1 tablespoon minced onion

½ cup flour

3 cups chicken broth

2 cups cooked wild rice (⅔ cup uncooked; see page 125)

⅓ cup minced ham

½ cup finely grated carrots

3 tablespoons chopped slivered almonds

½ tsp. salt

1 cup half-and-half (fat-free half-and-half works too)

2 tablespoons dry sherry, optional

An elegant soup created by the Byerly's chain of supermarkets, now part of Lund Food Holdings. You can buy this soup frozen but it's really easy to make at home. This is the most-requested recipe at the Wild Rice Council, sent to cooks all over the world.

Melt butter in saucepan; stir-fry onion until tender. Blend in flour; gradually add broth. Cook, stirring constantly, until mixture comes to a boil; boil 1 minute. Stir in rice, ham, carrots, almonds, and salt; simmer about 5 minutes. Blend in half-and-half. Add sherry, if using. Heat to serving temperature. Garnish, if desired, with minced parsley or chives.

WILD RICE BARON

2 cups wild rice, uncooked

6 cups water

2 pounds lean ground beef

1 pound fresh mushrooms

1 cup chopped onion

½ cup chopped celery

1 cup butter

¼ cup soy sauce

2 cups sour cream

2 teaspoons salt (or less)

¼ teaspoon ground pepper

½ cup slivered almonds

One of the top ten favorite recipes of Mary Hart. She featured it in her cookbook, Favorite Recipes, *published in 1979 and now a collector's item.*

Preheat oven to 350°F. Add wild rice to pot of boiling water. Return to boil; stir. Cover and simmer gently 45 minutes or until kernels just start to open. If you want the kernels to pop, simmer 1 hour. Drain rice if necessary.

Brown ground beef. Rinse briefly under cold running water and pat dry. Cut stems off mushrooms and slice caps. Stir-fry mushrooms with onion and celery in butter for 5 minutes.

Combine soy sauce, sour cream, salt, and pepper. Add cooked wild rice, browned beef, and onion mixture. Stir in about half the almonds. Place mixture in lightly greased 3-quart casserole.

Bake uncovered for 1 hour. Stir several times while baking. If mixture seems to be getting dry, stir in a little water. Garnish with reserved almonds.

1 ½ cups cooked wild rice
(½ cup uncooked)

⅓ to ½ cup brown sugar,
depending on taste

½ cup chopped dates

½ cup dried cranberries
(craisins)

½ cup golden raisins

¼ cup toasted chopped pecans

FANCY WILD RICE

MAKES 3 ½ CUPS, 6 TO 7 SERVINGS

This recipe is adapted from Wild Rice, Star of the North: 150 Minnesota Recipes for a Gourmet Grain, *published in 1986 by the 1006 Summit Avenue Society. 1006 Summit Avenue is the address of the Minnesota Governor's Mansion; the Society is a group devoted to raising funds for that stately home.*

Prepare recipe 2 to 3 hours ahead of time so that flavors can blend.

Combine wild rice, sugar, dates, cranberries, raisins and pecans. Cover and set aside until ready to serve. Serve as a topping for ice cream, ice milk (such as Dairy Queen soft-serve) or frozen yogurt. Also delicious served in small bowls and topped with real whipped cream.

---

1 cup uncooked wild rice

Water for cooking rice

½ cup sliced celery or
chopped portabello
mushrooms

½ cup sliced green onion
(1 bunch)

¼ cup chopped fresh parsley

1 cup dried cranberries, such
as craisins

⅔ cup cranberry juice

¼ cup white wine vinegar or
cider vinegar

¼ cup olive oil or other
vegetable oil

½ cup chopped pecans

CHIPPEWA WILD RICE SALAD

MAKES 8 SERVINGS

Cook rice according to one of the methods on page 125. In large bowl, combine cooked wild rice (3+ cups), celery, onion, parsley, cranberries, cranberry juice, vinegar, and oil; refrigerate. Just before serving, stir in pecans.

MEMORABLE PLACES

130 The American
    Swedish Institute:
    Mansion Museum
    Preserves Culture

135 BC Gardens—
    Woman-Powered and
    Community-
    Supported

141 Carlson's Apple
    Orchard and
    Bakery—Minnesota
    Apples Everywhere

147 Forest History
    Center—One Last
    Lumber Camp

151 Fine Food at
    Kavanaugh's Sylvan
    Lake Resort

157 Summer Fun—and a
    New Language Too

163 Schumacher's Hotel
    in the Heart of New
    Prague

169 Ironworld—How to
    Tour the Iron Range
    in Two Easy Hours

23
THE AMERICAN SWEDISH INSTITUTE
MANSION MUSEUM PRESERVES CULTURE

Over a million immigrants from Sweden—entire boatloads—came to this country between 1860 and 1910. Large numbers of them came to Minnesota, which so closely resembled their native land.

Among those immigrants was Swan J. Turnblad, just eight years old in 1868. Turnblad grew up to publish a national Swedish-language newspaper and made himself a millionaire. This cultured man was a marketing genius long before the phrase was coined.

In 1904, work began on his French chateauesque home at the corner of Park Avenue and 26th Street in fashionable south Minneapolis. The building took four years to build, thanks to its size—thirty-three rooms—and elaborately carved woodwork throughout. By 1908, the imposing place, topped by five chimneys and three turrets, was ready for Turnblad and his family to move in. Then in 1929, the family founded the American Swedish Institute and turned the mansion into its museum and cultural center.

This is the place that newcomers to Minnesota come to learn about their Swedish roots and get acquainted with others interested in Swedish culture. And the learning and the friendships flourish over Swedish food served, of course, with rich coffee. Whenever you visit the institute, there's usually something delicious to eat. After you tour the house—the dining room with its intricate woodwork, the eleven colorful porcelain tile stoves—head for the *Kaffestuga* (coffee shop) for sugar-crusted pastries.

The American Swedish Institute.

On Wednesdays, the museum's open evening, the *Kaffestuga* offers soup and sandwiches in cold weather, sandwiches and salads in summer. If time permits, visitors browse in the museum shop with its array of imports, crispbread and chocolate among them. And the *Bokhandel* (bookstore) carries books about Sweden and Swedish-American life, including *Var Sa God,* the institute's 1980 recipe collection.

And a Swedish smorgasbord is de rigeur. It is served one Sunday a month and reservations are a must, particularly for the Mother's Day meal. My advice: Go slow; there is much to sample. The menu changes every month, but the menu described here is typical.

As we waited for our number to be called out, the women at my table and I scanned the folk-art frieze in the lower-level auditorium. Titles are in Swedish, but even without someone to translate, it's easy to see that the scenes depict life in the Old Country, the trip to America, and the new life here. It's a unique touch.

The fish course is first. The buffet table held pickled herring, both creamed and plain, and salmon with a sweet, clear dill sauce. My favorite was a hard-cooked egg half coated with mayonnaise and generously garnished with baby shrimp. Boiled potatoes stand alongside—they're traditional—to balance the richness of the fish.

The groaning main-course board held Swedish meatballs, red cabbage, cold roast beef, cucumber salad (excellent!), potato salad, Swedish sausage, the creamy potato-anchovy casserole called "Jansson's Temptation," and elegant little veal birds (veal slices rolled to resemble birds) with parsley and lemon inside.

Not really ready for dessert, we chatted and rested, some sipping beer, others coffee. When our table was called, we gathered around the dessert buffet and found big bowls of ice cream, whipped cream, blueberries, raspberries, and strawberries from which we created our own desserts. The perfect finale for a festive dinner on a warm June Sunday.

The first weekend of November, institute members put on a Christmas fair, *konditori*. The rooms are decorated for the holidays and, after the tour, refreshments are served downstairs. The culinary star of the event is a luscious cream torte, alternate layers of cake and custardy whipped cream. Cookies and bars are offered, too, priced individually.

A second Christmas fair, the third weekend of November, is a bake sale for which volunteers prepare breads, cakes, and cookies. Specialties such as *sandbakkels*, so time-consuming to bake at home, are snatched up very quickly. People have trouble keeping the two fairs straight, says Jan McElfish, the institute's communications manager. "They call to ask, 'Is this the eating fair or the buying fair?'"

The institute's St. Lucia celebration on December 13 is a festival of light. A lovely young woman is chosen from among the institute's active families to represent Sankta Lucia, a fourth-century Christian martyr. Robed in white with a circlet of candles on her head, Lucia is the Queen of Light. A saffron-flavored sweet bread is traditional for Lucia day.

Besides being home to more than 7,000 artifacts and 15,000 reference materials, the institute is also home to the renowned American Swedish Institute Male Chorus. The men practice there weekly and perform widely. Singers who did not learn Swedish as children learn the songs phonetically. To raise funds for their travel, the men put on two bountiful breakfasts yearly (October and February). The menu, according to Jan, includes eggs, Swedish pancakes, hardtack with cheeses, a soufflé potato dish, and a "really good" almond kringle.

The institute took a bow nationally in 1998 when it was featured in an episode of *America's Castles* on cable television's Arts and Entertainment channel. So, come for the castle, stay for the food.

These recipes were adapted from *Var Sa God, Heritage and Favorite Recipes & Handbook of Swedish Traditions* published in 1980 by the American Swedish Institute.

SWEDISH PEA SOUP

MAKES 8 TO 10 SERVINGS

1 pound dried yellow peas,
  preferably split peas

2 quarts water

1 ham bone with some meat or
  smoked pork hocks

1 large carrot, grated

3 ribs celery, diced

1 medium onion, chopped

Salt and pepper to taste

This is the traditional meal for Thursday evening in Sweden and in Swedish homes in Minnesota. The dessert that typically follows the soup is Swedish Pancakes (tiny 'cakes much like crepes) with whipped cream and lingonberries. This filling meal was meant to sustain Swedes on Friday, which was a fast day, during the Middle Ages.

Place the dried peas in a large kettle with water to cover. Cook over medium heat and bring to boiling. Reduce the heat and cook a few minutes. Remove kettle from heat and let stand 1 to 2 hours.

Drain soaking water from peas. Add the 2 quarts water to peas in kettle and cook over low heat. Add the ham bone or pork hocks to the kettle. Simmer until peas are nearly soft, about 1 ½ hours. If whole peas are used, skim off skins of peas as they rise to the top.

Stir in carrot, celery, and onion. Cook until vegetables are done, 30 to 45 minutes. Remove the ham bone, cut off meat, and add to soup; discard bone. If using pork hocks, remove from soup and cut up meat, discarding the thick skin and bone. If desired, soup can be pureed in the blender, working with 2 to 3 cups of soup at a time. Season to taste with salt and pepper.

ROYAL SWEDISH MEATBALLS

MAKES 4 TO 5 DOZEN MEATBALLS

2 pounds lean ground beef

1 pound lean ground pork

2 eggs, beaten

1 cup mashed potatoes

1 cup dry bread crumbs

1 tablespoon brown sugar

1 cup milk

2 ½ teaspoons salt

½ teaspoon each, pepper,
  ginger, nutmeg, cloves, and
  allspice

Butter for frying meatballs

½ to 1 cup beef stock for fried
  meatballs

Meatballs have been called the heart of the Swedish kitchen. This recipe reportedly originated in the Royal Palace in Stockholm. This large amount allows enough to freeze for a second or third meal. Mashed potatoes are the typical accompaniment.

Combine all ingredients except cream; mix but do not overmix. Form into small balls (about 1 inch in diameter) with a wet hand and a spoon.

To bake meatballs: Preheat oven to 325°F. Dip lightly in flour, then brown in butter in large skillet. Put in baking dish. Cover and bake for 35 to 45 minutes—no liquid need be added.

To pan-fry meatballs: Make a trial meat ball; fry it, and check for seasoning. Fry meatballs in butter being careful not to fry too many at once. Shake pan frequently so meatballs stay round. Place cooked meatballs in a heavy saucepan or Dutch oven. Pour on beef stock to prevent sticking. Cover and cook on low 10 to 15 minutes.

JANSSON'S TEMPTATION

MAKES 6 TO 8 SERVINGS

1 cup sliced yellow onions
(1 ½ onions)

2 tablespoons butter

6 medium-size potatoes (about
1 pound)*

1 (3½-ounce) tin Swedish
anchovies

1 cup heavy whipping cream

¼ cup dry bread crumbs

*Do not use new potatoes.

You will find the Swedish anchovies, which are not as salty as other anchovies, in Scandinavian specialty shops. This is a typical smorgasbord offering, both at the American Swedish Institute and in Sweden.

Preheat oven to 375°F. Stir-fry onions in butter, but do not brown. Set onions aside. Peel potatoes and cut lengthwise into thin strips. In buttered baking dish, arrange alternate layers of potatoes, anchovies, and onion, ending with potatoes. Add cream to cover the potatoes. Sprinkle with bread crumbs. Bake, covered, for about 40 minutes. Remove cover and bake another 10 minutes, until potatoes are tender and top is golden brown.

SWEDISH SPICE CAKE

MAKES 20 SERVINGS

2 cups sifted cake flour

2 cups brown sugar

1 teaspoon baking soda

1 teaspoon baking powder

¼ teaspoon salt

2 teaspoons ground allspice

2 teaspoons ground cinnamon

1 teaspoon ground cloves

½ cup butter or margarine,
softened

1 cup sour cream

3 eggs

Powdered sugar

A tender cake that needs no frosting. Delicious served with a spoonful of vanilla or apple-flavored yogurt.

Preheat oven to 375°F. In large bowl of electric mixer, stir together flour, sugar, soda, baking powder, salt, allspice, cinnamon, and cloves. Add butter, sour cream, and eggs. Beat on low speed for 30 seconds, scraping bowl constantly. Then beat on high speed 3 minutes, scraping bowl occasionally. Pour batter into greased and floured angel food or Bundt pan.

Bake for 45 to 55 minutes, or until toothpick inserted in center comes out clean. Let cool on rack 15 minutes before removing from pan. Loosen cake from pan using flexible spatula or knife, then invert onto serving plate. Using a small sifter, dust the cake with a light coating of powdered sugar. Slice thin to serve.

24
BC GARDENS
WOMAN-POWERED AND COMMUNITY-SUPPORTED

Kathy 'n Ruth, tell the truth
What does your garden grow?
Peas and beans, herbs and greens,
And pepper plants all in a row.

Kathy Botten and Ruth Capp, owners and growers at BC Gardens near Belgrade, do indeed grow peas and beans (six varieties), herbs and greens (including fifteen lettuces), plus nine types of peppers. They grow a hundred varieties of vegetables, herbs, and edible flowers, including twelve types of succulent squash, many specialty potatoes, and over a dozen tantalizing tomato varieties. They do plants from A to Z—arugula to zucchini. They are proud of the fact that their little farm feeds seventy-five families, and provides fresh

BC has two meanings: Before Chemicals, signifying that plants grow naturally, and Botten and Capp, the surnames of partners Kathy and Ruth.

goods to several food co-ops and restaurants all summer long.

BC Gardens is short for "Before Chemicals" because theirs is an organic operation. The letters "BC" are also the initials of the gardeners, women who take health, the environment, and farming seriously. BC Gardens is part of a growing movement called community-supported agriculture, or CSA. It takes some of the risk out of farming because the crops grown are bought and paid for in advance. Typically, a family that is environmentally conscious and loves just-picked vegetables and herbs, but is not able to grow them themselves, buys a share in a CSA garden/farm. The fees are normally paid in late winter or early spring and the buyer gets produce every week, summer through fall. Most CSA farms follow organic practices.

The concept of CSA was started in Japan by women who wanted to both be self-sufficient and stay in farming, Ruth explains. The idea came to the United States in the late 70s. Both coasts had this type of farm before the idea came to the Midwest, she added. Minnesota is home to a dozen CSA farms, with another dozen across the river in Wisconsin within delivering distance to potential customers in the Twin Cities metro area.

Kathy and Ruth's farm is on the one hill around Belgrade. The property has many trees and a creek borders two sides. The land was bare when they came in 1997. They moved in a mobile home and got busy building a greenhouse out of recycled pallets. Kathy, a personal wellness and fitness consultant, continued her consulting work during the first year, while Ruth worked at a nearby sewing factory.

The third partner in the business is Kubby, their orange 25-horsepower Kubota tractor. Using it, they plow and plant a four-acre plot in the center of their twenty-acre farm. Three acres are devoted to long rows of vegetables; the fourth is planted in cover crops. Typical cover crops are rye and hairy vetch in spring and fall; buckwheat, clover, and flax in warmer weather. They mow these crops and plow them into the soil. Their philosophy: "We feed the soil and let the soil feed the plants."

The BC Gardeners plant for flavor and variety and are always on the lookout for appealing new plants. Studying the organic seed catalogs is one of their favorite wintertime activities. The planting of seedlings in their greenhouse starts in late March or early April. They grow different varieties of the same vegetable in order to offer unique flavors, they told me. For example, each color of pattypan squash has a slightly different flavor. One of the zucchini squash they raise has a nutty flavor. They grow both the Yukon Gold potato, which looks like it's already been buttered, and the all-blue heirloom potato from Peru.

Each partner is responsible for planting, growing, and harvesting a different list of produce. They work together on their big compost pile, which, according to new organic rules, has to be turned five times in each fifteen-day period. "We're always on the lookout for earthworms," says Ruth. "Earthworms are a sign of good soil. And more come all the time. Ladybugs are plentiful too."

Kathy and Ruth delivered their first produce in 1998—to just thirteen customers. Knowing people want convenience, Kathy and Ruth deliver right to the

Ruth Capp, left, and Kathy Botten at their four-acre farm with their trusty wheelbarrow and one of the waxed boxes they use to deliver fresh vegetables and herbs.

customer's door; other CSA farms use drop-off sites from which customers pick up their produce. Each BC Gardens family puts a 48-quart cooler containing a one-gallon jar of ice on their doorstep on the day of the weekly delivery. When the customer returns home, there's a waxed peck (8-quart) box of vegetables, herbs and, in season, melons, awaiting them inside the cooler. BC Gardens was the first Minnesota CSA farm to offer farm-to-door delivery and the first to offer a two-person share, rather than the larger family share.

"Delivery day is our day out," says Ruth. "We drive three hundred miles a week during delivery season." Now using a van, the women are looking for a refrigerated truck, big enough for the veggie boxes, but not too big for navigating city streets. Their early season is June 17 to 24. Main season runs July 1 to October 12, and late season is October 14 to 24. Customers buy one, two, or all three seasons.

"Green peas, sugar snap peas, and green beans are the most popular vegetables,'" the partners say. "We recommend just steaming all the vegetables. Greens are also very popular. Most of our customers say they will never eat iceberg lettuce again." In the early season, they label all the greens in the delivery box so customers know exactly what they're getting. They also offer a braising mixture of greens, grown together and meant to be cooked (briefly!) together. "The education part of the farm is a bigger part than we had thought," says Kathy.

Arugula, the leafy green with the mustardy flavor, has become a personal favorite of Kathy and Ruth. "We make a lunch of arugula, dark bread, and cheese that we take on the road," says Ruth. Their wild arugula winters over, they discovered. They call purslane, an edible weed with yellow flowers, their "wild child." "And what is tatsoi," I asked, after seeing the word on their produce label. "It's a dark, shiny green," they told me; it looks something like a rose and the leaf is shaped like a spoon. Yes, something new is always being added.

After the customer base grew from the first thirteen to the present seventy-five families, the two farmers needed more work space. In 2002 they built a combination packing and equipment shed that includes a produce washing area and a cooler.

Besides the considerable outdoor work of the farm, the two publish *BC Briefs*, a monthly newsletter. They also write up a timely recipe that is tucked into the weekly box of produce. "At first, everything was done by phone; now it's Internet," says Kathy. The year 2001 was a bountiful season, the partners say. "Sometimes we gave the customers an extra bag of produce or a second box of vegetables, just to keep up with the supply."

2001 was also the year that Kathy learned she had breast cancer. Wanting to have organic food all winter long, for health reasons, the two made canning and freezing a priority. "Nutrition is so important when someone is fighting cancer," says Ruth. Knowing that Kathy was ill, a group of women friends came in September to help the partners bring in their harvest. They worked all day Saturday and Sunday bringing in squash, pumpkins, etc. "It had rained just before the harvest," remembers Ruth. "One friend took over the food. We'd work about two hours, then go back to a warm house and food on the table. Sunday night there was a killing frost, but we had all the veggies under cover."

"Mother Nature has the last word," comments Kathy.

Here are some good ideas for using fresh garden produce.

6 to 8 green tomatoes
½ cup all-purpose flour
1 to 2 tablespoons chopped
   fresh herbs (whatever
   sounds good to you)
Salt and freshly ground pepper
   to taste
2 tablespoons milk
1 egg
Oil, preferable olive oil,
   for frying

FRIED GREEN TOMATOES

MAKES 6 TO 8 SERVINGS

Some folks like these tomatoes so much that they serve them all during the growing season; others turn to them in the fall when green tomatoes are plucked from the vines just before Jack Frost arrives.

Wash tomatoes, then cut into 4 to 6 slices each and set aside.

Mix flour, herbs, salt, and pepper together in wide, shallow bowl. Add milk and egg and mix batter with a fork or wire whisk until smooth.

Heat 2 to 3 tablespoons oil in large skillet over medium heat. Dip tomato slices into batter making sure both sides are covered. Fry in single layer, without crowding, 2 to 3 minutes on each side, until tomatoes are tender and coating is golden brown. Serve hot.

Potatoes, as needed
Oil-based cooking spray
Seasonings, as desired

OVEN FRIES

2 POUNDS WHITE OR RED POTATOES
MAKES 4 SERVINGS

Kathy and Ruth like to use colored potatoes—part Yukon Gold or Yellow Finn and part purple South American potatoes—for this side dish.

Peel the amount of potatoes desired. Cut into ⅜-inch-thick slices; if you have a food processor, try the slicing blade to save time.

Preheat oven to 400°F. Spray 13 x 9-inch baking pan with oil-based vegetable spray. Arrange potato slices in single layer on prepared pan, turning to coat with spray. Sprinkle with favorite seasonings, such as Mrs. Dash or a mixture of ground herbs. Bake potato slices 18 to 20 minutes, then raise heat to broil and broil 2 to 3 minutes, until crisp. Turn potatoes to second side, and repeat baking and broiling, cooking a total of 40 to 45 minutes or until fork tender.

¼ cup granulated sugar

½ teaspoon salt

1 clove garlic, mashed

⅛ teaspoon pepper

2 to 3 tablespoons vegetable oil, such as canola

¼ cup white or rice vinegar

BETSY'S SWEET GARLIC DRESSING

MAKES 6 SERVINGS

A wonderful dressing frequently used by the late Betsy Norum, a longtime friend of mine, and a colleague at Betty Crocker.

Mix sugar, salt, garlic, and pepper in oil to form a thick paste. Stir in vinegar. Serve on sliced tomatoes or tossed with green salad.

For sauce:

3 tablespoons hoisin sauce

⅔ cup water

3 tablespoons rice or white vinegar

3 tablespoons soy sauce

1 ½ tablespoons cornstarch

For stir-fry:

3 to 4 tablespoons vegetable oil

2 garlic cloves, minced or pressed

¼ teaspoon red pepper flakes or to taste

1 (12-ounce) cake silken tofu, cut into 1-inch cubes

5 cups bite-size pieces fresh broccoli

⅓ cup dry sherry

1 bunch green onions, cut into ¾-inch pieces

1 red bell pepper, cut into strips

Crushed salted or unsalted peanuts as desired

4 portions hot, cooked white rice

STIR-FRIED BROCCOLI, RED PEPPER, AND TOFU

MAKES 4 SERVINGS

A nutrition-packed main dish adapted from Gustie Gourmet Cookbook, *a recipe collection by Gustavus Library Associates, Gustavus Adolphus College, St. Peter.*

Combine hoisin sauce, water, vinegar, soy sauce, and cornstarch in a small bowl and set aside. Before starting to stir-fry, have all the ingredients ready near the wok or skillet.

Heat 2 tablespoons of oil in a Chinese wok or large skillet over high heat. Add the garlic and red pepper flakes; stir-fry half a minute. Add tofu; stir-fry 3 to 4 minutes until tofu starts to turn golden. Remove tofu and set aside. Add another tablespoon of oil, heat it, and add broccoli. Stir-fry 1 minute, then add sherry and stir-fry 3 minutes. Next add green onions and red bell pepper; stir-fry 1 minute. Finally, add tofu and sauce mixture, stirring carefully so as not to mash tofu. Reduce heat to low and simmer 3 to 4 minutes, or until bell pepper is tender-crisp. Top with peanuts. Serve over rice on individual bowls or plates.

25
CARLSON'S APPLE ORCHARD AND BAKERY
MINNESOTA APPLES EVERYWHERE

Apples, apples everywhere. Apples by the branchful in the orchard. Apples by the basketful in the salesroom. Apples in the muffins for a second breakfast. Apples in the warm, fragrant pies just waiting for a scoop of ice cream. Apples, apples everywhere is the way to describe the late summer and fall at Carlson's Orchard and Bakery, a few miles west of Winsted. Joe Carlson, partner with his wife Colleen, puts it this way: "We were growing the apples. We had to have a way to bring the people here. The bakery and the restaurant proved to be the way to do it."

Joe Carlson grew up on this McLeod County farm, but had left it to attend technical college in Portland, Oregon, in 1979. From there he traveled the Pacific Northwest, selling testing equipment to industries. Yet he hankered to return to the home farm. He dreamed of raising his own family on the fields bordered by beautiful 200-acre Butternut Lake. The Dakota had camped on the lake, and he had found their arrowheads. He hoped to continue the long history and traditions of the land with his own work. Not interested in growing row crops, he had begun to look for alternatives.

He and Colleen, his Winsted sweetheart who had just graduated from the University of Minnesota, were married in 1982. Little did she know how important her major in horticulture would be. It was also in 1982 that Joe was driving through central Washington's orchards on business when an idea hit him: maybe apples could be grown on his folks' farm in Minnesota. Before long he discovered the University of Minnesota Horticulture Research Center near the home place. The center's aggressive apple research program had developed cool-hardy apple varieties with excellent flavor.

In 1985, the Carlsons began a double life: Minnesota apple farmers in summer,

Picking and sorting the fruit of their orchard is a family affair for the Carlsons. From left: Dad/grower Joe; sons Nick and Noah, and mom/chef Colleen.

Pacific Northwest city dwellers in winter. They purchased the farm from Joe's widowed mother and planted the first fruit trees. From then on the Carlsons' vacations meant flying to Minnesota to plant, prune, and nurse their trees. By the end of the fourth planting season, they had 3,500 dwarf trees growing on twelve acres. (Dwarf trees mean easier picking.) Colleen and their sons, Nicholas and Noah, stayed all summer when Joe returned to his job in Washington. Thus, she was responsible for the farm, even installing fifteen acres of drip irrigation.

By 1992, the first planting of apple trees, at seven years old, were starting to bear. The Carlsons returned to Minnesota full time. As the orchard business grew, Joe's experience as a salesman, learning to treat the customer as king, served him in good stead. The first two years their garage, not far from the farmhouse, was the apple salesroom. The apples that fill the branches, baskets, and pie shells at Carlson's are Minnesota apples; that is, twelve varieties of Minnesota-developed apples. A top seller is Honeycrisp, developed in Minnesota twelve years ago, and it is perfect for eating raw. As the Carlsons had hoped, people were pleased to be able to buy quality Minnesota apples. But they also wanted pies. "You can't say 'no,' so you look for ways to say 'yes,'" says Colleen.

The couple decided to bake and sell pies themselves. The space needed for a salesroom, restaurant, and kitchen was standing empty right there in the barnyard: their red, poster-perfect, 1930s dairy barn.

"We gutted the barn and put in sheet rock," says Joe. While the barn was being redone, Colleen went on the auction trail buying restaurant and bakery equipment. By mid-August 1994—the earliest date of apple availability—the space was ready to make that first apple pie and squeeze that first gallon of cider. Some 75 percent of Carlson-grown apples plus all the cider and baked goods are sold in the barn. The remaining apples are sold wholesale to grocers and produce brokers.

Though most customers are happy to select apples by the bag or basket, some want to pick their own and, when the yields are high, the Carlsons offer that. On weekends, folks can take a free hayride through the orchard. And on weekdays they schedule school tours. The school children are given a fresh apple for eating, a face-painted apple, a sample of cider, and a minimuffin.

Most visitors think a piece of pie, preferably warm from the oven, is the perfect ending to a visit to the orchard. Colleen offers both French crumb-topped

Colleen Carlson adds the finishing touch, sugar and spice, to apple slices heaped in piecrusts in her efficient bakery kitchen.

pie and the traditional two-crust pie. There's always soft-serve ice cream for à la mode. And there's cinnamon "hard" ice cream for the pie during their popular grilled pork chop Sunday dinners. These dinners of pork, corn, cole slaw, and pie are served four or five Sundays during peak season. A retired farmer named Ambrose keeps the dinner hour lively with his accordion music. "Every day I go around the restaurant with coffee. I can't stand to see the bottom of a coffee cup," says Joe, who shifts smoothly from his role as apple farmer to that of host. He also offers all comers sample sips of his fresh-made cider.

Though cider-making is the messiest job in the place, Joe doesn't mind it. After washing the fruit, apples are dumped into a conveyor and enter a hammermill. There they are mashed to a fine pomace—seeds, stems, peels, everything. The pomace goes into a series of bags within the cider press and is compressed to extract the juice. The apple juice is filtered into a bulk tank, bottled, and refrigerated. It takes forty pounds of apples—an entire bushel—to make three gallons of cider. They do not pasteurize the cider; if not used in two to three weeks, it will turn to vinegar.

"The people who came to buy apples said: 'How about some soup?' and 'I think muffins would be good,'" explains Colleen. So they expanded the restaurant.

Colleen Carlson serves two customers in the converted 1930s dairy barn.

She serves soups, muffins (apple, of course), and salads. Her hefty meat and cheese sandwiches are made from fourteen-inch-round foccacia bread. "My food is accented with flavors we like; that is, heavy on the garlic and basil," says Colleen of her creations.

Seven waitresses keep the 116-seat dining room humming. Joe's mother, Madeline, is the full-time cashier. Everyone wears aprons with the Minnesota Grown logo—the Carlsons are proud to be part of that program of the state Department of Agriculture.

Colleen's sister, Denise Dostal, helps with the daily pie baking. No, they don't peel the apples—eight bushels a day for the kitchen—by hand. They use a stainless steel automatic peeler developed by Joe, and Colleen's brother Pat. Colleen, as the cook/baker and kitchen majordomo, gets her menu, the barn kitchen, and the gift-craft shop organized during June and July. From mid-August through the day before Thanksgiving, she works from 5:30 A.M. 'til 6:30 P.M. doing all the cooking and the bulk of the baking herself. That's a hundred-day marathon. "Between Thanksgiving and June, I just enjoy my family and being Mom," she says. And sometimes, to her family's delight, she experiments with new apple recipes.

Here's the sequence of ripening for the different apple varieties at Carlson's Orchard, starting in mid-August and ending in mid-October: State Fair, Paula Red, Zestar, Red Baron, Cortland, Honeycrisp, Haralson, Honeygold, Regent, Fireside, Connell Red, and Keepsake. Regent and Fireside are recommended for fresh eating only, while all the others are excellent both raw and cooked.

TWO VALUABLE HELPERS

Kitchen shears and kitchen parchment paper are two things I recommend for kitchen efficiency. Pairing the two together in a gift basket with a few favorite recipes makes a smart bridal shower gift.

The shears—mine are Fiskars—are easier than using a knife for so many tasks. I use them to trim fat from raw chicken, to snip open the liner in packaged foods, to cut away leaves of lettuce and cabbage that have seen better days, and to cut up dried fruits such as dates and apples.

The parchment—look for it near the foil at the store—saves scrubbing pans and casseroles. I especially like it for baking cookies. You cut (or fold) the parchment to fit the baking sheet, then place the shaped cookies on it for baking—no greasing of the sheet. When cookies are done you slide the sheet of paper onto the cooling rack.

The Carlsons chose to keep their original recipes, the basis of their successful restaurant, secret. They did, however, share recipes for a pancake, a Bundt cake, and a cheesecake, all of which they frequently give to customers. I liked all three. I've also tucked in a favorite apple treat, discovered while writing a children's cookbook.

3 tablespoons butter
2 cups peeled and sliced apples*
½ cup raisins
2 eggs
¾ cup water
¾ cup flour
¼ cup nonfat dry milk powder
2 tablespoons sugar
Pancake syrup

*If time is short, don't peel apples, just slice them.

APPLE PUFF PANCAKE

MAKES 4 SERVINGS

Much like the Dutch baby so popular at pancake houses.

Preheat oven to 425°F (400°F if using glass pan). Melt butter in 9-inch pie plate in oven.

Mix apples with raisins. Stir apple mixture into melted butter. Cover pie plate with foil. Bake 10 minutes.

Beat eggs with wire whisk or rotary beater. Add water, flour, milk powder, and sugar. Beat until blended. Pour egg mixture over hot apple mixture. Bake uncovered 15 to 20 minutes or until puffy and deep golden brown. Cut into wedges and serve with your favorite syrup.

2 cups granulated sugar
3 eggs
1 cup canola oil or other vegetable oil
2 teaspoons vanilla
3 cups all-purpose flour
1 teaspoon baking soda
1 teaspoon salt
3 cups chopped tart apples
1 cup chopped walnuts

APPLE WALNUT BUNDT CAKE

MAKES 16 SERVINGS

This cake keeps exceptionally well in the refrigerator—weeks, in fact.

Preheat oven to 350°F. Grease and flour 12-cup Bundt pan.

In large mixing bowl, beat together sugar, eggs, oil, and vanilla. Add flour, soda and salt; beat well. Fold in chopped apples and nuts.

Pour batter into prepared pan. Bake 55 to 65 minutes or until toothpick comes out clean and top of cake is well browned and springs back when touched.

Cool cake upright on wire rack 10 to 15 minutes. Invert and remove from pan. Finish cooling on a rack.

For crust:

1 cup graham cracker crumbs

3 tablespoons granulated sugar

½ teaspoon ground cinnamon

3 tablespoons melted butter

For filling:

8-ounce package cream cheese, softened

½ cup granulated sugar

2 eggs

½ teaspoon vanilla

⅓ cup granulated sugar

½ teaspoon ground cinnamon

4 cups peeled and thinly sliced apples

½ cup chopped pecans

AUTUMN HARVEST CHEESECAKE

MAKES 12 SERVINGS

Preheat oven to 350°F. Combine crumbs, sugar, cinnamon, and butter. Press crumb mixture onto bottom of 9-inch springform pan. Bake 10 minutes.

For filling: In medium bowl, combine cream cheese and sugar. Beat on medium speed of electric mixer until well blended. Add eggs and vanilla; mix well. Pour cream cheese mixture into prepared crust.

Combine sugar and cinnamon. Toss cinnamon sugar with apples. Spoon apple mixture over cream cheese layer. Sprinkle top with pecans.

Bake at 350°F 60 to 80 minutes, or until center does not tremble when cake is gently shaken. Cool, then chill in refrigerator.

---

3 eggs

1 cup granulated sugar

1 cup all-purpose flour

Enough slices of tart apple to cover bottom of 10-inch round pan, peeled

Powdered sugar

RUSSIAN APPLE CAKE-PIE

MAKES 6 TO 8 SERVINGS

I can't resist adding this super-easy—and yummy—apple dessert that I got from a Russian woman when she was teaching at Gustavus Adolphus College, St. Peter.

Preheat oven to 350°F. Spray a 10-inch round pie pan with nonstick vegetable oil spray.

Break eggs into medium bowl; beat well. Beat in sugar. Add flour; fold flour in thoroughly. Batter will be thick.

Peel and core apple(s). Cut into thin slices, then cut each slice in half. Arrange slices in a circle pattern in the pan, fitting in as many slices as you can. Pour the batter over the apple slices; use the back of a spoon to smooth the batter.

Bake 25 minutes or until cake is golden. Test the cake by sticking a toothpick into it to see if it comes out clean. Let cake cool 5 minutes.

Loosen cake around edge of pan with a table knife. Put a dinner plate upside down over the pan. Taking a hot pad in each hand, grasp both sides of the hot cake pan. Flip it all over so the plate is on the bottom with the cake-pie on it. Sprinkle cake with powdered sugar—a sieve or sifter works well for the sugar.

26 FOREST HISTORY CENTER
ONE LAST LUMBER CAMP

Back in 1900, there were three hundred logging camps scattered across vast northern forests in Minnesota. From early morning until sundown, November through March, some 20,000 rugged lumberjacks harvested the mighty white pine. The first northern camps opened in the 1860s. The last major logging season, or "drive," was in 1937. Production peaked near the turn of the century, when more than two billion board-feet of lumber were harvested from the snowy Minnesota forests in a single year.

Today one logging camp survives, an authentic re-creation of the Minnesota Historical Society. This camp, named the Forest History Center, is just southwest of Grand Rapids. Interpreters dressed like lumberjacks, cooks, and the camp blacksmith, tell how they lived and worked through the long, dark winters.

As our guide noted when we toured the camp, "The lumberjacks' pay was the same, the work was the same, the beds were the same. Only the food was different." These real-life Paul Bunyans had enormous appetites. Feeding the seventy-five to eighty 'jacks who lived in a typical camp was no easy task. A typical breakfast saw the eighty men rapidly devour nearly five hundred pancakes and dozens of jars of doughnuts (fried the previous day). The breakfast was washed down with gallons of coffee; thus the men fortified themselves before they headed for the woods.

The late Jalmar Johnson, whom I interviewed in 1977 when he was 86, cooked at a North Star Logging Company camp as a young man. Johnson termed the life of the lumberjacks hard, sometimes dangerous. Himself a first-generation Norwegian American, Johnson said the 'jacks were usually Scandinavians or French Canadians, young and not so young. After swinging an ax or manhandling a saw all day, they spent their evenings in the bunkhouse

playing cards, telling stories, and smoking. Their pay, withheld until the end of the season, was about a $1 a day.

Mealtimes were for eating, not socializing, Johnson explained. Conversation during the fifteen minutes spent at the long wood tables was usually limited to requests to the "cookees" (porters) for more food. And they ate their fill.

The noon meal was eaten in the woods, served from a one-bob (horse) sleigh called a "swing dingle." The sled was usually packed with a large kettle of beans and a kettle of boiled potatoes, as well as a huge roast. A roaring fire was built near the sleigh-riding buffet and a big horn was blown to call the men to eat. "Even if it was snowing, they went right on eating," Johnson said.

Top. This 1890 postcard photo, titled "Lunch time in the woods," shows lumberjacks taking their only break for a hearty lunch brought into the woods by a team of horses.

Bottom. Artist Carl Henrikson's "Gabriel's Horn. The Summons to the Cook-Camp for Meals."

Soup couldn't be served at noon because the broth would have spilled as the horse towed the sleigh. But soup was always served at night along with more meat and hot vegetables. Supper for the eighty lumberjacks also meant that thirty loaves of bread and twenty pies would disappear. Though no fresh fruit was available in these deep woods, dried fruit came in by the barrel. Cooked prunes, called "logging berries" were consumed at every meal and were used in desserts.

The logging camp cooks, clad in ankle-length white aprons, were nothing if not busy. The head cook had three or four cookees, who helped with preparation and served at the table. Together they butchered the meat and scaled the fish, which they bought from Native Americans by the sackful. They peeled the potatoes, carrots, and rutabagas stored in the root house behind the camp. They stirred vats of soup, split pea or vegetable, so good for warming men who'd worked outside nine or ten hours. Another task was "boiling up": washing aprons and dish towels. Afterward, the hot water was used by the loggers for their personal laundry.

The frying of pancakes and doughnuts and the baking of bread, pies, cakes, and cookies were coveted jobs because the kitchen became cozily warm.

These recipes are from *Cookshack Cooking,* a pamphlet published by the Forest History Center. No, Virginia, you don't need eggs and milk to make delicious snacks and desserts, as these recipes from northern Minnesota prove. The original recipes were made with lard; the modernized recipes substitute margarine or hydrogenated shortening, such as Crisco.

RIVER DRIVER'S GINGERBREAD

MAKES 15 TO 18 SERVINGS

1 cup granulated sugar
1 cup molasses
1 scant cup lard or other shortening
1 cup cold water
4 cups all-purpose flour
1 tablespoon ground ginger
1 teaspoon baking soda
1 scant teaspoon cream of tartar
1 teaspoon salt

Preheat oven to 350°F. Stir together the sugar, molasses, and lard until smooth. Stir in water. On a sheet of waxed paper, combine the flour, ginger, soda, cream of tartar, and salt.

Stir the dry ingredients into the molasses mixture. Turn batter into a greased 13 x 9-inch pan or two 8-inch square pans. Sprinkle batter lightly with more granulated sugar.

Bake for 25 to 35 minutes or until gingerbread pulls away from sides of pan.

DRIED APPLE CAKE

MAKES 9 TO 12 SERVINGS

1½ cups chopped dried apples
1 cup light molasses (part honey may be used)
3 tablespoons shortening
¼ cup granulated sugar
2 cups all-purpose flour
1 teaspoon baking soda
¼ teaspoon ground cinnamon
¼ teaspoon ground cloves
½ cup water

This unusual cooked-then-baked dessert has a flavor similar to fruitcake.

Preheat oven to 350°F. Simmer the dried apples in the molasses for 15 minutes. Allow to cool.

Grease a 9-inch square or 10-inch round layer cake pan. Stir together the apple mixture, shortening, sugar, flour, soda, cinnamon, cloves and water; beat vigorously for 30 seconds. Spread batter in prepared pan.

Bake at 350°F for 10 minutes. Then reduce heat to 325°F and bake 35 to 40 minutes longer, until toothpick inserted in center comes out clean.

COOKEES' RAISIN OATMEAL COOKIES

MAKES ABOUT 4 DOZEN COOKIES

¾ cup soft shortening, such as Crisco
1 cup brown sugar
½ cup granulated sugar
1 tablespoon plus 1 teaspoon water
1 teaspoon vanilla
3 cups regular or quick rolled oats (uncooked oatmeal, not instant)
1 cup all-purpose flour
1 teaspoon salt
½ teaspoon baking soda
1 cup raisins

Preheat oven to 350°F. Combine shortening, sugars, water, and vanilla. Stir in the oats, flour, salt, soda, and raisins. Dough may be crumbly; if so, work dough with your hands to aid mixing. Drop dough by rounded teaspoonfuls onto ungreased baking sheet (or cover sheet with kitchen parchment paper). Bake for 12 minutes until set but not hard.

FRUIT-TOPPED CAKE

½ cup + 1 teaspoon soft
shortening
½ cup granulated sugar
2 cups all-purpose flour
2 ½ teaspoons baking powder
¼ teaspoon salt
½ cup + 1 tablespoon water
2 cups drained, cooked fruit
(dried plums, dried apricots,
raisins, or similar mix)

For streusel topping:
½ cup all-purpose flour
½ cup granulated sugar
½ teaspoon ground cinnamon
¼ cup firm margarine

Prunes (now labeled dried plums) were often used for this easy cake. For testing this delicious cake, I used a mixture of prunes, dried apricots, and raisins, but any cooked or canned fruit would work.

Preheat oven to 350°F. Combine the shortening, ½ cup sugar, and 1 tablespoon water. Add the flour, baking powder, and salt to the shortening mixture, adding dry ingredients alternately with the ½ cup water. Pour into greased 9-inch square pan. Arrange fruit on top. Make streusel by mixing the ½ cup flour, ½ cup sugar, and cinnamon, then cutting in the margarine until chunky. Sprinkle streusel over fruit. Bake for 45 to 50 minutes.

LARRIGAN PIE

1 cup granulated sugar
3 tablespoons cornstarch
3 tablespoons cider vinegar
¾ cup water
½ teaspoon lemon extract
1 unbaked 8-inch pie shell

Larrigan is the name of woodsmen's moccasins—the connection to this particular pie escapes me!

Preheat oven to 350°F. Stir together the sugar and cornstarch. Add the water, vinegar, and lemon extract; mix well. Pour vinegar mixture into pie shell. Bake for 45 minutes or until mixture sets and crust is brown.

FINE FOOD AT
KAVANAUGH'S
SYLVAN LAKE RESORT

Sherman Kavanaugh was justly proud of his wife Mae's cooking. And he shared her dream of opening a fine restaurant. A successful salesman, he had his own dream of running a resort somewhere amid the beautiful woods and lakes of northern Minnesota.

In 1969, Sherm and Mae purchased a place on the shore of lovely, serene Sylvan Lake, north of Brainerd near the little town of Pillager. The land-locked lake of 880 acres is spring-fed and extremely clean. "I was three and a half when we moved here," says Tom Kavanaugh, youngest of their six sons, now executive chef at Sylvan Lake Resort. The Kavanaughs were thrilled with their new location with its 1,000 feet of lakeshore and set to work with a will to make their business a success. "Dad was always building," recalls Tom. One year they would expand the resort, the next year they would add on to the restaurant.

The first restaurant—capacity 35—occupied the lower level of the home that had been on the property when the family took over. Today's dining room, with its white tablecloths and full bar, faces Sylvan Lake and accommodates 170; 190 on a busy Saturday. Four of the original nine cabins, though completely redone, are still in use. All told, Kavanaugh's now has fifty-five units to rent. All are equipped with kitchens and chef Tom estimates that families spending a week there may eat at the resort once during that time.

In the early days of the business, Mae handled the restaurant herself, teaching the art of cooking to sons who were interested, and employing both family members and neighbors as servers. "Mom loved cooking," says her proud son, Tom. "She had cooked for threshers when she was growing up on the farm." Year by year, the resort and the restaurant prospered. The boys married and, often, their wives and, sometimes, their children worked at the ever-growing family business.

In 1994, four of the sons—John, Dave, Mark, and Tom—bought the property from their father—who by then had been named Minnesota Resorter of the Year. John is the president and day-to-day manager. His wife, Vicki, manages the office, gift shop, and reservations. "John deals with the vendors, the banks; he stays busy," explains Tom. Dave had been Mae's right hand in the kitchen for twenty years. Then about ten years ago he took over buildings and maintenance, keeping everything working, from docks to locks.

Mark is the people guy, according to youngest brother Tom. Mark manages the restaurant and handles all the conference services. His wife, Sue, is restaurant hostess. Tom, who had started cooking as a teenager and learned meal planning at his mother's side, has been head chef since '91. "The majority of our dinner guests are seasonal residents and vacationers." There's many a summer home hidden through the woods, not to mention other resorts and the eighteen golf courses nearby.

Recently Chef Tom trimmed the "Classics" menu and added two new menus: "Italian" and "Pacific Rim." He says a change was in order. "There are so many places vying for the food dollar." The evening of our interview he was serving a new Asian salmon dish to a conference group that was arriving for three days of meetings. "I tease them; I say they're my guinea pigs," comments Tom, grinning.

Walleye is the dish Kavanaugh's is famous for. You can get it deep-fried, almondine, or topped with a delicate shrimp sauce—a treatment called Vanessa. Though the walleye for the restaurant once came from Red Lake, it now comes from one of the four commercial fishing lakes in Canada. "We get walleye three times a week," says Tom. "It gets here the day after it's

Chef Tom Kavanaugh offers steak with mushrooms and mixed vegetables (left) or walleye with wild rice and broiled tomato. The upright garnish on the beef is a sprig of rosemary.

Lovely grounds surround
Kavanaugh's Sylvan Lake Resort
near Brainerd.

caught." But the chef himself prefers ocean fish to walleye. He's happy to have swordfish on his Pacific Rim menu. "I try to push fresh seafood, things like marlin and mahimahi. Our supplier is American Fish and Seafood in Minneapolis. They guarantee that the fish not be more than thirty-six hours out of the ocean."

Kavanaugh's has been an à la carte restaurant since 1999. "Salad comes separately," explains Tom. So does soup. "We do serve quite a plate of food. Vegetable and starch are included with the entrée." And portions are generous. "I cook with cream and butter. I don't worry about calories and neither do my diners. They can worry about that at home." The restaurant always has a nightly soup plus the popular French onion soup. "My mother made pretty good soup, but I do even better," he brags. "I love to make soup. I decide what the soup of the day will be when I come to work. During a season, I'll serve sixty-five or seventy different soups, most of which I've never written down."

Chef Tom's day starts at 7:30 A.M. when he walks from his home, right across the road, to the restaurant to check on the advance preparation for the evening meal. Then he leaves for about three hours, running errands, sometimes squeezing in a round of golf. He's always back in the kitchen by 11:30 A.M. The restaurant opens at 5 P.M. and closes at 8:30 P.M. "I love to cook on the line. And the kitchen is small enough that I can see everything that's going on," says the chef. "No, I don't go into the dining room to greet people. My apron is a mess." Tom stays until the job is finished. He usually gets home to wife Jenni, a nurse, and their daughters in time for the 10 P.M. news. Mention of his wife reminds Tom to tell me about his wedding day. He prepared all the food for the reception himself, then got ready and went to church to say his vows.

Kavanaugh's Restaurant opens each year on Memorial Day and closes Labor Day. Dinner is served daily except Sundays. During the rest of the year—fall is especially lovely—the resort hosts conferences for up to 125 participants.

Chef Tom and his crew serve conference attendees a breakfast buffet, a nice lunch, and a dinner with two entrée choices. "We get a lot of state and education

The skill that home cooks can learn from trained chefs is *presentation*—how to make a food look impressive when you bring it to the table. Parsley sprigs, once so common, have been replaced by fresh herbs, such as a piece of rosemary used by Chef Tom Kavanaugh (page 152). But the plate or platter and how you arrange the food is key. Rather than passing rice or mashed potatoes in a separate bowl, press them into a ring mold or a well-shaped bowl and invert on the serving plate, then surround with a stir-fry or a creamed mixture. To focus on presentation, think about taking a cooking class from a chef and seeing presentation first hand.

groups," says Tom. "Some like the facilities so well they have returned for ten or eleven years in a row. They can be here four days and never get the same bread, salad, entrée or dessert—everything is different."

The quieter weeks in the winter allow Tom to slip away for further training, whether to Napa Valley for a Culinary Institute of America session or to the Twin Cities to work side by side with a chef friend. And then there's his alter ego: coach for the junior high school girl's basketball team at Pillager, the school he and his brothers attended when they were kids.

There's every indication that Kavanaugh's will continue as a top Minnesota resort and restaurant well into the twenty-first century. The four brothers are in charge, and a new generation is learning the ropes.

You can sample the resort's fare by preparing these recipes from *Kavanaugh's Cookbook* by Mae Kavanaugh.

Walleye fillets
Butter
Toasted almonds
Clarified Butter (see below)

WALLEYE ALMONDINE

3 TO 4 SERVINGS PER POUND OF WALLEYE FILLETS

Season fillets of walleye. Line broiler pan with foil; butter the foil. Arrange fillets on foil in broiler pan. Brush fillets generously with melted butter.

Broil until fish flakes or bake in 450°F oven 10 to 15 minutes. Watch carefully so that fish does not overcook.

Serve with toasted almonds and clarified butter.

½ pound butter

CLARIFIED BUTTER

MAKES ¾ CUP

This is sometimes referred to as drawn butter.

Place butter in heavy saucepan over lower heat. Cook until butter is melted. As butter melts, use a ladle—working with a circular motion—to skim off the foam that rises to the top.

Remove pan from heat. Let butter stand until all milk solids have fallen to the bottom of the pan. Using a ladle, remove the clear liquified butter; use immediately or refrigerate. Discard the remaining milky residue.

RELISH BAR HERRING SALAD

MAKES 8 TO 10 SERVINGS

1 cup sour cream
1 tablespoon granulated sugar
2 onions, thinly sliced
1 apple, cored and thinly
   sliced
1 lemon, thinly sliced
1 (12-ounce) jar herring in
   sour cream or wine sauce

A favorite when Mae Kavanaugh offered a relish bar to her diners.

Combine sour cream and sugar in medium bowl. Add onion, apple, and lemon slices; mix well. Gently stir in herring. Cover and chill at least 2 hours.

VICHYSSOISE

MAKES 12 SERVINGS

4 leeks, sliced, white part only
1 medium onion, sliced
4 tablespoons butter
5 medium potatoes, peeled
   and chopped
1 quart chicken broth
2 to 3 teaspoons salt
3 cups milk
2 cups heavy cream
Chopped chives for garnish

The thought of enjoying a bowl of this velvety potato soup while looking out at lovely Sylvan Lake is most appealing.

Brown the leeks and onion in butter. Add potatoes, broth, and salt. Cook until potatoes are tender, about 40 minutes.

Puree mixture in blender or food processor. Chill well.

Add milk and cream to chilled soup. Season to taste. Serve sprinkled with chives.

RATATOUILLE

MAKES 5 CUPS, ABOUT 10 SERVINGS

1 small eggplant (about
   1 pound)
2 small zucchini (about
   1 pound)
1 large onion
1 large green pepper
⅓ cup olive oil
1 clove garlic, finely chopped
2 medium-size ripe tomatoes,
   chopped
2 tablespoons chopped
   parsley*
1 teaspoon salt
¼ teaspoon pepper
1 teaspoon leaf oregano,
   crumbled
1 teaspoon leaf basil, crumbed

*Use kitchen shears if you
   have them.

A French classic if there ever were one.

Cut eggplant into ½-inch thick slices, then cut into ½-inch cubes. Cut zucchini into ¼-inch slices; slice onion thinly. Cut green pepper into ¼-inch strips.

Stir-fry eggplant cubes in 2 tablespoons of the oil in a large skillet until lightly browned, about 5 minutes. Remove to large saucepan or Dutch oven.

Add 1 tablespoon more of oil to skillet. Stir-fry zucchini until almost tender; remove to saucepan. Add remaining oil to skillet; stir-fry onion, green pepper, and garlic until tender; add to saucepan. Add tomatoes, parsley, salt, pepper, oregano, and basil. Stir gently to mix.

Simmer mixture, covered, over low heat 15 minutes. Remove cover; stir in parsley. Simmer 10 minutes longer, or until most of the free liquid has cooked away. Taste; add more seasonings, if you wish.

1 cup sour cream

2 tablespoons packed brown sugar

1 to 2 tablespoons orange liqueur such as Grand Marnier or Triple Sec

DEVONSHIRE-STYLE CREAM

Resourceful Mae Kavanaugh worked out a quickly made topping reminiscent of the prized thick cream served over fresh fruit in Britain.

Mix together sour cream, brown sugar, and liqueur; cover and chill to blend flavors.

Serve as a topping for strawberries, raspberries, grapes, or sliced peaches.

28 SUMMER FUN
AND A NEW LANGUAGE TOO

Young people at the Concordia Language Villages talk, sing, dance, play—and eat—in the culture they are studying. Whichever of the villages they're living in, campers enjoy culturally authentic food.

The Language Villages began in 1961 with a two-week session for would-be German speakers. Immersing oneself in a language while enjoying summertime in the pristine north woods was the idea of Gerald Haukebo, a professor at Concordia College, Moorhead, a private, four-year, liberal arts college.

The idea caught on and soon villages were being held in rented "Y" and Scout camps all over central and northern Minnesota. The quality and success of the program have brought renown to its sponsor. There are thirteen villages; the most recent is the Italian village, Lago del Bosco. Five of the villages (Spanish, Norwegian, German, French, and Finnish) have permanent facilities around Turtle River Lake fifteen miles north of Bemidji.

The number of villages and villagers (as campers are called) was growing steadily in 1981 when David Erceg of the food service staff began to replace typical kids' camp fare with authentic ethnic foods. The foods of the various countries soon became a regular part of the language immersion experience.

The food they are going to be served is presented to the villagers before each meal, says Jodi Nordlund, Bemidji, food coordinator for the Language Villages. This is done as a skit with each food named and an example shown, all in the target language. Such skits are usually put on by the counselors, some of whom are native speakers who have come to Minnesota to work at the villages. Occasionally, a villager will perform the food skit, and, very occasionally, someone on the kitchen staff will come out. "Sometimes they really ham it up," Jodi says, grinning.

A costumed counselor zeroes in on a tray of crispbread, along with cheeses, mustard, and dark bread, set out for a snack at Salolampi, the Finnish Language Village.

Though the campers are encouraged to speak the target language at the table, they are not reprimanded if they don't, according to Jodi. The whole staff is committed to passive language learning. When a camper says, "Please pass the bread," in, for example, French, the counselor repeats the sentence. "The aim is to get the language and culture into their lives," she explains.

While living in St. Peter, I was told this little story, in which a Concordia Village-learned language influenced a life. As a teenager, Christine Gray went to the Swedish Language Village with her best friend, whose father had been born and raised in Sweden. They learned easily, became counselors, and traveled in Sweden. Christine's sister was the activity director at the St. Peter Community Care Center. An elderly patient had not spoken a word since coming there and it worried the staff. They knew she had come from Sweden and wondered if speaking to her in Swedish might elicit a response. Christine was summoned and came to meet the old woman. Sure enough, the woman's English had slipped away but she had retained her native language. After months of silence, she was finally able to converse, to everyone's delight.

As can be expected, meals are an important part of the day at the villages. Hours of swimming, boating, hiking, and craftwork, all in a new language, make the villagers hungry. "It turns out that fresh fruits and vegetables are really offbeat for today's kids," explains Jodi. "They come from a tradition of fast and processed food. At camp they learn to enjoy fresh produce. And they love our homemade bread."

Though a one-week exploratory session is offered, a two-week immersion session is most common, according to Jodi. "We try to build with the children. The first part of the stay we serve foods that are authentic but kid-friendly." Many two-week villagers return later as four-week campers. These campers earn high school credit, while advanced speakers of French, German, or Spanish who are juniors or seniors in high school can opt for college credit.

Though there are many Minnesotans among the campers, they come from all over the world. The food staff tries to learn each group's tolerance for hot, spicy foods, typical in Asia and Spain. "We try not to put too much spice in a dish, but occasionally we slip up," admits Jodi. "We put bottles of Tabasco on the tables in the Spanish Village for those who want more heat. And there are containers of chili paste on the tables in the Asian villages." They have kimchi (fiery cabbage pickle) at nearly every meal in the Korean Village.

The kitchen crew fills serving bowls for each table of villagers at Sup Sogŭi Hosu, the Korean Language Camp.

When they enter camp, passport and all, young people exchange their money for authentic currency of the country they're studying. And buying snacks is a way to learn to handle that money. Norwegian and Swedish chocolate is excellent, notes Jodi. Asian snacks include sweet potato chips, rice crackers with seaweed, and fish crackers made with dried shrimp. A particularly exotic Asian snack is crunchy, dried green peas seasoned with powdered wasabi (a fiery seasoning like horseradish).

Each camp's head cook plans his or her own menus. "We give them that responsibility and power," says Jodi. "It lets them make choices they feel good about. Some menus are repeated every session because both the counselors and the campers would be disappointed if these favorites weren't served. "Cooks are given a lot of leeway. They're told to trust their palates. Some are college kids, a few are as young as twenty."

The food service part of the villages' support staff includes fifteen or sixteen head cooks, eighty to a hundred kitchen helpers, cooks, and bakers. Daniel Eastman, who is Jodi's assistant, trains cooks during June and July. Food production

Norwegian villagers show off their *vafler* in the kitchen at Skogfjorden.

manager Donna Kastner plans menus for weekend programs and special events. "We run very clean kitchens. All the head cooks are certified food service managers. And we have in-house sanitation classes." Jodi sees the training as an important preventative measure, knowing the kitchens will pass muster when the health inspector drops in.

The Asian villages are a big challenge foodwise. Choosing and preparing foods that are authentic Japanese, Chinese, or Korean *and* kid-friendly takes work. A library of cookbooks at the Bemidji head office is helpful. The best help, though, comes from native-born staffers from that particular country or those that have studied extensively in that part of the world.

Another challenge for the food staff has been the French Voyageur program, which started in 1979. The group does a grand portage, or extended canoe trip, so foods need to be light, which means dehydrated foods and items like smoked jerky. And everything is cooked over a fire. "It's important that the voyageur cook be a French speaker, because they are very involved with the villagers, who help with some food preparation on the trip," says Jodi.

Jodi has found that one of the joys of her job as food coordinator is seeing cooks grow in their abilities. "For example, we had a young kid who started out as a kitchen helper," says Jodi. "After a few summers working in the Language Village kitchens, he decided to study culinary arts at the Hibbing Technical College. After graduation he spent a month at a cooking school in Seoul, Korea. Dr. Ross King, dean of the Korean Village, was able to procure grant money to help make that happen. The leadership of the villages is hoping that more head cooks will be able to do something similar." She adds: "He and his staff prepared some fabulous food at Sup sogŭi Hosu [Korean Language Village]."

She is convinced that kids learn the language through the food. "This is a wholistic approach to learning about another culture. This food is fresh and good and prepared with love." One young villager put it another way: "It may look weird but it tastes great."

Jodi Nordlund passed along these recipes from the Concordia Language Villages files.

VEGETABLE MAFÉ

3 large onions, finely chopped

½ cup olive oil

1 butternut or buttercup squash, peeled and chunked

4 turnips, peeled and chunked

4 potatoes, washed and quartered

1 small cabbage, coarsely chopped

3 tomatoes, chunked

1 bunch leaf spinach, stems removed

4 serrano hot peppers, sliced

3 cups tomato sauce

1 cup water

1 cup creamy peanut butter

Salt to taste

10 portions hot cooked rice

A lovely dish, says Jodi. From French-speaking Senegal, it is served at Lac du Bois, the French Village. This is a culinary cousin of the chicken-tomato-peanut butter stew served in other parts of Africa, a longtime favorite of mine.

Brown the onions in the olive oil in a large braising pan. Add the squash, turnips, potatoes, cabbage, tomatoes, and spinach. Stir-fry 10 minutes.

Add the hot peppers, tomato sauce, and water. Simmer until vegetables are tender, about 15 to 20 minutes.

Mix in the peanut butter; heat briefly. Serve over rice.

CHINESE SPICY PORK AND TOFU

For sauce:

3 to 4 tablespoons soy sauce

2 to 3 tablespoons cornstarch

1 to 2 tablespoons cider vinegar

Pinch each of sugar, salt, and ground white pepper

For main dish:

1 pound ground pork

2 tablespoons minced ginger

2 cloves garlic, minced

1 tablespoon hot pepper sauce

1 tablespoons crushed Sichuan peppercorns*

1 medium white onion, minced

12 ounces firm or extra-firm tofu, cut into 2-inch squares

3 green onions, cut diagonally in ½-inch pieces, for garnish

Hot cooked rice

*If you cannot buy peppercorns already crushed, do it yourself with a mortar and pestle.

This is a great way to introduce healthful tofu to your family.

Make sauce: Combine soy sauce, cornstarch, vinegar, sugar, salt, and pepper; set aside.

Fry the ground pork. Remove the pork from the skillet, leaving the fat; set pork aside.

Add ginger, garlic, hot pepper sauce, and Sichuan peppercorns to the pork fat and stir-fry 5 to 10 seconds to flavor the oil.

Add the onion and stir-fry 2 more minutes.

Add the tofu and cooked pork. Stir-fry another 2 to 4 minutes, stirring gently.

Add the sauce mixture. Cook and stir until sauce thickens. Top mixture with green onion. Serve with rice.

SWEDISH SEAMAN'S BEEF

MAKES 10 SERVINGS

2 pounds boneless beef chuck
    or round
1 ½ teaspoons salt
1 tablespoon freshly ground
    black pepper
6 bay leaves, crumbled
12 ounces beer or ale
1 cup flour for coating meat
⅓ cup butter
2 pounds potatoes (about 5
    medium), peeled and sliced
3 large carrots, sliced
3 large onions, sliced

An oven-easy one-pot meal that will warm the hearts of your family during cold weather.

Cut beef into 1-inch cubes. Place in deep container. Sprinkle with salt, pepper, and crumbled bay leaves. Pour on the beer. Marinate overnight in refrigerator, or for at least 4 hours.

Preheat oven to 325°F. Drain the meat, reserving the beer marinade. Coat the meat with flour. Melt the butter in a large skillet and brown the beef cubes; set aside. Fry potatoes, carrots, and onions separately, frying them just enough to color the surface. Grease a large casserole. Dividing potatoes in half, arrange alternate layers of potatoes, meat, carrots, onions and potatoes in casserole (first and last layers should be potatoes). Pour the beer marinade over layers.

Cover and bake 1 ½ hours, until meat and vegetables are fork tender.

RUSSIAN OLIVIER SALAD/BALAKSHA

MAKES 10 SERVINGS

2 cooked chicken breasts,
    diced (about 3 cups)
6 boiled potatoes, diced (4 to
    5 cups)
2 medium cucumbers, peeled,
    seeded, and diced (2 cups)
2 green pepper, seeded and
    diced
2 carrots, cooked and diced
1 cup cooked peas
6 hard-cooked eggs, finely
    chopped
Salt and pepper to taste

For dressing:
6 tablespoons mayonnaise
6 tablespoons sour cream
2 teaspoons sugar
2 teaspoons ketchup
2 teaspoons lemon juice

This shows the French influence in Russian cooking. The chicken breasts, potatoes, carrots, peas, and eggs need to be cooked ahead of time.

Have chicken, vegetables, and eggs cut; chill until ready to serve.

Combine mayonnaise, sour cream, sugar, ketchup, and lemon juice. Cover and chill until needed.

Just before serving, combine all salad ingredients. Taste just before serving, adding salt and/or pepper, if desired.

20 SCHUMACHER'S HOTEL
IN THE HEART OF NEW PRAGUE

Schumacher's Hotel in New Prague is, indeed, the house that John built. In the hospitality business, "house" refers to a restaurant or hotel or both. John's house has sixteen guest rooms, a lobby, a bar, a large restaurant, even a gift shop.

Chef-hotelier John Schumacher decorated the lovely rooms, creates the elegant menu offerings, and dreams up the annual innovations that keep the New Prague experience fresh. He also promotes his establishment with his State Fair restaurant, cookbooks, and television appearances.

Granted, John did not build the hotel per se. It had been built in 1898 as the Hotel Broz. The attractive brick building was designed by famed architect Cass Gilbert, who later designed the State Capitol in St. Paul and other landmarks. John and his first wife, Nancy, bought the hotel in 1974. He renamed the place after the town: Schumacher's New Prague Hotel (later shortening it to Schumacher's). He featured Czech and German entrées with rich gravies. He and his bakers perfected the beloved Czech fruit-filled roll called *kolache* that they put it in breadbaskets for breakfast, lunch, and dinner.

Schumacher's Hotel, designed by famed architect Cass Gilbert, is a New Prague landmark.

He also adapted the unique Czech sausage called *jiternice*. "The original was something you had to grow up with to like," John explains. "I went to Frank Mach, the butcher at Montgomery Meat Market, for help in making it more appealing. We added garlic and barley and used a lighter casing." The updated *jiternice* makes a great sandwich on rye bread to sell at the State Fair or a filling meal with kraut and dumplings for the restaurant.

Oh, yes, the fair. Chef John opened a booth at the Minnesota State Fair in 1975. "I've got the best place at the fair," he announces, beaming. And that place keeps growing. He started with a ten-foot space in the Food Building and over time it grew to thirty feet. Then he moved to an outside corner of the Food Building where there had been little business. He made the corner work and won ribbons for best booth in his seven years there. In 1997, he purchased a steel building and transformed it into a mini-Schumacher's Restaurant, complete with a replica of the New Prague hotel on the façade. John and a crew of seventy-five run the State Fair restaurant, which seats 125.

While John is at the fair or off on a book signing or a cooking demo, the New Prague hotel-restaurant is in the capable hands of his wife Kathleen. They've been married since 1986. "I call her an in-trepreneur," he says. "She deals with the details of the house. She gets the credit for my survival during the hectic growth years of the business. " (In the mid-'90s they bought the building next door and nearly doubled the hotel in size.) Pretty and petite, a trained dietitian, Kathleen developed the gift shop, choosing exquisite items for display and sale. She has even been known to select a particular beer stein or vase for special customers while she is on buying trips to eastern Europe.

The Schumachers once lived in the hotel but now have a home around the corner. The retrofitting of their house included the design and building of the light, open kitchen where the chef films his fish-and-game cookery spots for Ron Schara's outdoor TV show, *Minnesota Bound*. Tall and broad shouldered, John is a natural born showman. "The camera crew comes once a month," says the chef. "We do four segments, one each for the next four weeks." It goes without saying that the family and crew have a feast after the video has wrapped.

The Schumachers' standards for their "house" are high. "There is no bar smell here," John says, gesturing toward the quaint bar adjacent to the lobby. Standards for food are high too. "When we make a Rueben, we slice our own corned beef," he continues. "And we make our own kraut." Standards for the staff are just as high. "I expect the staff on the first shift to be respectful of the people on the second shift. A cook should leave the oven clean, the pans on the rack, so that the next cook coming in finds things where they should be." His

John Schumacher, in his chef's toque, and outdoorsman Ron Schara present a platter of whole fish garnished with lemon baskets. The two have been filming one of weekly cookery segments for Schara's *Outward Bound* television program in the demo kitchen of Schumacher's home.

crew numbers seventy, including the three it takes to answer the phone. "It rings all the time," he notes, his tone one of pride, not exasperation.

John also takes pride in his rural Minnesota roots. He grew up milking cows on his family's dairy farm in Traverse County. He was in the first grade, in 1940, when the REA (Rural Electrification Association) came to his county and his parents got a refrigerator. "Then the country women could make Jell-O like the town gals," he says, grinning.

His mother, Helen Schumacher, is of Norwegian descent and "the best cook in the world." He gets his self-discipline from her. "You did well because you kept trying," he explains. He learned to cook by watching his mother and Grandma Blenda in the kitchen. He was an attentive listener at school. Watching and listening and remembering helped him move from Wheaton High School to Minneapolis's Dunwoody Institute to study baking, on to the Navy, and finally to chef training at the famed Culinary Institute of America (CIA). He's a classically trained chef but he cannot read. He is dyslexic, one of some twelve million learning-disabled Americans.

"Dyslexia is a pain in the neck," says John. "I've learned to draw my initials, but I cannot really read or write." For years, he hid his disability. Yet he had always wanted to share his recipes in a cookbook. He knew how costly it was to publish a book of 200-plus pages. Still he was determined, knowing every top chef had written a signature book.

So he had the cover designed. It features an excellent likeness of himself, mustache, toque, and all, in front of the hotel. The cover mock-up was placed prominently in the hotel gift shop. "Buy the book now," read the sign. "It will be autographed and mailed to you when it is published." Nearly a year later, in 1991, when the sales total matched the printer's bill, *John Schumacher's New Prague Hotel Cookbook* by International Cuisine Publishers came out. The chef had dictated the 212 recipes, then had the transcriptions read aloud to him as he reworked the copy. The flurry of publicity about the book proved the perfect time for John to admit his dyslexia. "I wanted people like me to have some hope, to have a chance. It took me twenty years to get here," he admits.

Earlier, John had wanted a spread in the magazine *Country Inns & Bed & Breakfast*. So he had a note sent to several of his most loyal guests suggesting that they write to *Country Inns* recommending the hotel. He gave them the editor's name, the address, everything but the stamp. Sure enough, the magazine bit. The multipage, four-color story featured the Christmas holidays at the hotel and brought inquiries from across the United States. And so impressed were the editors who came to write the piece that Schumacher's was named one of the top twelve inns in America in 1991.

More books have followed: *Wild Game Cooking Made Easy* (1997) and *Fish Cooking Made Easy* (1999) plus two books with Ron Schara: *Minnesota Bound Game Cookbook* and *Minnesota Fish Cookbook* (2000). The latter cookbooks, compilations of recipes featured on television, become dual promotions for the show and the hotel.

John tries to add something new to his operation every year. In 2001, it was fondue on the front porch; in 2002, a little indoor herb garden. Repeat customers want the familiar, with the touch of something new, he finds.

THOUGHTS ON BUYING COOKBOOKS

Though I once interviewed a woman who said she was happy if she found one wonderful recipe in a new cookbook, most of us hope to find a variety of interesting dishes in any cookbook we're buying. Now that so many cookbooks are being published, and there are so many titles on the same topic—be it vegetarian or bread machines—I recommend doing some homework before spending your money. Go to the library; check the book out, and give it a trial. Or head to a bookstore where you can sit in a comfy chair and give the author's ideas a serious read.

P.S. Used bookstores have been a source of many of my "finds," some of them last year's "in" books.

Chef John shared these popular "house" recipes.

WIENER SCHNITZEL/ VIENNA CUTLETS

MAKES 4 SERVINGS

2 eggs

½ cup flour

1 teaspoon salt

Dash of white pepper

2 cups fresh bread crumbs

1 pound veal loin, cut into
12 slices at the market

¼ cup Clarified Butter (see
page 154)

2 tablespoons fresh lemon
juice

12 lemon slices

Instead of veal, you may use pork tenderloin, sliced turkey breast, or chicken breast. You could use venison slices, moose tenderloin, or caribou loin, too, but you would need to soak the game in milk for two hours before cooking to sweeten the game taste.

Preheat oven to 350°F. Beat eggs and set aside.

Stir together flour, salt, and white pepper in shallow bowl wide enough to place a veal slice. Line up two more bowls of the same size; pour beaten eggs into one and put the bread crumbs in the other. Coat veal with flour, shaking off excess. Then dip into beaten egg, and then into bread crumbs.

Heat butter in a 12-inch skillet. When butter starts to bubble, add coated veal slices and brown. Turn them over and splash with lemon juice. Arrange in shallow baking pan. Cover and bake about 15 minutes, or until cooked through.

Serve 3 schnitzels on each plate. Garnish with lemon slices.

ENDLESSLY EASY CHICKEN BREASTS

MAKES 4 SERVINGS

4 boneless, skinless chicken
breast halves, about 6 to 7
ounces each

3 eggs

½ cup fresh grated Parmesan
cheese

1 cup flour

2 teaspoons salt

⅛ teaspoon white pepper

¼ cup clarified butter

2 tablespoons fresh lemon
juice

8 lemon slices, ¼-inch thick

Preheat oven to 350°F. Stir together eggs and Parmesan cheese, and whip smooth with wire whip. The egg batter should be of medium consistency (not too thick, not too thin).

Stir together the flour, salt, and white pepper. Spread in a pie plate. Meanwhile, heat the butter in a heavy 12-inch, oven-proof skillet. (Cast-iron works well.)

One at a time, dredge the check breasts in flour, then dip in Parmesan/egg mixture, coating well, then dip back into flour. Place in butter in the heated skillet. Brown lightly, turning once and splashing with lemon juice.

Cover the skillet full of chicken with oven-proof lid or heavy-duty aluminum foil. Place in preheated oven and bake 30 to 40 minutes. Remove and serve each breast garnished with 2 lemon slices.

6 cups grated potatoes, raw
2 teaspoons fresh lemon juice
½ cup diced onion
½ cup heavy cream
1 teaspoon salt
½ teaspoon white pepper
¼ cup butter

GRANDMA SCHUMACHER'S HASH BROWNS

MAKES 4 SERVINGS

"These are simply the best hash browns you will ever taste," boasts Chef John.

Potatoes can also be shredded. If you have one, a food processor works well for the shredding. Place prepared potatoes and lemon juice in a bowl, and let stand 10 minutes. Add onion, cream, salt, and pepper; mix well.

In a 10-inch nonstick frying pan, bring butter to a fast bubble. Add the potato batter—it will be thick—and cover. Cook 5 minutes on medium heat until potatoes are brown. Using spatula, push potato mixture toward center leaving ½-inch rim. Cut potato mixture into quarters. Turn potato quarters, cover, and steam 10 minutes. Potatoes should be light brown on both sides. Remove from pan to plate.

---

1 cup raisins
1 cup water
¼ cup Kahlua
1 cup granulated sugar
½ cup soft shortening, such as Crisco
2 eggs
2 cups all-purpose flour
1 teaspoon baking soda
1 teaspoon ground cinnamon
¼ teaspoon ground cloves
1 teaspoon vanilla
Pinch of salt
Cream Frosting (recipe follows), optional

FROSTED KAHLUA CREAMS

MAKES 12 LARGE BARS

Here Chef John embellishes a simple raisin spice bar that homemakers—my own mother included—have used for many a year.

Preheat oven to 350°F. Place raisins, water, and Kahlua in a saucepan. Simmer 5 minutes. Remove from heat and cool to room temperature. Drain and save raisin liquid.

Meanwhile, grease and flour a 13 x 9-inch baking pan. Put sugar and shortening in a mixing bowl and mix on high speed of electric mixer for two minutes. Scrape sides of bowl, and add eggs. Mix at medium speed for one minute. Scrape down sides of bowl. Add flour, baking soda, spices, vanilla, salt, and 1 cup of liquid from raisins; mix at medium speed one minute. Set beaters aside and stir drained raisins into batter by hand. Spread batter in prepared pan.

Bake for 25 to 30 minutes, or until golden brown. Cool to room temperature before frosting.

---

5 tablespoons brown sugar
3 tablespoons butter
¼ cup heavy whipping cream
1½ cups sifted powdered sugar
1 teaspoon vanilla

CREAM FROSTING

Put brown sugar, butter, and cream in a saucepan. Bring to a boil. Slow boil for one minute. Remove from heat and add powdered sugar and vanilla immediately. Stir until smooth. Top cooled bars with frosting.

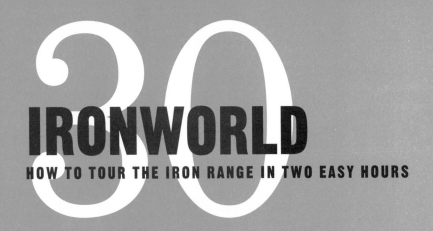

30 IRONWORLD
HOW TO TOUR THE IRON RANGE IN TWO EASY HOURS

On the Iron Range, at the turn of the *other* century, when iron mining was in its heyday, housing was scarce. Very, very scarce. So scarce that single miners had to rent sleeping space on the floor of the homes of married miners. In one home—now open for tours by Ironworld visitors—five single miners slept on the kitchen floor, sharing the one-bedroom home with a family of seven.

Five! Five grown men asleep on the floor of this not-very-large kitchen. Even with the furniture pushed back to the wall, each man would barely have room to stretch out, much less roll over. But mining was hard work; they probably slept soundly.

By day, the kitchen with its black wood-burning stove was the heart of the home. Cooking and baking were done here, perhaps some mending, too, while the bread rose and the soup bubbled. And all the canning was done—after the garden nearby had brought forth its fruit.

You get a glimpse of the activities of the Iron Range wife and mother (played by an interpreter in period costume) when you tour this very basic wooden house on the Glen Location at Ironworld Discovery Center, the museum at Chisholm. You come in the back door, just as the children would have come in from school, the miners from the pit. Despite having

This three-room home on the Glen Location is part of Ironworld, Chisholm. It housed twelve people in the early 1900s, the peak of iron mining in northern Minnesota.

An underground ore miner on the Range in 1906.

to tend the bacon she was frying, the friendly mother showed me the bedroom shared by the parents and the baby. And I peeked at the small living room where the four older children slept and where the family gathered in the evenings.

The washtubs with the wringer between them were standing near the little back porch. The outhouse (or do you call it the privy?) was not far beyond the back door.

But—more amazement!—the house was not stationary. The guide/mother says that the house was built so that it could be moved. Thus, the valuable ore could be dug from the soil below it. According to the guide, the children might come home from school and discover that their house had been moved three blocks. The houses were rolled on the huge logs that held them up.

Ironworld's two-car trolley, its cars beautifully preserved, carries visitors around the mine that, so long ago, was busy with digging and moving iron. There's a deep lake where nature has filled in what once was an ore pit. And there are tall trees where regrowth has covered the hills.

The conductor on the trolley (also an interpreter) explains how important these iron mines were to the winning of World War II. Metal much needed for tanks, ships, and guns came from the mines of the Range. Workers put in grueling shifts all during the war.

During those peak years in the early 1900s, the Iron Range became the home of people from forty-three nations of the world, with eastern Europe, Scandinavia, and Italy heavily represented. A man need not have been a miner in the Old Country. If he could swing a pickax or handle heavy equipment, he could find work on the Range. Men were hired for their brawn. These many national groups are now intertwined by marriage. For example, Amy Carlson, my museum guide, is Italian on one side and Polish on the other; and she's married to a German.

All summer long Ironworld offers daily self-guided tours and demonstrations. The Interpretive Museum itself offers much to see—and a welcome respite from a sudden rain or the hot sun. Rock hounds and wannabe geologists can lose themselves in the rock hall. Exhibits tell the stories, not only of mining, but of logging and immigrant life. And don't miss the observation deck looking out over a former open-pit mine.

There's an all-modern "Ethnic Kitchen," too, where volunteers demonstrate old-time recipes. The day I stopped by, it was Norwegian food day with *krumkake* (sometimes called Scandinavian ice cream cones) and rice pudding being prepared.

The late Rudy Perpich, who was born in Carson Lake, near Hibbing, is memorialized in a painting-lined room at the museum. As a two-time governor of Minnesota and an international businessman, this tall man with the big smile was instrumental in bringing new business to northeastern Minnesota after mining slowed.

Individuals who have traced their family roots to this area will find records to search at the Iron Range Research Center, an inviting, quiet library attached to the museum. This center is open year-round.

When you catch sight of the huge statue of an iron miner that marks the entrance, you know you're near Ironworld. The complex also includes the Minnesota CCC History Museum and the Mineland Reclamation Division. Happily, Chisholm has ample lodging for visitors—you won't have to sleep on the floor.

NIFTY, THRIFTY SOUP

You can make a pot of soup *and* clean out your refrigerator—a good Saturday morning job, even if you have a no-defrost fridge.

Start with the vegetable drawer; pull out any carrots, celery, or peppers that are getting wobbly, and chop them. Next mince some onion and mash some garlic. Stir and cook these veggies in a little oil in a heavy saucepan. Next add any cooked vegetables, that is, green beans, peas, tomatoes, a stray potato—dibs and dabs you've put away in the freezer or shoved back in the fridge. While you're at it, pull out a bottle of pickles. Toss the vegetables in the pan, add some water or broth (I like a mixture of beef and chicken broth) and start things cooking. When it's bubbling nicely, throw in leftovers du jour—using your taste sense, of course. Then add a handful of pasta (elbow macaroni or rotini, perhaps) plus a tablespoon or two of pickle juice—that helps meld the flavors. Bring to bubbling, cook 7 to 10 minutes, or until pasta is tender. Serve topped with grated Parmesan or croutons.

The Old Country Cookbook: Iron Range Ethnic Food, a cookbook published by volunteers for the Iron Range Interpretative Center (forerunner of Ironworld), provided the inspiration for this selection of recipes.

ITALIAN PORKETTA

MAKES 8 SERVINGS

4-pound boneless pork butt
roast

½ cup chopped fresh parsley
or 2 tablespoons dried
parsley flakes

¼ cup fennel seeds

2 teaspoons salt

2 teaspoons freshly ground
black pepper

½ teaspoon garlic powder

½ teaspoon onion powder

This boned, seasoned pork roast has become so popular in the Twin Cities that it is now available, ready to roast, in the meat departments of the larger supermarkets.

Preheat oven to 350°F. Cut the roast in half lengthwise and open it like a book. Combine the parsley, fennel, salt, pepper, garlic powder, and onion powder. Rub it over both sides of the meat, pressing the fennel seeds into the meat. Fold the meat back together and secure the roast with a string (or thread).

Place in a shallow roasting pan. Roast for 45 to 60 minutes or until temperature on meat thermometer reads 150 to 155°F. Let roast rest 5 to 20 minutes before slicing.

(Traditionally, porketta is roasted until meat falls apart. To serve Old World style, pull pork apart with fork.)

ENGLISH MEAT PASTIES

MAKES 6 SERVINGS

For pastry:

3 cups all-purpose
unbleached flour

1 ½ teaspoons salt

1 cup soft shortening, such
as Crisco

6 tablespoons cold water

For filling:

2 cups ½-inch cubes beef
chuck steak

2 cups cubed potatoes

1 cup chopped onion

1 cup finely chopped rutabaga
or diced carrots

Minnesota iron miners took these hearty turnovers, called pasties, often wrapped in newspaper for insulation, to the mines with them for a nutritious lunch. And the miners' children carried pasties to school instead of sandwiches. Lead miners liked pasties as much as iron miners did, according to my late mother, who had lead miners on her family tree. Those forebears took pasties to the mine each day, first in the Old Country, Cornwall, and later in the New Country, Spring Green, Wisconsin.

Preheat oven to 375°F. Combine flour and salt in mixing bowl. Using pastry blender or two knives, cut shortening into flour mixture until size of peas. Blend in water until slightly sticky. Gather dough into a large ball. If you wish, pastry dough can be wrapped and refrigerated until ready to roll and bake.

Divide dough into 6 equal parts. Toss together the meat and vegetables. Season with salt and pepper and toss again.

For each pasty: Roll one part of dough into a 9-inch circle, roughly the size of a dinner plate. Place a scant cupful of the filling on one side of the pastry. Fold one side of pastry circle over filling. Press edges together carefully. Crimp or flute edges to seal tightly. For easy handling, line the baking sheet with kitchen parchment paper before placing the filled pastry on the baking sheet. Bake for 45 to 55 minutes, or until filling is fork tender and pastry is golden brown. Use a wide spatula to move pasties from baking sheet to plates after baking—they are tender and break easily. Often served with mustard, ketchup or tomato sauce.

CZECH KOLACHES

Two or three fillings (recipe follows)*
2 envelopes active dry yeast (4½ teaspoons)
½ cup warm water (110 to 115°F)
1½ cups lukewarm milk (scalded then cooled)
½ cup sugar
1 teaspoon salt
2 eggs
½ cup oil or soft shortening
6 to 7 cups all-purpose unbleached flour
Oil for brushing buns after baking

A fruit-filled roll that has become popular all over Minnesota since Czech immigrants brought it to the area.

Preheat oven to 400°F. Have fillings ready ahead of time.

Dissolve the yeast in the warm water.

Using a large mixing bowl, stir the milk, sugar, salt, eggs, oil or shortening and half the flour together. Mix until batter is smooth. Stir in the dissolved yeast. Add just enough of the remaining flour to make a dough that handles easily. Try to add flour only until the dough passes the sticky stage. Flour a work surface or spread out a pastry cloth. Dust surface lightly with flour. Knead the dough 5 to 10 minutes, or until smooth. Place dough in a greased bowl; turn the ball of dough once to put the greased side up. Cover bowl with a cloth. Let dough rise in a warm place, 1 to 1½ hours.

Punch yeast dough down and divide in half; cover remaining half to shape later. Cut or pull off small portions of dough the size of a walnut. Shape dough into balls. Arrange balls of dough on greased baking sheets about 9 balls per sheet. If the room is warm, dough balls will have risen almost enough to be filled by the time you have rolled the first batch—24 or 25 rolls.

Using both hands to shape two kolaches at a time (it's speedier!), push your second and third fingers down into the center of each ball of dough, forming a rim about half an inch wide. Fill each indentation with a heaping tablespoon of filling. Let kolaches rise briefly.

Bake rolls for 10 to 12 minutes, or until golden. Watch carefully as rolls brown quickly. Remove from oven and brush with oil. Place kolaches on wire racks to cool.

Repeat the shaping and filling process with second half of dough using another flavor of filling. These rolls freeze beautifully.

DRIED FRUIT FILLING

12 ounces pitted dried plums or apricots
Water
About ¼ cup sugar

Cook plums or apricots in water to cover until soft. For plums, mash cooked fruit with a fork, then sweeten with sugar. If desired, half a teaspoon of cinnamon can be added to plums. For apricots, blend with sugar in food processor or blender to form a thick mixture.

*Canned apricot and poppy seed fillings made by Sokol & Co. under the Solo brand work well in kolaches.

NORTH STAR COOKS

176 Leeann Chin: Mother,
Caterer, Teacher,
Restaurateur

182 Hockey Mom Beth
Dooley Puts Health
on the Menu

188 Marie Vogl Gery,
Breakfast Queen

193 Al Sicherman, a.k.a.
Mr. Tidbit

199 Grais Notes on
Minnesota Jewish
Cooking

205 Ginny Hoeschen: Live
from the Test Kitchen

210 Lynne Rosetto Kasper
and Her Splendid
Table

215 Bea Ojakangas:
Cookbook Writer Is a
Favorite Finn

220 State Fair Judge Jan
Stroom Finds the Best

226 Eberhard Werthmann:
The Dean of Cooking
Teachers

LEEANN CHIN
MOTHER, CATERER, TEACHER, RESTAURATEUR

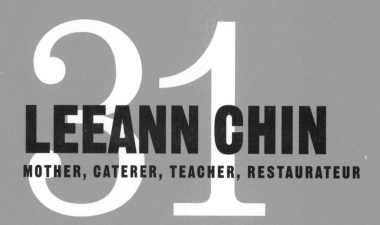

When she left China for Minnesota in 1956, Leeann Chin began a new chapter of her personal life. And when she opened her first restaurant in 1980, she began a new chapter of her professional life.

Wai-Hing (she chose the name Leeann when she came to this country) was born and raised in Canton, part of a large close family. Her father ran a grocery store. She worked at the store after school, figuring accounts on the abacus and delivering heavy bags of rice on her bicycle. There she became acquainted with China's fruits and vegetables, meats and spices. At mealtime, she worked alongside her mother or the family's cook, learning how to prepare the delicious foods of her native province.

Wai-Hing (Leeann Chin) at sixteen (far left) with friends in China.

At seventeen, Wai-Hing was sent to Hong Kong, where she married Tony Chin, as their parents had arranged. This was the period when the Communist regime controlled every aspect of the lives of the Chinese. Not long after her marriage, the border between Hong Kong and China was closed, making it impossible for the young wife to visit her family in Canton. (Reunited after thirty-five years, she now visits them annually.)

In 1956, when Wai-Hing was twenty-three, the Chins boarded ship for the United States, immigrating to Minneapolis where Tony's sister and her family lived. Leeann became the mother of five children, four daughters and a son.

Though many of the ingredients used in their homeland were not yet available in Minnesota, Tony expected Chinese fare and Leeann created it with local foods. Her guiding principles were (1) use the freshest, best ingredients you can find, and (2) balance the color, flavor, and texture of the food.

As her children were growing up, Leeann began taking in sewing and alteration work to help the family budget. As a gesture of appreciation for her women customers, now friends as well as clients, she hosted a luncheon featuring some of her specialties. They loved her food—the lightness of the batters on the meats, the delicacy of the sauces. And they began asking her to cater parties for them and to put on classes to teach them her skills.

Before long Leeann was catering and teaching all over town. We met for the first time when she included me in a Chinese New Year celebration at her home. She packed the first floor of the house with chairs and tables and fed us royally. Though she had prepared many platters of colorful food and seen to every detail of the party herself, the petite Leeann was the picture of the gracious hostess, perfectly groomed in a simple silk sheath.

Leeann Chin, in 1985 at her first Leeann Chin's Chinese Cuisine eatery in the Bonaventure shopping center in Minnetonka.

Then I began to hear rumors that Leeann was starting a restaurant. Adding glamour to the enterprise, movie actor Sean Connery was among her first investors. He had met Leeann and been impressed with her food when she had catered parties at the home of Carl Pohlad, then-new owner of the Minnesota Twins. Pohlad, too, invested in the new venture.

Her lovely restaurant, Leeann Chin's Chinese Cuisine, opened in Bonaventure shopping center in Minnetonka in 1980. Open and airy, decorated with beautiful Chinese art, the restaurant was a world away from the typical Cantonese eatery, all done in heavy black and red. Chin's food was delicious, fresh, and healthy, particularly the lemon chicken—lightly battered pieces of tender chicken breast in a tangy sauce garnished with slices of lemon—which quickly became one of her signature dishes. Service was buffet style, which customers liked because they could try a little of a new food—spicy Szechuan perhaps—while serving themselves more of a favorite.

Leeann plunged wholeheartedly into her new business. Her family kept busy, too: son and daughter William and Jean in college, daughter Linda practicing law in New York City, younger daughter Katie busy with high school, and husband Tony involved in his own career. Daughter Laura, continually interested in the business, helped Leeann open the new restaurant. Leeann followed the work ethic she had learned at her father's store. Her reputation for excellent food grew steadily.

Also in 1980, General Mills asked her to create recipes for a cookbook. The dishes already popularized in her cooking classes formed the core of *Betty Crocker's Chinese Cookbook, Recipes by Leeann Chin* published in 1981. (A bestseller, the book's second edition appeared in 1990.)

She soon opened restaurants in the Union Depot Place in St. Paul and the International Centre in downtown Minneapolis, both with larger buffets and more seating than the one in Bonaventure. Amazing to me, these spacious restaurants are quiet, even when full, thanks to Leeann's attention to acoustics and space and her use of carpeting and other sound-absorbing elements.

Then Leeann Chin, Inc., began building a freestanding carryout restaurant in virtually every Twin Cities suburb. Diners could eat in—there's a serving line and in-store seating—or take out, choosing from among her most popular items: potstickers, Peking chicken, Young Jewel Fried Rice. I found visits to her restaurants a delightful way to learn about Chinese ingredients. For example, *fun see*, used in soups and stir-fries, is cellophane noodles. And I'm very fond of oyster sauce, thanks to her Chicken Wings with Oyster Sauce.

The company also added deli-style carryouts selling her specialties in supermarkets. For example, most the Byerly's and Lund's stores feature a Leeann Chin counter. Shoppers have found it very convenient to buy their groceries, then select a hot Chinese meal to enjoy as soon as they get home. Customers in the Marketplace section of the downtown Minneapolis Marshall Field's department store can buy a Leeann Chin meal too. All told there were fifty places to buy Leeann's food by 2002.

Two of Leeann's daughters, Laura and Katie, are following in her footsteps. (Of her other children, one daughter is an attorney, another, a physician, and her son is a math professor.) Laura, a chef, is involved with local and national community affairs. Katie, an entertainment consultant in Los Angeles, co-wrote *Everyday Chinese Cooking: Quick and Delicious Recipes from the Leeann Chin Restaurants* (2000) with Leeann. The idea for the book came when Leeann discovered that Katie's cupboard was all but bare and set about to teach her daughter some basics. The book, with over 150 recipes (including tofu ideas for vegetarians), is dedicated to Leeann's seven grandchildren.

THANK YOU FOODS

When someone has done you a good deed, there's no better way to say thanks than to prepare a treat for them. A big batch of cookies can fill the family cookie jar *and* show appreciation to a helpful neighbor, the mechanics who service your car, or your mail carrier. I've taken bags of goodies to the beauty school where I get my hair done and to the audiologist who adjusts my hearing aids. Recycle take-out containers for safe take-along.

Here is a sampling of the everyday Chinese recipes from this recent cookbook.

HONEY BARBECUED PORK

3 pounds boneless pork butt or shoulder

For marinade:

¼ cup ketchup

2 teaspoons salt

4 teaspoon sugar

2 teaspoons minced garlic

2 teaspoons brandy

1 teaspoon five-spice powder*

½ cup honey

*a mixture of ground cinnamon, cloves, fennel seed, star anise, and Szechuan peppercorns

The mother-daughter writing team suggests serving sliced barbecued pork atop hot cooked rice with oyster sauce for a Chinatown rice bowl.

Trim all fat off pork; cut pork into six 1-inch-thick slices. In a glass bowl, combine the ketchup, salt, sugar, garlic, brandy, five-spice powder, and honey. Add pork slices and rub this mixture on the slices, covering all sides. Cover the pork and marinate in the refrigerator at least 2 hours.

Preheat the oven to 425°F.

Place the pork on a rack in a roasting pan and roast 20 minutes. Turn the meat and cook another 20 minutes. Reduce the oven temperature to 350°F and cook 20 minutes more, or until pork reaches an internal temperature of 170°F. Remove from oven. Brush any remaining sauce from roasting pan over pork before serving.

CHICKEN SKEWERS

12 (6-inch long) wooden skewers

1 pound skinless, boneless chicken breasts

For marinade:

1 tablespoon vegetable oil

2 teaspoons dry white wine

1 teaspoon peeled and finely chopped fresh ginger

1 teaspoon cornstarch

1 teaspoon salt

1 teaspoon dark soy sauce

½ teaspoon sugar

½ teaspoon ground white pepper

¼ teaspoon dark, oriental sesame oil

The Chins suggest marinating the chicken in the refrigerator during the day so that it will be ready to cook that night. Serve either as an appetizer or as a main course. They add that any leftovers make an excellent salad tossed with greens the next day.

Soak the wooden skewers in water for 30 minutes before broiling (so they won't catch fire in the broiler).

Cut the chicken into 2 x ½-inch strips. Mix the vegetable oil, wine, ginger, cornstarch, salt, soy sauce, sugar, pepper, and sesame oil in a glass or plastic bowl. Add the chicken strips and stir. Cover and refrigerate at least 30 minutes.

Preheat the broiler. Thread 3 chicken strips onto each skewer. Repeat until all skewers are prepared. Broil about 4 inches from the heat, keeping your eyes on the chicken, which can overcook quickly. Cook about 5 minutes, turning once.

GREEN BEANS WITH CASHEWS

MAKES 4 SERVINGS

1 pound fresh green beans

2 tablespoons vegetable oil

2 teaspoons minced garlic

2 tablespoons hoisin sauce

2 tablespoons oyster sauce

2 ounces roasted cashews (about ½ cup), coarsely chopped, if desired

Hoisin is a sweet and spicy, reddish brown sauce; oyster sauce is dark brown and lends richness without overpowering other flavors. Both are sold bottled. Buy them for these recipes, then be adventurous: add them—sparingly—to other foods.

Rinse the beans with cold water; drain. Snap off both ends. Break beans in half or in 2-inch pieces.

Heat a wok or skillet over high heat. Add the vegetable oil and beans; stir-fry for 2 minutes. Add the garlic, hoisin sauce, and oyster sauce; cover and cook until tender-crisp, about 4 minutes. Remove to a serving platter. Garnish with roast cashews. Serve immediately.

YEUNG CHAU FRIED RICE

MAKES 2 TO 3 SERVINGS

3 tablespoons vegetable oil

1 large egg, slightly beaten

4 cups cooked white rice

½ cup peas

½ cup ½-inch diced carrots, blanched in boiling water 1 minute

½ cup diced fresh mushrooms

¾ cup cooked shrimp

¾ cup diced barbecued or cooked chicken

2 green onions, with tops, diced

1 tablespoon oyster sauce

Colorful vegetables add vibrancy to this popular recipe, noted the cookbook authors. I recommend barbecued chicken rather than just plain cooked chicken.

Have all ingredients cut, measured, and assembled near the wok or skillet.

Heat a wok or nonstick skillet over high heat, add the vegetable oil, and stir-fry the egg. Cook the egg to soft scramble. If the rice has just been cooked, fluff with a fork to allow steam to escape and rice to cool before adding to the wok. After the rice is added, stir constantly and cook 2 minutes (turn heat down if rice starts to stick).

Add the peas, carrots, mushrooms, shrimp, chicken, green onions, and oyster sauce. Stir until well mixed and vegetables are hot, about 1 minute.

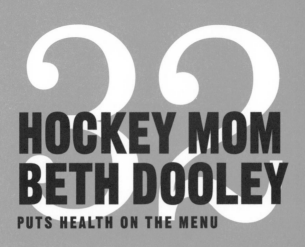

HOCKEY MOM BETH DOOLEY

PUTS HEALTH ON THE MENU

"Behind every hockey kid is a hockey mom"
—motto for the Minnesota Hockey Mom Competition, 2001.

And behind Matt, Kip, and Tim Dooley is Beth Dooley of Minneapolis, a hockey mom, a soccer mom, and a ski mom. What's more, she's an early-morning runner, supercook, frequent hostess, cookbook writer, and restaurant reviewer. Discussing her role as a hockey mom, Beth adds that she's also a hockey sister and a hockey wife. "My brothers and I went to St. Lawrence (the university, in Canton, New York)," she says. "It's a big hockey school." That's where her husband Kevin went—and skated—too. Kevin, then just out of law school, also played pick-up hockey here after the couple moved to Minnesota from the East. They have season tickets for the University of Minnesota Gopher hockey team as well and Kevin takes their sons to the games at Mariucci Arena when school schedules permit.

"On hockey days, I feed the boys about 4:30 in the afternoon. They're starved then. Oh, something like my barley soup or corn chowder," she explains. "Then it's off to New Hope or Columbia Heights (or wherever) for a game. Sometimes Matt (the eldest) plays three to five nights a week. We may not get home 'til 10 o'clock and they may have cereal, some oatmeal, something easy to go to sleep on."

All sorts of physical activities fill the Dooley calendar year-round. They skate, ski, swim, bike, and play soccer because it's fun, and because it gives them rosy cheeks and good appetites. Never mind that the back hall is almost impassable thanks to three kids' worth of skates and hockey gear in winter; bats, tennis rackets, and balls of all sorts in summer. There's a closet, sure, but it's

mighty hard for the boys to hang up their stuff when their eager dog is jumping all over them, wanting some action.

Matthew Dooley was just two years old and Kip (short for Christopher) was just home from the hospital in fall 1989, when I started spending Monday nights with the Dooley family. (Third son, Tim, was born four years later.) When I was moving to St. Peter to start my bed-and-breakfast, Beth said, "You know, we've got a grandmother's room and you're welcome to use it whenever you want." Thus began weekly visits that continued for five-plus years as I worked both at the *Star Tribune* in Minneapolis and at my four-room inn in Nicollet County.

On my in-town nights, I enjoyed the bountiful and healthy meals that Beth serves her family. Sometimes I helped taste-test recipes she was developing for one of the cookbooks she produced during those years.

Just as the Dooleys skate and swim because it's fun, they eat lots of fruits and vegetables because they're good—and good for you. Beth has long been an advocate of community supported agriculture. She was a member of Red Cardinal Farm (now defunct) for several years, eagerly preparing meals with the bumper crops that came in her weekly vegetable-and-herb share. These days the family participates in the Lake Country Land School, a teaching farm in Wisconsin operated by Lake Country Day School in Minneapolis, which the boys attend.

She prefers organic products and shops regularly for them at the Wedge Community Co-op, just a good walk from her home in Kenwood. With the store so close, she shops every day or so for fresh foods. Before her sons were born, Beth worked with fresh fruits and vegetables every day as a publicist for Sno-Boy products, a major player in the Midwest produce market. It was through Sno-Boy that I met Beth. Her office was a wonderful resource for clear photos—and the recipes that went with them—when I was featuring a certain fruit or vegetable in Taste, the weekly food section in the *Star Tribune*.

Beth is one of those women who, when she gets an idea, just goes for it. That's how she wrote her first cookbook. I had mentioned that a Chanhassen company was seeking manuscripts for cookbooks as part of a series of state-themed gift lines. A few months later, she brought me one of the first copies of *Recipes from Massachusetts . . . with love*. She had cowritten it with her mother, Liz Anton of Short Hills, New Jersey. That was in 1985. I was amazed at how speedily they had pulled it off. And she'd kept it light, doing fun things like naming their version of Red Flannel Hash, Red Bandana Hash.

Writing cookbooks works for her and gives her the flexibility so desirable with a growing family. Between books, she also writes cookery articles and restaurant reviews for national and regional magazines. Her background at Sno-Boy served her well in writing *It's the Berries* in 1988 and *Peppers, Hot & Sweet* in 1990. They are part of an A, Apples, to Z, Zucchini, cookbook series by Garden Way.

Beth and Lucia Watson, chef/owner of Lucia's Restaurant in Minneapolis (a favorite of mine) spent months on the testing and writing of their cookbook *Savoring the Seasons of the Northern Heartland*. It was published in 1994 and is part of the prestigious Knopf Cooks American series. Lucia often joins Beth on early morning runs and the two have collaborated on features for *Fine Cooking* magazine.

Next came an Italian period as Beth did the recipe testing and copy writing for *Quick & Healthy Low-Fat Cooking Featuring Pasta and Other Italian Favorites* (1996). She was back in the familiar Midwest for *The Heartland*, which came out in 2001, part of the Williams-Sonoma New American Cooking Series.

Beth's writing, whether books or articles, is often marked by lively personal vignettes, glimpses of her growing-up years or her current family life, that pull the reader into her subject. She writes with ease about "sun-ripened appetites" and "two-fisted meat turnovers," a skill based not only on her master's degree courses in creative writing but also her genuine love of healthy living, friends, and family.

Try these Beth specials, chosen from her cookbooks.

2 tablespoons butter
2 cups peeled, diced onions
2 cups diced carrots
3 cups diced celery
2 cloves garlic, peeled and
  diced
1 ½ cups peeled, diced russet
  potatoes
½ cup pearled barley
8 cups homemade chicken
  broth or low-salt canned
  broth
2 bay leaves
1 teaspoon dried thyme or
  1 tablespoon fresh thyme
½ cup white wine
½ cup heavy cream
2 cups diced, cooked chicken
  or turkey meat
Salt and freshly ground pepper
  to taste
Fresh parsley for garnish

CREAMY CHICKEN AND BARLEY SOUP

MAKES 8 TO 10 SERVINGS

This is one of the delicious, filling soup recipes that are standbys for hockey kids and their busy parents. It is from Savoring the Seasons of the Northern Heartland. *I consider a container of this soup in the freezer something akin to an insurance policy, ready when you need it.*

In a large stockpot, melt the butter and stir-fry the onions, carrots, celery, and garlic until soft.

Add the potatoes, barley, stock, bay leaves, and thyme. Cook, partially covered, 1 hour or until potatoes and barley are tender. Add the wine, cream, chicken, and salt and pepper to taste. Heat to serving temperature. Serve garnished with minced parsley.

2 tablespoons butter

1 medium onion, chopped
  (about ¾ cup)

2 cloves garlic, minced

1 ½ cups diced, canned roast
  red peppers*

2 tablespoons all-purpose flour

2 cups chicken stock

¾ cup heavy cream**

Salt and freshly ground black
  pepper

*4 medium red bell peppers
  before roasting

**To save some calories, use
  ½ cup fat-free half-and-half
  plus ¼ cup lowfat milk in
  place of cream.

RED PEPPER SOUP

MAKES 4 SERVINGS

Here is my simplified version of Beth's colorful pepper soup. The original version, in which you roast the peppers yourself, was published in her cookbook, Peppers Hot & Sweet.

In a medium-size saucepan over low-medium heat, melt the butter and stir-fry the onion and garlic until transparent. Add the peppers and cook 5 minutes. Stir in the flour and cook about 2 minutes—do not brown.

Slowly whisk in the chicken stock and bring the mixture to a boil. Reduce the heat and simmer gently 15 to 20 minutes.

In a blender or food processor fitted with the steel blade, puree the pepper mixture until smooth. Return the mixture to the saucepan. Whisk in the cream and cook until hot through—do not boil. Add salt and pepper to taste. Serve hot, or chill and serve cold.

¼ cup fresh bread crumbs

½ cup grated Colby cheese

8 large ears of corn, husks
  and silk removed

3 shallots, minced

1 cup heavy whipping cream,
  lukewarm

3 dashes Tabasco or other hot
  pepper sauce

1 teaspoon salt

¼ teaspoon freshly ground
  pepper

6 eggs, lightly beaten

2 teaspoons chopped fresh dill
  or thyme or ¾ teaspoon dried

Boiling water, as needed

FRESH CORN PUDDING

MAKES 4 TO 6 MAIN-DISH SERVINGS,
8 SIDE-DISH SERVINGS

For a hot dish occasion—potluck, church supper, covered-dish party—try cutting down the cut corn to 3 cups (1 to process until creamy, 2 to combine with eggs, thyme, and cheese) and add 1 cup of diced ham or leftover turkey.

Preheat oven to 350°F. Butter a 2-quart baking dish. Sprinkle with bread crumbs and 2 tablespoons of the cheese and tilt to coat the bottom and sides evenly.

Resting an ear of corn on its stalk end in a shallow bowl, cut down along the ear with a sharp knife, stripping off the kernels and rotating the ear with each cut. Then run the flat side of the blade along the ear to remove any "milk." Repeat with as many ears as necessary until you have 4 cups corn kernels. Set aside.

In a food processor, combine 1 cup of the corn, the shallots, cream, hot pepper sauce, salt, and pepper. Process until creamy.

Turn the corn mixture into a large bowl and stir in the eggs, the remaining 3 cups corn, dill, and cheese. Pour into the prepared dish. To cover the dish, coat one side of a piece of aluminum foil generously with butter and place it, butter side down, over the dish. Put the dish in a deep roasting pan and fill the pan with boiling water to reach two-thirds of the way up the sides of the dish.

Bake for 45 minutes. Remove the foil cover and continue baking until the pudding is lightly browned on top and a knife inserted into the center comes out clean, about 15 minutes longer. Serve immediately.

For filling:

3 cups homemade chicken
  stock or low-salt canned
  chicken broth
3 carrots, diced
2 medium potatoes, peeled
  and diced
2 ribs celery, diced
4 tablespoons (½ stick) butter
1 cup chopped, peeled onions
4 tablespoons all-purpose
  flour
½ cup whole milk
½ teaspoon dried thyme
¼ teaspoon ground nutmeg
¼ cup green peas
¼ cup corn kernels, fresh or
  frozen
Salt and freshly ground pepper
  to taste
2 ½ cups diced cooked
  chicken or turkey

For crust:

1 ½ cups all-purpose flour
½ teaspoon baking powder
½ teaspoon baking soda
¾ teaspoon salt
4 tablespoons (½ stick) butter,
  cut into bits
⅓ cup grated sharp Cheddar
  cheese
1 egg
½ cup buttermilk
Egg wash: 1 egg yolk mixed
  with 1 tablespoon milk

CHICKEN (OR TURKEY) POT PIE   MAKES 6 SERVINGS

Another wonderful example of the hot dish so long popular in Minnesota. Meat, vegetables, and bread all in one satisfying dish. From Savoring the Seasons.

Bring the chicken stock to a low simmer in a large stockpot. Add the carrots, potatoes, and celery, and simmer until the vegetables are soft, about 5 minutes. Drain the vegetables and reserve the stock; set the vegetables aside.

Melt the butter in a deep skillet and stir-fry the chopped onions over medium heat until they are soft, then sprinkle in the flour and cook some more, stirring, 3 to 5 minutes. Add the milk and 2 cups of the chicken stock in a stream, stirring, and bring to a boil. Add the thyme and nutmeg and cook about 5 minutes—mixture should be thick. Add the peas and corn. Taste and adjust with salt and pepper. Add the chicken and vegetables that were cooked in broth; stir to combine. Turn the filling into a large casserole dish. Cover to keep warm while making the crust.

For crust, sift together the flour, baking powder, baking soda, and salt. Cut in the butter until the dough resembles coarse meal, then toss in the grated cheese. Whisk the egg with the buttermilk. Add to the flour mixture and gently stir to make a soft dough. Turn the dough out onto a lightly floured surface and pat it into a large round.

At this point, preheat oven to 425°F. Cut the dough into 2 ½-inch circles with cookie cutter or the top of a drinking glass. Place the biscuits on top of the chicken filling. Brush with egg wash.

Bake for 20 to 25 minutes or until crust is golden brown and filling is bubbling.

33 MARIE VOGL GERY

BREAKFAST QUEEN

After serving 4,923 breakfasts in eleven years at her Martin Oaks Bed and Breakfast in Dundas, Marie Vogl Gery could certainly write the book on being a B&B cook and hostess. But, no, she would rather write poetry and scripts. Like hundreds of B&B owners, Marie exemplifies Minnesota hospitality. And like many multitalented hosts, Marie is active in the community. She is a member of Northfield Women Poets, who recently published *Tremors, Vibrations Enough to Change the World*, an anthology. And she writes scripts for the storytelling programs she performs. One of the women whose story she delights in presenting is Juliet Low, the wealthy widow who founded the Girl Scouts. Another is Zerelda Samuels, mother of Jesse James, whose botched hold-up gave rise to the annual Northfield celebration, the Defeat of Jesse James Days.

When I stayed the night at Martin Oaks, Marie and I explored the house while she told me a bit of its history. The original portion, built in 1869 (remember, Minnesota became a state in 1858) was just two rooms—living space downstairs and a bedroom upstairs, a pattern used for many a frontier cabin. It was built for Sara Etta Archibald Martin, just a few years after her family had founded the community of Dundas on the banks of the Cannon River. They ran a mill on the river, a mill whose patents were bought by the company that's now General Mills. In 1876, the house was enlarged. The original rooms were encircled by kitchen, living room, dining room, and staircase on the main floor and three more bedrooms on the second floor.

The multitalented Marie Vogl Gery on her porch.

Marie and her husband Frank bought the attractive house on the riverbank in the friendly little town of 400-plus in 1990. They opened it as Martin Oaks B&B (Martin for the original family, oaks for the surrounding trees) a year later. Frank taught economics at St. Olaf College in nearby Northfield. Business was good, particularly when there were events at St. Olaf or neighboring Carleton College. (The Gerys retired and closed the B&B in 2002; they now live in Northfield.)

Though pretty plantings are a feature at many B&Bs, Marie's garden was very large, all but replacing the lawn. Flower beds completely surrounded the house. Marie was passionate about her flowers, spending hours on her knees with trowel and pruning shears. She took breaks from her work only to check the answering machine for messages from would-be guests.

After the garden tour, we took our ease on the big wraparound porch. It's a lovely space, naturally cooled by the ancient oaks. A commodious porch is a feature of many historic B&Bs (my own included), but the Gerys' was more, really a porch room.

Upstairs, I found two treats in my pretty antique-filled bedroom. The first: books she had selected just for me. Second: a big chocolate-covered strawberry, a little glass of sherry, and one of her Killer Brownies. The next morning, when I opened the door heading to the bathroom, there was a tray with a fancy white coffeepot and a demitasse cup for that important first cup of coffee in the morning. Marie must have tiptoed to the door very early because I had heard no sound.

At Martin Oaks, breakfast was served by candlelight. When they realized their dining room was rather dark (due to the wide staircase between that room and the bank of windows) the Gerys filled the room with candles. The buffet, the sideboard, and the table itself all held candles. The candlelight was inviting, with light glinting off the elegant china and glassware.

At her candlelight breakfasts Marie served all sorts of special egg entrées, homebaked bread or muffins and, usually, a dessert. Many guests returned again and again, so Marie tried not to repeat breakfast menus. Perfecting new recipes was no hardship, because she loves to cook. And her kitchen was roomy and well equipped. The day I was there she made a quiche with lots of sharp Cheddar and big chunks of ham. Alongside were mini cinnamon rolls made slightly risqué by the brandy flavoring in the currants.

Marie is an avid reader and collector of all sorts of books, including cookbooks. She also carries on a lively recipe exchange with friends, family, and other B&B owners. She admits to changing printed recipes—even before she

FOODS TO SHOW YOU CARE

Preparing food for friends and neighbors when a family member is ill or a new baby has arrived is a wonderful way to be "Midwest nice." I'll not soon forget how happy I was when Muriel Johnson, a fine Swedish cook, arrived to see our newborn daughter bringing a deep bowl filled with her delicious, tiny meatballs—so easy to reheat, so satisfying. During the years that I worked at home, I always kept tuna, cream soup, and cashews in the cupboard so that I could put together a favorite tuna casserole to take to someone. Nowadays, I keep cans of pumpkin and cream cheese frosting handy to make pumpkin bars for giving.

tries them. The cookbooks that Marie likes best are those that carry stories along with the directions.

Marie gladly released these directions for several of her creations.

1 (17-ounce) package frozen
    puff pastry sheets
½ cup currants
Brandy for marinating currants

For caramel:
⅔ cup butter
1 cup packed brown sugar
2 tablespoons white corn
    syrup

To complete recipe:
¾ cup finely chopped pecans
Grated lemon rind
¼ cup melted butter
1 tablespoon cinnamon
½ cup granulated sugar

TINY CARAMEL ROLLS

MAKES 12 ROLLS

This recipe is adapted from one by Northfield's Ruthanna Gustafson.

Ahead of time: Place puff pastry package in refrigerate to thaw (overnight works well). Pour brandy over currants; cover and set aside.

Preheat oven to 350°F. For caramel, combine the ⅔ cup butter, brown sugar, and white corn syrup in medium saucepan. Bring to a boil and simmer 1 minute.

Drizzle the caramel all over the bottom of a 13 x-9-inch oblong pan.

Sprinkle each sheet of puff pastry with ½ teaspoon finely grated lemon rind. Roll lemon rind into sheets with rolling pin. Spread each sheet with 1 tablespoon of the melted butter.

Mix the cinnamon into the granulated sugar. Sprinkle cinnamon sugar over each buttered sheet of puff pastry.

Drain currants and divide evenly, spreading them over the two sheets of puff pastry. Place one sheet on top of the other

and roll tightly. If puff pastry has gotten warm, place in refrigerator to cool before cutting. Cut into 12 equal parts. Place in prepared pan atop caramel.

Bake 30 to 35 minutes or until rolls are puffed and golden brown. Tip rolls out of pan onto wax paper as soon as removed from oven. Let cool a few minutes. Using a spatula, transfer rolls to a serving platter and drizzle remainder of the caramel from pan over them. Serve warm.

Variation: Pour a little of the caramel mixture into bottom of each of 12 custard cups, dividing evenly. After cutting the rolls, place in custard cups atop caramel. Place the filled cups in a larger pan. Bake as directed. Tip rolls out of cups onto a platter after removing from oven.

Note: This caramel bubbles up quickly, so place a larger pan below baking pan to catch any spills.

1 loaf French bread, crust
   removed

For syrup:

½ cup unsalted butter
1 cup packed brown sugar
2 tablespoons white corn
   syrup

For batter:

5 eggs, preferably jumbo
1 ½ cups half-and-half
1 teaspoon vanilla
1 teaspoon Grand Marnier
Powdered sugar, violets, and
   mint leaves for garnish

CRÈME BRULÉE FRENCH TOAST   MAKES 6 SERVINGS

An easy do-ahead recipe from the B&B grapevine. It originated at the Inn at Sunrise Point, Camden, Maine, and was published in Gourmet *magazine in July 1998. It was given to the Gerys by the owners of Twin Gables Inn, Saugatuck, Michigan.*

Cut trimmed loaf of French bread into one-inch thick slices.

Make syrup by melting butter in small saucepan with brown sugar and corn syrup. Cook over moderate heat, stirring until smooth. Pour into a 13 x 9-inch baking dish. Arrange bread slices in single layer over syrup in baking dish. You may need to squeeze them slightly to fit.

Whisk eggs, half-and-half, vanilla, and Grand Marnier together in large bowl until smooth. Pour evenly over bread. Cover baking dish with plastic wrap. Chill at least 8 hours or up to one day.

Before baking, remove dish from refrigerator and bring to room temperature.

Preheat oven to 350°F. Uncover baking dish and bake 35 to 40 minutes, or until puffed and edges are golden brown.

Remove from pan, divide into 6 individual servings. Dust with powdered sugar. Garnish with violets and mint leaves. Serve immediately.

Brownie batter made from your
   favorite recipe or a mix
2 teaspoons rum flavoring
1 cup raisins
1 cup chocolate chips
1 cup shredded coconut

THOSE KILLER BROWNIES   MAKES 50 TO 60 SERVINGS

Marie cut the moist, super-rich brownies about one-inch square and served them in the fluted papers sold for baking mini muffins.

While preparing the brownie batter, place raisins in small bowl and pour the rum flavoring over the raisins so that it can soak in.

Stir the flavoring-soaked raisins, chocolate chips, and coconut into the brownie batter. Spread the batter in prepared pan and bake according to recipe or package directions.

For crepes:

2 jumbo eggs

⅓ cup water

⅔ cup milk

½ teaspoon vanilla

¾ cup sifted all-purpose flour

1 teaspoon baking powder

2 tablespoons powdered sugar

Oil for frying crepes

For filling:

1 (3-ounce) package cream
cheese, softened

¼ teaspoon vanilla

2 teaspoons powdered sugar

1 egg yolk

Raspberry jelly or raspberry
pie filling

Butter for frying

For topping:

Chocolate syrup, canned or
homemade

Bottled raspberry syrup

Fresh raspberries and mint
leaves for garnish

RASPBERRY CHEESECAKE CREPES

**MAKES 7 TO 8 BREAKFAST SERVINGS
OR 14 TO 16 DESSERT SERVINGS**

A versatile recipe that can be an entrée at breakfast or a dessert with dinner.

To make crepes: Beat eggs until frothy. Beat in the water, then the milk. Add the vanilla. In a separate medium bowl, stir together the flour, baking powder, and powdered sugar. Pour in the egg mixture and whisk together. Ignore the lumps. Let this batter sit for at least 15 minutes before using and whisk again.

Heat a crepe pan or 7-inch skillet over medium-high heat. Grease with a few drops of oil. Add a small amount of the batter and rotate the pan so that the bottom is covered. Cook over moderate heat. When brown on one side, turn it over. These are almost paper thin and cook quickly.

This recipe makes 14 to 16 crepes. If you make crepes ahead of time, store them with pieces of waxed paper between crepes.

To serve: Whip together the softened cream cheese, vanilla, powdered sugar, and the egg yolk. Spread each crepe with flavored cream cheese, then cover lightly with raspberry jelly or raspberry pie filling. Roll tightly or roll as you would a blintz.

Melt 1 tablespoon butter in a large skillet. Fry filled crepes to a golden brown, turning once. Place on individual plates using two per serving as a breakfast entrée, one as a dessert. Drizzle rolled crepes with chocolate and raspberry syrups. Garnish with fresh raspberries and fresh mint leaves or sweet woodruff.

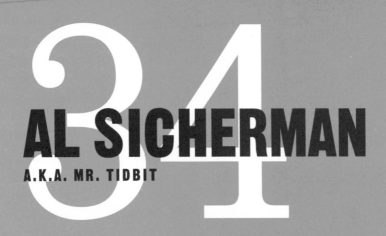

34 AL SICHERMAN
A.K.A. MR. TIDBIT

In the case of food columnist Al Sicherman, engineering's loss is journalism's gain. Al holds a degree in electrical engineering. But when he started working in the field, he found it "kind of boring." He adds: "It's a great hobby, though."

"Journalism seemed interesting. I enrolled at the 'U' [University of Minnesota] as an adult special and took five history courses. That was a disaster; the first quarter, there were thirty-seven books to read. But I'd taken a journalism course earlier, and I really liked that. So I decided to become a copy editor. I was attracted by all the variety; every day something new. I never wanted to be a reporter."

The *Tribune,* then the morning half of the two jointly run Minneapolis newspapers, hired Al as a copy editor. Since a morning paper goes to press in the late (sometimes very late) evening, Al worked nights. Management noted his engineering expertise and tapped him to work on the computerization of the newspapers. "I really enjoyed working days, but it meant I was sidetracked from journalism for four years." Then, during much of 1978, he lived in Paris, working on the *International Herald Tribune.* "Paris is where I learned how to eat," he has written.

Al was back in Minneapolis when one of the *Tribune* food writers became ill, and their mutual boss asked other writers to fill in for her in a rotation—a different person writing a food story each week. Al had an idea for the first week. Then next week he had another, and so on, and eventually, he just had the job (the other writer didn't come back).

"My first cover story was 'Splendor in the Grease.' It featured every fatty thing I could think of. The entrée was roast duck with hollandaise sauce," he recalls. At our interview, he smiles, remembering the fun of putting those rich foods together. Tribune readers howled with laughter as they mentally digested the "splendor" he described. And they begged for more. Thus began his seven-year series of pun-theme stories. Each cover story featured a meticulously planned meal and its recipes. He created (and kitchen-tested) dinners like the Orange and Black Meal (for Halloween) and the Earl and Winegar dinner (a repast of oil and vinegar combinations dedicated to two popular *Strib* staffers, the late Earl Seubert, a photographer, and Karen Winegar, a feature writer). His following grew as readers stifled their giggles long enough to phone friends to share pun-rich passages. "Each cover idea was peculiar," says Al. Working at a desk across from him after the *Star* and *Tribune* merged in 1982, I remember overhearing him say: "I look for story ideas under every rock." And he found them.

Early on, Al developed a unique voice. He writes as if he were talking one-on-one to the reader. He anticipates the reader's response and answers it—in his inimitable way. Here's a sample, from the 1992 State Fair recipe booklet:

Yes, this does say Broccoli Fudge Cake. Don't look so surprised. You've eaten zucchini bread and you might have eaten chocolate sauerkraut cake. They're all nice and moist. But this chocolate broccoli cake recipe is perhaps the best heavy-moist chocolate cake I've ever made. If you like your cakes to float off the plate, don't make this one.

Then a reporter from the *Wall Street Journal* called, asking to interview him. The result was a long feature article that called Al "the Woody Allen of food writing" and included a recognizable head-and-shoulders sketch. The feature alerted the publishing world to his book, *Caramel Knowledge,* a 1985 collection of pun-laden articles, published under his own imprint, Pants Press. Within days, his phone was ringing off the hook as major publishers vied to buy the book and sell it nationally. Within weeks, the book was auctioned off to the highest bidder: Harper & Row.

Meanwhile, Al was also writing a column called "Tidbits," a collection of short takes and follow-ups. The format required a small illo (illustration: piece of line art). Full of confidence on paper, Al was somewhat reticent about pressing the paper's artists to produce these tiny works. A top hat had appeared at his desk (a press gift probably) and he found that wearing it, as "Mr. Tidbit," gave him the panache he needed when dealing with the "artistes," as he called them. When we saw him wearing the top hat, we knew it was "Tidbits" time. Alas, the illustrations have disappeared, as has the top hat.

As the column has evolved, Al's persona has become Mr. Tidbit. His columns often deal with line extensions of best-selling products, usually investigations of flavors above and beyond the ubiquitous "original" flavor, or size and packaging concerns. Every time the newspaper gets a redesign Al's writing assignments gets a redesign too. Way back when, he made every effort to solve what he called "Little Mysteries." These were unfathomable questions such as which is larger: a mammoth olive or a colossal olive? As readers, we loved having him delve into issues like this, ones we had never given a moment's thought.

At one point, Al was doing weekly in-print "Cooking Lessons." These proved most helpful, especially to cooks who had not had that kind of grandmotherly, side-by-side lessons in the kitchen. He wrote careful step-by-step directions accompanied by clear black-and-white pictures, which he set up for the photographers in his home kitchen. "Just Desserts" became his theme in 1999, a most appropriate one for a man who admits to having "a monumental sweet tooth." Al tests and rhapsodizes about a wonderful dessert every week. A tough job, but someone's got to do it.

Al Sicherman of the *Star Tribune* writes the "Mr. Tidbit" column in the weekly Taste section. An admitted chocoholic, Al also does the "Just Desserts" column.

A STATE FULL OF CHOCOLATE LOVERS

A food rep once told me that this is prime chocolate and cocoa country. He maintained that we bought more cocoa than any other area. I'll share these chocolate tips: (1) The addition of coffee points up the flavor of chocolate, so use coffee instead of water in making cookies and sauces. If there's no water, stir in a tablespoonful of instant coffee powder. (2) If the recipe calls for unsweetened chocolate, but all you have is cocoa: replace 1 ounce (square) unsweetened chocolate with 3 tablespoons cocoa plus 1 tablespoon oil or melted shortening. (3) Chocolate can "bloom" if it is stored at warm temperatures. This greyish cover to the squares is the cocoa butter rising to the surface. It's fine to cook with—just looks funny. In summer, you might want to store chocolate in the refrigerator.

Al indulged his chocoholic tendencies in this selection of pet recipes.

1 cup chopped pecans

⅔ cup (10 ⅔ tablespoons) butter

2 (12-ounce) bags (4 cups) semisweet chocolate chips*

1 cup minus 2 tablespoons sugar

4 eggs

2 teaspoons vanilla

1 cup plus 2 tablespoons flour

1 teaspoon baking powder

½ teaspoon salt

*If you like, substitute 1 cup of (Hershey's) raspberry chocolate chips for half of the chips stirred into the batter at the last step.

EXTREME BROWNIES

MAKES 12 TO 15 SERVINGS

Al says, "This is my favorite brownie recipe. The brownies are intensely chocolate."
Author's note: This is now my favorite brownie recipe. It will be yours as soon as you try it.

Preheat the oven to 350°F. Lightly grease a 13 x 9-inch pan.

Toast the pecans in a heavy frying pan about seven minutes, stirring occasionally, until they become fragrant and begin to color. Set aside.

Melt together the butter and 2 cups of the chocolate chips. Beat in the sugar, then the eggs (two at a time), and vanilla. Sift together the flour, baking powder, and salt and stir into the batter, along with the pecans and the remaining two cups of chocolate chips. Bake about 35 minutes until a toothpick inserted in the center (try several places—you might hit a chocolate chip) comes out clean.

If you like—and you should—top with a recipe of Chocolate Ganache.

2 ripe avocados

2 (10 ¾-ounces) cans condensed chicken broth

1 ½ cups milk

2 cups fat-free half-and-half

½ cup dry white wine

½ tablespoon lemon juice

Salt and white pepper to taste

¼ to ⅓ cup lime juice of 2-3 fresh limes

AVOCADO-LIME CREAM SOUP

MAKES 8 SERVINGS

"I made this up," explains Al. "I like it best chilled, but it's surprisingly nice hot too."

Peel and pit the avocados. Puree the avocado flesh in a food processor (or mash it by hand) until smooth. Gradually add the broth, beating or processing until the mixture is smooth. Stir in the milk, wine, lemon juice, salt, and pepper. Then add the lime juice, a little at a time, tasting as you go.

Heat gently (do not boil), stirring occasionally, and serve hot or chilled.

1 ½ cups heavy cream
4 tablespoons (½ stick) butter
12 (1-ounce) squares
  semisweet chocolate or
  2 cups semisweet chocolate
  chips

CHOCOLATE GANACHE

Put the cream and butter in a saucepan and bring to a boil over medium heat, stirring until the butter is melted. Remove from heat.

Put the chocolate into the small bowl of an electric mixer and add the hot cream mixture. Stir until the chocolate is fully melted, then beat at low speed until it is completely smooth. At this point you can just pour the ganache as a deep, dark glaze over the brownies. But it can also be whipped and piped as rosettes, and that's pretty great, too.

GANACHE ROSETTES

Prepare Chocolate Ganache (above). Place the bowl (with the beaters in it) in the refrigerator. Chill, stirring occasionally to speed cooling, half an hour or so, until the mixture is the consistency of very thick cream. If you accidentally let it get fully hard, let it warm up until you can just stir it.

When the mixture is nicely thickened, whip it as you would whip cream, until it is stiff. The color gets lighter, but the flavor remains dark and wonderful. Scrape the bowl periodically (you'll be able to spot less-beaten portions because they are darker). When it holds stiff peaks, pipe the whipped ganache as rosettes or use two spoons to form dollops of ganache onto brownies, cakes, pies, your hand . . . Keep refrigerated.

¾ pound (3 sticks) unsalted
   butter
2⅔ cups (16 ounces)
   semisweet chocolate chips
1 cup milk
7 egg yolks
Heavy cream, whipped, for
   topping

CHOCOLATE GOO CAKE

Al describes this dessert as a very nice flourless chocolate cake, almost more fudge than cake—but better than fudge.

Preheat the oven to 350°F. Melt the butter over low heat and allow it to cool to room temperature.

Cut a round of waxed paper to fit the bottom of a 9-inch springform pan. Butter the sides of the pan and one side of the waxed paper. Place the paper in the pan, buttered side up.

In a saucepan over very low heat, heat the chocolate and milk, stirring constantly, just until the chocolate is melted. (You will note that at every step the batter for this cake smells even better than it did at the last one.) Pour the mixture into the large bowl of an electric mixer.

Beat on low speed, just to smooth out any bits and lumps of chocolate. With the mixer running at low speed, add about a seventh of the melted butter (a shy ¼ cup) and beat at low speed only until the butter is fully absorbed. Then add an egg yolk and beat, at low speed, just until the mixture has fully absorbed it. Don't raise the speed of the mixer, because we don't want to beat in any air. It's not supposed to be a fluffy cake; it's supposed to be a fudgy lump of goo.

Continue to alternate additions of butter and egg yolk until all are used up, scraping the bowl with a rubber spatula and beating after each addition only until incorporated. When the mixture is smooth, pour it into the prepared pan.

Set the pan on a cookie sheet (it might weep a bit). Put the whole thing in the oven (not near the top).

Bake for 25 minutes. It will be soupy in the middle and look like a mistake, but unless you forgot to turn the oven on, it is done. (You'll see the cake does not rise!)

Allow it to cool on a rack, then refrigerate a few hours, until firm. It may be kept refrigerated a day or two.

When ready to serve, cut around the side of the pan with a small, sharp knife and release and remove the side of the pan. Cover the dessert with a flat plate and invert.

Carefully (it takes a bit of doing) pry up and remove the bottom of the pan and the waxed paper.

Decorate with whipped cream. (I like to make a simple lattice pattern that lets the dark, dark chocolate show through.)

35 GRAIS NOTES
ON MINNESOTA JEWISH COOKING

"Shabbat dinner at 7 P.M. on Friday evening is always the best meal of the week," says Etheldoris Grais of St. Louis Park. She goes on:

Etheldoris (Stein) Grais at the well-stocked perfume counter at her father's Stein's Drug Store in Hibbing in 1940.

There is a ritual with Shabbat [Hebrew for Sabbath]. First a blessing over the candles, then a glass of wine. Next the challah bread [an egg-rich yeast braid] is blessed and we tear off a piece. The challah could be served with the soup course or with the fish course. We start with a good soup, usually a chicken soup made with a heavy, meaty bird. When I was still at home in Hibbing, it was usually chicken noodle soup.

The second course would be gefilte fish or a cold poached fish served with a sauce. My mother usually served a salad tray along with the fish.

The meat course might be roast chicken or it might be prime rib or short ribs. Accompanying the meat would be two vegetables and a starch. The starch was often rice or potatoes, but sometimes it would be something more unusual like couscous. You know, I am from the Iron Range. All the different nationalities came together there. We might serve kasha [buckwheat groats] or bulgur wheat. Our Italian friends taught us their way of cooking rice, cooking it in broth to make risotto. And, of course, wild rice. I remember when we still got the wild rice in a gunnysack from the family that harvested it.

Dessert for Shabbat is not elaborate, according to Etheldoris. A fruit compote, perhaps, or an angel food cake.

"Yes, we keep kosher," she says, referring to following Judaism's dietary laws. "We never mix meat and milk in the same meal." Etheldoris belongs to Adath Jeshurun Congregation in Minnetonka. "It's a conservative temple. We're middle of the road," she adds.

Fishman's Kosher Market and Deli in St. Louis Park is the source of many of the products that Etheldoris uses, including the meaty chickens for soup and bouillon cubes for enriching broth. (Supermarkets also carry many kosher foods.) While Shabbat is a weekly holiday for Jewish families like the Graises, Passover, which recalls the Jews' exodus from Egypt, is the annual celebration to which both friends and family are invited. "Passover Seder depends on who the guests will be," explains Etheldoris. "If it is someone who is traditional, you will serve the dinner you have always served. But if it is someone who is adventurous, you will try new things."

"Matzah [also spelled matzo] ball soup is always the first course," she continues. Matzah, made of flour and water with no leavening, commemorates the speed with which the Jews fled their captors—there was no time for bread to rise. Matzah, in thin, brittle sheets, and matzah meal, a granular substitute for flour, are used exclusively during Passover. "For a long time, red wine was traditional for Passover. But, more often than not, someone would spill some wine and stain the tablecloth. Now it is perfectly acceptable to serve white wine. Then, if someone spills wine, it will wash out."

"The second course for Passover is gefilte fish [prepared cakes or ground fish balls]. My family makes gefilte fish out of whitefish, Lake Superior trout, and northerns—you need a fat fish for flavor. We would make a big batch, then we would have them for the festive dinner and the next day we could have them for lunch, covered with a chunky tomato-vegetable ragu."

(Her how-to video of making gefilte fish with Minnesota lake fish was part of an exhibit, "Unpacking On the Prairie," at the Minnesota Historical Society. The exhibit describes the ways Jews adapted to life in rural Minnesota. The Jewish Historical Society of the Upper Midwest put the video on the Web.)

Roast turkey or chicken with a delicious sauce is the third course for the first Passover Seder, according to Etheldoris. "My favorite with poultry is a duck sauce made with orange or peach marmalade." And, of course, mashed potatoes and gravy with the roast bird. She sensed that I was picturing the meal as she described it and warned: "Remember, you could not put milk in the mashed potatoes." Oh, that's right, keeping kosher means no milk in a meat meal.

A compote of dried fruit cooked with fruit juice or red wine and flavored with cinnamon and allspice is a typical Passover dessert. "I like my compote sweetened with honey. It's one of the many food ideas I brought from Hibbing," she adds.

Because Passover continues for eight days, there is ample time to enjoy other specialties. Etheldoris confesses a fondness for Passover tzimmes made with new potatoes and prunes (now called dried plums) and flavored with just a little chunk of beef short ribs. Every family, every region, seems to have its own version of tzimmes, all combining vegetables and fruits and slow-baked to combine the flavors. Kugel may also be served at Passover, but it's a wonderful comfort food all year long. Kugel is a baked pudding made with noodles (sometimes potatoes) served as a side dish. A sweet version made with noodles, fruit, raisins, and spices makes a lovely dessert.

Etheldoris started her adult life as a jazz pianist, then ran the cosmetics department of her father's Hibbing drugstore, but it is as a homemaker, culinary historian, and cooking teacher that she found her lifework. An intrepid traveler, she finds someone to teach her the foods of the region wherever she goes. And she sandwiches taking classes between teaching them. She taught her first classes under the aegis of Stanley and Marvel Chong, the Chinese couple who, in the 1950s, taught Minnesotans to love chow mein and fortune cookies.

"All my teaching is volunteer," she explains. Her most recent class—featuring cold soups—was for friends of Brandeis University in Massachussets. "My grandson Jason helps me with the classes. I always have him taste the foods before I serve them. I think his taste buds are better than mine," says Etheldoris, confiding that she is now, admirably, in her eighties.

Etheldoris Grais in the '70s.

CHICKEN SOUP WITH MATZAH BALLS

MAKES ABOUT 12 CUPS OF CHICKEN BROTH

1 (3+-pound) chicken, including giblets
3 to 4 quarts water
3 carrots
3 ribs celery with leaves
1 large onion, slashed
2 sprigs parsley
1 bay leaf
2 whole peppercorns
½ parsnip (3 to 4 inches)
½ clove garlic
Salt to taste
Matzah Balls (recipe follows)

The nutritious soup that has been called "Jewish penicillin." Etheldoris prefers a plump hen for this soup, but sometimes they are difficult to obtain.

Cut chicken into pieces; clean and scald it, rinsing first with tap water, then boiling water. Place chicken and the 3 to 4 quarts cold water in a large kettle. Bring slowly to a boil, skimming foam that rises to top. Simmer 45 to 60 minutes.

Add carrots, celery, onion, parsley, bay leaf, peppercorns, parsnip, garlic, and salt. Simmer another hour, or until chicken is very tender—time depends on tenderness of the chicken. (A 4-pound stewing hen would take 3 hours.) Strain the broth, discarding the vegetables and spices. Refrigerate broth overnight; chill chicken for another use.

Remove broth from refrigerator and skim fat. Reheat and serve with matzah balls. Soup is also excellent with small pieces of tender chicken or noodles added.

MATZAH BALLS

MAKES ABOUT 16 MATZAH BALLS, ENOUGH FOR 8 (10-OUNCE) SERVINGS OF SOUP

4 eggs
½ cup water
⅓ cup canola oil
1 cup matzah meal
1 teaspoon salt
White pepper and nutmeg to taste
2 to 3 quarts salted water for boiling

When shaping balls, remember that they will swell during cooking.

Beat eggs slightly. Add water, then oil, matzah meal, salt, white pepper, and nutmeg. Refrigerate the matzah mixture 30 minutes so that the meal can absorb the liquids.

Start heating a kettle of 2 to 3 quarts salted water. Using wet or oiled hands, form the matzah mixture into balls the size of walnuts. Drop the matzah balls into the boiling water. Let water come to a boil again. Cover and reduce heat; let matzah balls cook 20 minutes.

Remove the balls with a slotted spoon and transfer to the kettle of heated chicken soup. Cook balls another 10 to 15 minutes in the soup so that they take on the flavor of the soup.

MEAT BLINTZES

MAKES 8 BLINTZES

For blintzes:

3 eggs

1 cup water

½ cup milk

1 cup all-purpose flour

1 teaspoon salt

½ to 1 teaspoon sugar

¼ teaspoon baking powder

For meat filling:

½ cup minced onion

Oil for frying onion

1⅓ cups roast beef, ground

5 tablespoons minced parsley

1 egg, lightly beaten

Nondairy margarine or
    rendered chicken fat for
    frying blintzes

The blintz is close culinary kin to the French crepe. Other names for it are leaves, blintz wrapper, or blintz pancake. "Schmaltz, the fat made by rendering chicken fat, is the perfect fat for frying these luncheon blintzes," says Etheldoris.

First, prepare blintzes: Place eggs, flour, salt, water, milk, sugar, and baking powder in electric blender. Blend until smooth. (Batter can also be beaten with electric mixer or a wire whisk.) Refrigerate batter 30 to 60 minutes.

Heat a 7- or 8-inch nonstick skillet with sloping sides. Grease lightly with vegetable oil—a kitchen brush works well for this.

Pour just enough batter—about 2½ tablespoons—into skillet to cover bottom. Tip from side to side to spread batter until bottom of pan is completely covered. If there is too much batter, pour off the excess. Cook the blintz on one side only, cooking until slightly brown and dry on top. Use a spatula to loosen edges.

Drop the blintz on a white tea towel fried side up. (Blintz will be thin.) When it is cool, put on a square of wax paper and stack fried blintzes until ready to fill.

For filling: Stir-fry minced onion in a little oil. Combine beef, fried onion, parsley, and egg.

To finish blintz: Place 2 tablespoons of filling on lower half of the browned side of the blintz.

Turn the opposite sides in and roll up like an envelope. Fry on both sides in margarine or oil. Serve with beef mushroom gravy.

KIBBUTZ FRESH VEGETABLE SALAD

MAKES 10 SERVINGS

3 ripe tomatoes

2 medium cucumbers

1 green bell pepper

1 red bell pepper

2 green onions, tops included

2 medium carrots

½ head lettuce

For dressing:

2 tablespoons fresh lemon
    juice

2 to 3 tablespoons good
    quality olive oil

2 to 3 cloves garlic, minced

Salt and freshly ground pepper
    to taste

When a nephew of the Grais family returned after living in a kibbutz—a communal farm—in Israel, he brought directions for this refreshing, nutritious salad. Etheldoris makes it in quantity for parties.

Dice tomatoes, cucumbers, peppers, and green onions. Shred carrots. Coarsely shred lettuce.

Put vegetables into a large salad bowl; toss to mix.

Stir together lemon juice, olive oil, minced garlic, salt, and pepper in small pitcher or 1-cup glass measuring cup. Pour dressing over mixed vegetables. Toss salad until vegetables are coated with dressing. Serve immediately.

EASY CARROT TZIMMES

MAKES 6 SERVINGS

2 (16-ounce) cans sliced carrots, drained
1 (23-ounce) can sweet potatoes, cut in chunks
½ cup pitted prunes, diced
½ cup dried apricots, diced
⅓ cup orange juice
¼ cup honey
½ teaspoon cinnamon
1 to 2 tablespoons margarine, optional

Tzimmes is traditionally served on Rosh Hashana. A big thank-you to Judy Goldfein, Golden Valley, who shared this recipe when I was doing an Arab-Israeli peace meal for the Taste section. This vegetable dish carries and reheats well.

Preheat oven to 350°F. In a casserole, combine carrots, sweet potatoes, prunes and apricots, orange juice, honey, cinnamon, and, if desired, margarine.

To cook conventionally: Bake covered for 25 to 30 minutes, then remove cover and bake another 10 minutes.

To microwave: Cover microwave-safe casserole with plastic wrap folding back one side to provide an air vent. Microwave on high (100 percent power) 4 minutes, then turn casserole ¼ turn and cook another 2 to 3 minutes until mixture is bubbling. Remove plastic wrap cover and let stand 3 to 5 minutes before stirring and serving.

If you wish to use fresh carrots and sweet potatoes, simply precook them before combining them in the casserole.

STRAWBERRY CHANTILLY SOUP

MAKES 6 TO 8 SERVINGS

1 pound fresh strawberries
2 ounces (¼ cup) kirsch (cherry brandy)*
⅓ cup water
1½ cups heavy whipping cream or half-and-half
⅔ cup sour cream
¼ to ½ cup sugar, to taste
Strawberry slices and mint leaves for garnish

*Brandy may be omitted if soup is preferred alcohol-free.

This dessert soup was served at Etheldoris's fiftieth birthday party. I adapted her amounts in order to fit the mixture into the electric blender.

Wash and stem berries and place in blender container. Add water and kirsch. Blend until smooth.

Add heavy cream, sour cream, and ¼ cup of the sugar to blender. Let stand 10 minutes, then blend again. Taste and correct flavor, which varies according to natural sweetness of berries.

Refrigerate covered overnight.

Serve in individual dessert bowls garnished with strawberry slices and mint leaves.

36

GINNY HOESCHEN

LIVE FROM THE TEST KITCHEN

After working in a test kitchen for thirty years, Ginny Hoeschen of Burnsville calls the work challenging, both mentally and physically, yet very rewarding. And what exactly does a test-kitchen home economist do? She tests recipes created by others; she creates new recipes; she develops product prototypes; and she prepares the company's products for demonstrations. She thinks nothing of juggling the preparation of six or eight different foods on a given day. This is a heads-up, back-straight job requiring confidence and capability.

"I would meet with the product managers," explains Ginny, referring to her work at Pillsbury (now a part of General Mills). "They would say: 'This is what we need. We need five foods with wheat and millet.' That's just an example. At the end of the workday, they would come and see what I had prepared. After tasting my creations, they might say 'This is fabulous' or 'No dates in this.' They always trusted me. And they always got good results."

"You have to work," she continues. "You can't be dilly-dallying. I knew that R&D [research and development] had to have a recipe by such-and-such a date. Or a mix had to go into production on a certain date. Some days there was little contact between the managers and me, but I went right on."

She worked virtually full time, but she was always a consultant—hired for a particular project—not a regular employee. "During the '80s, I worked on a lot of long-term projects." One was developing a line of hearty grain refrigerated products. "They were low in fat and full of fiber, but they were way ahead of the times." Sales were disappointing and the line was dropped.

Another project of Ginny's was the development of single-serving items, sold refrigerated or frozen, both desserts (Pillsbury's forte), and meals. I remember buying a toothsome dessert, a Bake-Off winner, all done up in a see-through package. It was delicious, perfect for a single like me. "But it never flew, never went national," says Ginny shaking her head.

One of her biggest projects was the introduction of the Pillsbury lines to potential customers in South America in 1996. "They wanted South Americans—distributors and supermarket owners—to sample a whole range of Pillsbury products." The company was then owned by the Britain-based Diageo conglomerate. "The products were shipped to the hotel or restaurant where the presentation would be given and I would prepare the foods there. We served pizza, Green Giant vegetables, Old El Paso salsas, and Pillsbury cakes and brownies." Ginny did presentations in Lima, Peru; San Jose, Costa Rica; Managua, Nicaragua; and San Juan, Puerto Rico. "Those were long days, 7 A.M. to 10 P.M.," she recalls. "I baked the cakes and brownies in kitchens which, even with the fans on, were 112 degrees." Another overseas assignment took Ginny to London and Edinburgh to bake for sales meetings.

Cy DeCosse, Inc., Minnetonka, was another test kitchen where Ginny developed recipes in the late 1980s and early '90s. Company founder Cy DeCosse changed the world of food photography by introducing spectacular food close-ups in fine-art format, showing only the finished food and a serving spoon or fork. "He is the most creative man I have ever known, a real artist."

Cy DeCosse's Microwave Cooking Library eventually grew to twenty-four titles, selling millions of volumes. Ginny describes her role:

> The editors spelled out exactly what was needed. For the microwave book on cooking fresh produce, they told me what fruits to use and asked me to create four appetizers and four salads.
>
> Four of us worked in one big room. They put the groceries on the wide worktable in the center and it was every woman for herself. When the foods were ready, we tasted and conferred, making suggestions. Sometimes a food had too much of a certain flavor. Sometimes it wasn't appealing-looking (every recipe was photographed). We just cranked out recipe after recipe, book after book.

Ginny is also one of many Twin Cities home economists who have done one of the popular monthly Pillsbury Classic Cookbooks. These photo-filled, magazine-rack booklets are sold at the supermarket checkout counter. She packed her *Country American Cookbook*, published in 1983, with family favorites. "It was a keeper. It sold out within weeks," she says with pride.

When Ginny began cooking at age ten, her mother, a talented cook and

A larger-than-life Pillsbury dough-boy gets chummy with home economist Ginny Hoeschen of Burnsville.

baker, was her mentor. College took her to Menomonie and the University of Wisconsin–Stout, where she majored in foods and nutrition. Her first job was with Northern States Power in Minneapolis. This was 1961 when "electricity was penny cheap." "We did cooking shows to demonstrate the electric range. What to bake. How to freeze it. We worked with small appliances, too, like the toaster oven. We also had a phone service, helping customers with recipes and menus. We even answered offbeat questions such as how to get gum out of a child's hair," Ginny remembers. She and her co-workers also gave demos at schools and advised families on redoing their kitchens. "There was always something new to learn," adds Ginny.

Marriage—to financial analyst Dick Hoeschen—and motherhood kept Ginny home for several years. Her son was a toddler and her daughter just six months old when she got a call from Karen Johnson. Karen, a college friend, wanted Ginny to work on the Pillsbury Bake-Off, promising that the project would take only six weeks. With the baby in a neighbor's care, Ginny headed downtown to the test kitchen. She did enjoy it, especially the camaraderie around the kitchens. She says, "I like to be in a joyful mood."

"I worked right next to Elaine Christiansen (later a Bake-Off manager). We were doing the scratch baking, and we made the flour fly," recalled Ginny. "There was one beer-cheese bread; I'm sure I made it fifty times." She worked on seven Bake-Offs, and then was persuaded to get into new product development.

Whether at Pillsbury or Cy DeCosse, at Old Home (where she recorded radio spots for dairy products) or at a photo studio for a food shot, she found friends. Typical Ginny is her habit of preparing Brandy Alexanders (rich with Häagen Dazs ice cream) on New Year's Eve afternoon for the few Pillsbury people still at work.

Reviewing her career, Ginny says, "Working on models for new products was especially rewarding. Afterward you see what you did on the product as a baby step. And now the product is walking out of the store. That's fun."

Ginny selected these recipes as favorites from her test-kitchen work.

HAM ROLLS WITH ZIPPY SAUCE

MAKES 12 SERVINGS

For rolls:

1 pound ground cooked ham

½ pound ground pork

1 pound lean ground beef

1 ½ cups graham cracker crumbs

1 cup milk

1 egg, well beaten

¼ teaspoon salt

¼ teaspoon pepper

For sauce:

1 (10 ¾-ounce) can condensed tomato soup

1 cup firmly packed brown sugar

⅓ cup cider vinegar

1 teaspoon dry mustard

A party special from her Country American Cookbook.

Preheat oven to 350°F. In large bowl, combine ham, pork, beef, crumbs, milk, egg, salt, and pepper; mix well. Using about ⅓ cup mixture for each, shape into 24 rolls, about 4 inches long. Place in 13 x 9-inch baking pan.

In medium bowl, combine tomato soup, brown sugar, vinegar, and dry mustard. Pour over rolls. Bake for 50 to 60 minutes or until thoroughly cooked.

Note: The ham rolls can be prepared ahead, unbaked and without sauce, and frozen. Thaw slightly and proceed with saucing and baking as directed.

CINNAMON CREAM CHICKEN FRUIT SALAD

MAKES 6 SERVINGS

For dressing:

⅔ cup light sour cream

¼ cup apple juice

1 tablespoon sugar

¾ teaspoon cinnamon

⅛ teaspoon salt

For salad:

6 ounces (2 ½ cups) uncooked rotelle (large spiral pasta), wagon wheel pasta, or radiatore (pasta nuggets)

2 ½ cups cubed cooked chicken

1 cup sliced strawberries

2 plums, sliced (1 cup)

¾ cup seedless green grapes, halved

¾ cup seedless red grapes, halved

½ cup sliced star fruit

⅓ cup thinly sliced red onion, separated into rings

6 large lettuce leaves

This unusual salad is a taste of summer; my friends and I love it. It's an ideal use for star fruit, an apple-like tropical fruit that produces star-shaped slices.

In medium bowl, make dressing by combining sour cream, apple juice, sugar, cinnamon, and salt. Cover dressing; refrigerate while preparing salad.

Cook pasta to desired doneness as directed on package. Drain pasta; rinse with cold water. In large bowl, combine drained pasta, chicken, strawberries, plums, grapes, star fruit, and onion. Stir chicken mixture gently. Pour dressing over salad.

Place lettuce leaves on individual salad plates. Spoon 1 ½ cups salad onto each plate.

CALYPSO PORK ROAST

MAKES 8 SERVINGS

4- to 5-pound boneless pork
    loin roast
2 large cloves garlic, each
    peeled and cut into 8 pieces
¾ cup packed dark brown
    sugar
1 teaspoon ground ginger
½ teaspoon ground cinnamon
½ teaspoon salt
¼ teaspoon freshly ground
    pepper
2 tablespoons dark rum
1 cup pineapple juice
½ cup water
Pork Gravy (recipe follows)

This is the main dish from the "Island Dinner" Ginny developed for Easy Microwave
Menus *from the Cy DeCosse Microwave Library. The menu included the kabobs below
and a cabbage salad embellished with roasted cashews and sliced bananas.*

Preheat oven to 325°F. Cut 16 1-inch slits
in pork roast. Insert garlic pieces. Place
roast, fattiest-side-up, on rack in large
roasting pan. Insert meat thermometer.
Roast 1 hour 30 minutes.

In small mixing bowl, combine brown
sugar, ginger, cinnamon, salt, and pepper.
Mix well. Add rum and mix thoroughly.

Remove roast from conventional oven.
Spread roast evenly with brown sugar mixture. Add pineapple juice and water to
bottom of roasting pan. Continue roasting
30 to 50 minutes longer, or until internal
temperature registers 165°F. Let roast
stand 10 minutes before carving. Strain and
reserve pan juices for gravy.

PORK GRAVY

MAKES ABOUT 2 CUPS

2 cups pan juices (see above)
1 tablespoon plus 1 ½
    teaspoons cornstarch

Place drippings in 4-cup measure. Place
cornstarch in small bowl. Add small amount
of pan juices to cornstarch. Stir until mixture is smooth. Add cornstarch mixture to
remaining pan juices, stirring with whisk

until smooth. Microwave on high 4 to 5
minutes, stirring twice, or until mixture is
thickened and translucent. Reserve 3
tablespoons gravy for kabobs (see below).

SWEET POTATO AND PINEAPPLE KABOBS

MAKES 8 SERVINGS

8 (6-inch long) wooden
    skewers
1 red pepper, seeded and cut
    into 16 chunks
4 fresh pineapple slices, about
    ¾-inch slices, each cut into
    fourths
1 (23-ounce) can sweet
    potatoes, drained
3 tablespoons Pork Gravy
    (recipe above)

On each skewer, thread 1 red pepper
chunk, 1 pineapple wedge, 1 sweet potato,
a second pineapple wedge and last,
another red pepper chunk. Repeat using
remaining ingredients. Arrange kabobs in
an even layer in a 10-inch square casse-

role. Drizzle with gravy. Cover casserole
with plastic wrap. Microwave at High 3 to 5
minutes or until hot, rotating once. If
desired, arrange kabobs around Calypso
Pork.

37
LYNNE ROSSETTO KASPER
AND HER SPLENDID TABLE

Lynne Rossetto Kasper's home and husband (not to mention her range and computer and Minnesota Public Radio's microphones), are in St. Paul, but her heart is in Italy. Cook and hostess, teacher and author, raconteur and radio personality, the indefatigable Lynne became an authority on Italian cooking via two intertwined routes.

Personally, she loved Italian food from babyhood. The grandchild of Italian immigrants, she had learned to speak Italian at home. Professionally, she studied, then taught Chinese cooking, moving on to classical French cooking. Then her husband Frank's transfer to Brussels in 1981 brought her within driving distance of Tuscany and her extended family there. She embraced Italian cuisine and never looked back.

After college, where she majored in theater and art, Lynne became the sous chef for a Chinese woman who entertained frequently. "I just immersed myself in that culture," says Lynne. She started teaching Chinese cooking in 1968. Next came French cooking. "I wanted to understand *why* something was done, as opposed to *how* it was done," explains Lynne. "That was really great, understanding the why. In teaching, I wanted to invite people on the journey." Through teaching, Lynne found that she could engage people. "I came to appreciate how that ability was a part of what I was." She views her books and her radio broadcasts as a unique way of teaching.

Lynne leaped from being a popular local cooking teacher and writer to being a national food celebrity in 1992 when her first book, *The Splendid Table*, won the double crown of cookbook awards. It won both the James Beard and the Julia Child/IACP Cookbook-of-the-Year Awards. (IACP is International

Lynne Rossetto Kasper exudes charm via the airwaves on her popular public radio program, *The Splendid Table*.

Association of Culinary Professionals, a worldwide organization of cookery teachers, food writers, food scientists, and manufacturers.).

"I spent ten years on *Splendid* (her nickname for the book), then seven years on *Country Table* (*The Italian Country Table*, 1999)." To give me an idea of how time-consuming her book research is, she adds, "For example, I have seen prosciutto made a hundred times, but these men are not scientists." To write about the famous Italian ham knowledgeably required serious study. She is a master at weaving together the background information and wonderful anecdotes.

"How did you come up with the name, *The Splendid Table*?" I ask. "It's perfect for both the book and the radio show." Lynne answers: "I was writing about a place (the Emilia-Romagna region of Italy) that no one had heard of. I wanted a title that suggested scope. We [longtime assistant Judy Graham and her recipe testers] kept throwing names into the computer. I'm very visual. I view the book as a tapestry with overlays of pattern and color that would represent this place, Emilia-Romagna. I envisioned a table reaching back in time, covered with foods, a splendid table."

Having invited myself to her kitchen, I was leaning on the work island while Lynne made a pot of dark, rich coffee. With the coffee she offered cream and a trio of new sugars she was taste-testing (her gourmet picks are on www.zingermans.com).

As you tour her no-nonsense kitchen, you're introduced to Babe, her restaurant-size gas range. The American-made Wolf range has six burners, each large enough to hold a 12-inch sauté pan. Also on hand is Toby, a tea cozy that looks remarkably like a brown-striped cat. Nearby is a pink pig. Its "skin" is diagrammed to show the typical pork cuts, all in French. Says Lynne: "It's papier-mâché, twenty years old."

Just off the kitchen is a snug eating area decorated with sketches from poultry books published in nineteenth-century England (farmers studied the books before ordering new breeds). "Frank surprised me with the chicken prints one Christmas," she says. Introducing her white-mustached husband, Lynne refers to him fondly as "the dear man." He tells me he's on sabbatical, having sold his international export firm.

Lynne's computer lives in the office near the eating area. That and the telephone are Lynne's link with Judy, who continues to work with Lynne despite living in Maine. "Judy has a home economics degree. She does what I'm lousy at. The administrative stuff. She can handle people. She understands what a deadline is," says Lynne. "We phone and e-mail constantly. And she stays here with us about ten days a month."

The Splendid Table, an award-winning radio show, aired by Public Radio International, is produced by Sally Swift. The popular food show has acquainted listeners nationwide with Lynne's personal warmth and her liquid voice quality. I'm sure I'm not the only one who can identify her voice on-air at twenty paces.

Guests on *The Splendid Table*—foodies from many areas of expertise—are amazed that Lynne rarely scripts her radio show. Relying on her seemingly inexhaustible food knowledge and her considerable abilities as a storyteller, she talks away, one eye on the clock, and seldom gets caught mid-word. Screening the questions that listeners send for the Q&A segment of the show is another of Judy's jobs. "Some of those questions are used for Boiling Water 101," explains Lynne. "We record eight questions for each program, then use four or five. I enjoy talking to people. They can be funny, intense. And some just want to schmooze."

MAMA D: EARLY TEACHER OF ITALIAN COOKING

Long before Lynne Rossetto Kasper, Mama D (Giovanna D'Agostino) taught Minnesotans about Italian cuisine. A widow from Chicago, she's an Italian matriarch right out of central casting: black dress, bountiful bosom, and hair back in a bun. She came to lend a hand at her son Sammy's sandwich shop (now defunct) near the University of Minnesota's Minneapolis campus. Students loved this generous woman with her wonderful laugh. Then she offered an Italian cooking class as a fundraiser for a member of the Minnesota Orchestra who was very ill. The classes led to her first book, *Cooking with Love and SPOG* (salt, pepper, oregano, and garlic). I still make a side dish of green peppers and mushrooms from it. When General Mills republished her book, her class size grew to include the entire country. For years, she has given back to her community by serving a free St. Joseph's Day all-you-can-eat dinner to any and all.

So, listen to Lynne and her guests schmoozing on Minnesota Public Radio every weekend, then get busy in the kitchen with these recipes from her book, *The Italian Country Table.*

MARCHE WEDDING SOUP

MAKES 6 TO 8 SERVINGS

10 cups canned low-sodium
   chicken broth
¼ cup dry white wine
Salt and freshly ground black
   pepper
2 large eggs, beaten
2 tablespoons water
1 cup freshly grated
   Parmigiano-Reggiano
   cheese
Shredded zest of ½ large
   lemon
Pinch of freshly grated nutmeg

This method—cooking beaten egg in broth—is also used in Greek egg-lemon soup and in Chinese egg-flower soup.

In a 4-quart saucepan, simmer the broth and wine 5 minutes, partially covered. Season to taste with salt and pepper.

Meanwhile, in a bowl, blend the eggs, water, cheese, lemon zest, nutmeg, and about ⅛ teaspoon pepper.

Take the soup off the heat. With a fork, gently stir in the egg mixture with long slow strokes until it firms into pale shreds floating in the broth. The long strokes lengthen the shreds slightly. This should take 10 to 15 seconds. There will be a moment when the Parmigiano and lemon release their fragrances—enjoy it. Quickly taste the soup for seasoning and serve it while it's still very hot and fragrant.

LINGUINE WITH PESTO OF PISTACHIOS AND ALMONDS

SERVES 4 TO 6
AS A MAIN COURSE;
8 AS A FIRST COURSE

Scant ½ cup unblanched
   whole almonds, toasted
Scant ½ cup shelled salted
   pistachio nuts, toasted
⅓ cup pine nuts, toasted
1 large clove garlic
Pinch of hot red pepper flakes
2 ½ to 3 ½ tablespoons extra-
   virgin olive oil or more to
   taste
40 large mint leaves*
Salt and freshly ground black
   pepper
1 pound linguine, spaghetti, or
   bucatini pasta
1 ⅓ pint baskets (1 pound)
   cherry tomatoes,
   quartered**

*⅔ to ¾ cup loosely packed
mint leaves

**part grape tomatoes,
halved, may also be used

A delicious pasta that Lynne discovered on the Lipari Islands, off Sicily's northeastern coast. Though mint and cherry tomatoes are available all year round, this is excellent during late summer when both ingredients are fresh from the garden or the farmers' market. No cheese is used here.

Mix the cooled toasted nuts. Coarsely chop about one quarter of them; set aside. In a mortar (a processor is second choice) pound (or grind) the garlic to a paste with the pepper flakes and 2 to 3 tablespoons of the olive oil. Work in the remaining whole nuts and a little more than half the mint leaves until the mixture looks like very coarse meal, with pieces of nuts at about ⅛ inch—this is the pesto. Season to taste with salt and pepper. Tear up remaining mint leaves.

Cook the pasta in 6 quarts fiercely boiling salted water, stirring often, until tender yet firm to the bite. As the pasta cooks, gently blend the pesto, tomatoes, and ½ tablespoon of the oil in a deep pasta bowl. Skim off ½ to ¾ cup of the pasta water just before draining, and drain the pasta in a colander. Add the ½ to ¾ cup pasta water to the bowl. Add the pasta and chopped nuts and toss. Then toss in the reserved torn mint. Taste for seasoning, adding extra oil, mint, salt, and/or pepper if needed. Serve hot or warm.

ROMAGNA ROAST POTATOES

MAKES 4 TO 6 SERVINGS

Extra-virgin olive oil
2 ½ to 3 pounds medium
  Yellow Finn or red-skinned
  potatoes
2 thick slices (2 ounces)
  pancetta, cotechino
  sausage, or soppressata,
  chopped
Leaves from a 6-inch branch
  fresh rosemary
Salt and freshly ground black
  pepper
1 ½ cups halved cherry
  tomatoes
6 cloves garlic, coarsely
  chopped

Potatoes and rosemary are a winning combination. Lynne wrote: "These potatoes are good with nearly everything—from a green salad to chicken or seafood. The chopped pancetta provides zing." Pancetta is an Italian bacon often found in delis.

Preheat oven to 425°F. Generously oil a large shallow baking pan (such as a 15 x 10-inch pan or broiler pan). Cut the potatoes in half or into quarters and place them in the pan, rolling the pieces around to coat with oil, ending cut side up. Make sure they are in a single layer and barely touching. Drizzle the potatoes with another tablespoon of oil, then sprinkle with the pancetta, rosemary, and salt and pepper.

Roast 30 minutes, turning once or twice. Blend in the tomatoes and garlic. Roast another 40 minutes, basting with the pan juices and turning for even browning. Once the potatoes are crisp and easily pierced with a knife, they're done. Serve hot or warm.

PANNA COTTA

MAKES 8 SERVINGS

1 ¾ teaspoons unflavored
  gelatin
2 tablespoons cold water
3 cups heavy whipping cream
½ cup sugar, or more to taste
Pinch of salt
1 ½ teaspoons vanilla
1 cup sour cream*
2 cups pitted fresh cherries,
  strawberries, raspberries, or
  sliced peaches or pears,
  optional

*Be sure the sour cream is
  only cream and culture, no
  other additives.

A wonderful dinner-party dessert. The name means "cooked cream."

Sprinkle the gelatin over the cold water. Let stand 5 minutes. In a 3-quart saucepan, warm the cream with the sugar, salt, and vanilla over medium-high heat. Do not let it boil. Stir in the gelatin until thoroughly dissolved. Take the cream off the heat and cool 5 minutes.

Put the sour cream in a medium bowl. Gently whisk in the warm cream a little at a time until smooth. Taste for sweetness; it may need another teaspoon of sugar. Rinse 8 ⅔-cup ramekins, custard cups, or coffee cups with cold water. Fill each one three-quarters full with the cream (a soup ladle works well for filling cups). Chill 4 to 24 hours.

To serve; either unmold by packing the molds in hot towels and then turning each out onto a dessert plate, or serve in their containers. Serve alone or with the fruit.

BEA OJAKANGAS

COOKBOOK WRITER IS A FAVORITE FINN

Duluth's Beatrice Ojakangas (often called Peaches) has *"sisu."* Thanks to her Finn forefathers and her *sisu,* she has become an international authority on Finnish food. She was nicknamed Peaches as a babe. Her Finnish-born grand-father couldn't say Beatrice in English, saying "peatsis" instead. His pronuncia-tion quickly became Peaches (Peach for short), the name her entire family calls her and the one she identifies herself with.

Sisu, a characteristic much in evidence in her career, is a Finnish word for "enduring energy." Finns are born with it, she has written. It means they have the physical energy and mental endurance to do a job and do it well. *Sisu* can be determination with a dash of stubbornness. I see *sisu* in the story of Peaches and her Finnish cookbook.

Here's how she tells it:

Dick [her husband] got a Fulbright to study geology in Finland in 1960 and '61. We were living in a tiny apartment on the third floor in Helsinki. Every day I carried my two babies and a pail of milk up those stairs.

When it began getting dark at 3 P.M. and staying dark until 9 or 10 the next morning, I simply had to do something. I had to do something to stay sane during that long, dark winter.

So I went to the USIS [United States Information Service] and told them I spoke Finn, that I was a home economist and I'd like to demon-strate American food to Finns. They thought it was a great idea. Each weekend I flew around Finland teaching the Finns to bake apple pies, pop popcorn, and cook hamburgers.

She spoke in Finnish to members of Marttaliitto, an organization much like the county extension groups in this country. After telling them about our foods, she asked them about their foods. "I asked what the food words meant that Grandmother had used. They showed me how to bake their breads, how to use the dairy products, everything. I asked about holiday foods and how foods had changed over the years. I took extensive notes about each region of Finland."

She wanted to write a book, but hardly knew where to start. Her mother (home in Minnesota) helped: "She said, 'Peach, pretend I'm a birdie on your shoulder and you're describing everything to me,'" Peaches recalls.

Back in the United States, the family lived in Menlo Park, California, while Dick earned his doctorate at Stanford and Peaches worked as a food editor at Sunset magazine. Her colleagues at Sunset encouraged her, and she worked away slowly turning that pile of notes into a book. "I turned in my manuscript and Dick's doctoral dissertation, which I had typed, the same day," she recalls. While earning his Ph.D., Dick had been both guinea pig and sounding board for the cookbook.

In 1964, the Ojakangases returned to their home state of Minnesota, where Dick joined the University of Minnesota–Duluth faculty. And, in 1964, *The Finnish Cookbook* was published by Crown. It is in its twenty-fifth printing and is recognized as the definitive source on Finnish cooking, both here and in Finland.

The Finnish menu is rich with fish and game, dairy foods, and root vegetables, according to Peaches. Summer, with lots of sunlight, is the time to enjoy lettuces and baby vegetables. Winter, with candlelight for color, brings simmered stews and yeast-raised breads. Rye is frequently used in breads because wheat is harder to grow. Strong coffee is served from morn to midnight.

Since writing that first highly successful book, Peaches has written twenty-three more cookbooks. "It's just fun being in this field," she says. "The biggest challenge is finding my niche. Scandinavian cooking is a narrow field. It somehow pushes me into the baking category, which then pushes me into desserts." Typically, she is almost constantly testing recipes for one topic while mulling ideas for the next.

Her beautiful *Scandinavian Feasts* was published in 1992. I consider this book her tour de force. She presents thirty-four festive menus from Denmark, Finland, Norway, and Sweden, with wonderful color photographs and her always carefully detailed recipes. The food names—some in all four languages—appear in the bottom corner of the page.

Breads have long been a specialty of hers; she uses them as creative party fare. For example, when a pastor friend was married, Peaches and Dick hosted a reception at their home outside Duluth. She set up interesting breads and matching foods at "stations" (much like chefs set up stations with different foods at big receptions) all around the yard of their sprawling home. The offerings included bread and salad at one station, bread and soup at another, bread with cold meats, bread with cheese, and others.

Peaches, with her strong *sisu,* continues to write proposals for new cookbooks and submit them to her agent. At the time of our interview, she was starting some creative writing, possibly a personal memoir. Perhaps, as Laura Esquivel did in her novel, *Like Water for Chocolate*, she will weave recipes into her chapters.

It was hard to pick a handful of recipes from the nine books of hers in my library. The soup and bread recipes are from *The Finnish Cookbook*. The vegetable and dessert appeared in *Scandinavian Feasts*.

2 packages active dry yeast

½ cup warm water (120 to 130°F)

2 cups milk, scalded and cooled

1 cup sugar

2 teaspoons salt

1 teaspoon freshly crushed cardamom

4 eggs, slightly beaten

8 to 9 cups all-purpose unbleached flour

½ cup (1 stick) butter, melted

1 egg beaten with 2 tablespoons milk

½ cup sliced almonds

½ cup pearl sugar or coarsely crushed sugar cubes

SCANDINAVIAN COFFEE BREAD

MAKES THREE LOAVES

For the holidays, writes Peaches in Scandinavian Feasts, *Norwegians and Danes add candied fruit and nuts and shape the dough into round loaves. The Swedes use essentially the same recipe but substitute saffron for cardamom to make their holiday bread.*

In a large bowl, dissolve the yeast in the warm water. Let stand for 5 minutes, until the yeast bubbles. Stir in the milk, sugar, salt, cardamom, eggs, and 4 cups of the flour. Beat until smooth. Add the butter.

Gradually stir in enough of the remaining flour to make a stiff dough. Turn out onto a floured board. Cover and let stand 15 minutes. Wash and grease the bowl and set it aside.

Knead the dough, adding flour as necessary, until it is smooth, about 10 minutes. Place the dough in the prepared bowl, turning the dough to grease it on all sides. Cover and let rise in a warm place until doubled in bulk, 1 ½ to 2 hours. Punch

dough down. Turn the dough out onto an oiled surface and divide into three parts. Divide each part into three or four portions. Roll each portion into a 30-inch-long rope.

Braid three or four ropes together to make a loaf. Pinch the ends together and tuck them under the loaf. Place on a lightly greased baking sheet and repeat with the remaining portions of dough. Let rise in a warm place, until almost doubled, about 45 minutes.

Preheat oven to 375°F. Brush the loaves with egg-milk mixture and sprinkle with almonds and/or sugar. Bake 25 to 30 minutes, or until lightly browned. Do not overbake. Cool on racks.

15 tiny new (or 2 or 3 larger) carrots

2 cups tiniest new potatoes (or larger potatoes, cubed)

1 cup sweet new peas (or frozen)

2 cups tiny snap beans (or larger beans cut into 2-inch pieces)

3 green onions, chopped

1 tablespoon sugar

1 teaspoon salt

2 tablespoons flour

4 cups milk (or, for an elegant version, half-and-half)

2 tablespoons butter

Chopped parsley

SUMMER VEGETABLE SOUP

MAKES 4 TO 6 SERVINGS

The recipe for this colorful soup, published in 1964, predated the baby-vegetable trend by many years.

Clean the carrots (cut large carrots into 2-inch pieces and quarter them lengthwise). Scrub the new potatoes to remove the thin peel (peel the large ones). Put the carrots, peas, beans, onion, and potato into a soup kettle. Add boiling water just to cover.

Cook for 5 minutes or until vegetables are almost tender. In another pan, combine the sugar, salt, flour, and milk and bring to a boil. Pour into the kettle of vegetables and simmer 10 minutes.

Pour into a soup tureen, dot with butter, and garnish with parsley. Serve hot.

MASHED POTATO AND RUTABAGA CASSEROLE

MAKES 12 SERVINGS

2 pounds thin-skinned boiling potatoes

Salt

1 pound (about 1 medium) rutabaga

¼ cup flour

2 eggs

2 teaspoons salt

½ to 1 cup hot milk or half-and-half

1 tablespoon butter

¼ cup fine dry bread crumbs

This is a delightful combination, golden in color and very nutritious. It can be put together a day in advance, if you wish, and refrigerated until ready to bake.

Put the potatoes in a large pot and cover them with water. Add 1 teaspoon of salt for each quart of water. Heat to boiling and cook 20 to 25 minutes, until the potatoes are tender. Drain, peel, and mash the potatoes.

Meanwhile, pare the rutabaga and cut it into 1-inch pieces. Place in a saucepan, cover with water and bring to a boil. Simmer until tender, 25 to 30 minutes. Drain and mash the rutabaga. Add the mashed rutabaga to the potatoes. Beat with an electric mixer until the potatoes and rutabagas are smooth and fluffy. Beat in the flour, eggs, salt, and milk.

Preheat oven to 350°F. Butter a 3-quart shallow baking dish. Turn the vegetable mixture into the dish. Using a spoon, spread out the mixture, making indentations in the top. Dot with butter and sprinkle with bread crumbs. Bake uncovered for 1 hour, or until lightly browned.

APPLE CRANBERRY PUDDING

MAKES 12 SERVINGS

6 cups bottled cranberry juice

½ to ¾ cup sugar, depending on the sweetness of the juice

4 Granny Smith apples, pared, cored, and sliced crosswise

½ cup cornstarch or potato starch

⅔ cup apple juice or cold water

Whipped cream or half-and-half

Puddings made with fruit juices are popular in Scandinavia.

In a 3-quart saucepan, heat the cranberry juice and sugar. Add the apple slices and simmer for 10 minutes, or until the apples are tender. With a slotted spoon, transfer the apples to a dessert bowl.

Mix the cornstarch (or potato starch) with the apple juice (or water). Reheat the cranberry juice to a boil and slowly add the starch mixture, stirring with a whisk. Reduce the heat and simmer until the juice thickens and becomes transparent. Pour the juice over the cooked apple. Cover and let cool. Serve warm or chilled with whipped cream or half-and-half.

39

STATE FAIR FOOD JUDGE
JAN STROOM
FINDS THE BEST

"It gets in your blood," says Jan Stroom of St. Anthony Village. When she says "it," she means the Minnesota State Fair in general and the food competition in particular. As a longtime food judge, she sees the streams of cooks—some of whom have been up all night baking—bringing their products to the Creative Activities Building for judging.

"Some bring in 30 or 40 entries," says Jan, referring to cooks for whom winning a ribbon on their pie or pickles, bread or jam has become a be-all and end-all. "They come from all over the state; some drive from two hundred miles away. Between the canning and the baked goods, there are thousands of entries all coming in at once; it's wild."

Entry day for baking is Monday morning a week and a half before the Fair opens. (The Fair opens on Thursday of the third week of August and closes twelve days later on Labor Day.) Jan describes the excitement:

> We start judging at 1 P.M. that Entry Monday. There's a big area set up with tables and a kitchen. The clerks arrange everything on plates. We work 'til 5 or 6 P.M. on Entry Day, then we judge 8 A.M. to 5 P.M. the next day.
>
> Each judge has a clerk right at her elbow, taking everything down. No one but the judges and the clerks are allowed in the room during judging. We dig through it all and find the best. We fill out a big judging sheet. It's all done by numbers—we have no idea who entered what.

Judges award ribbons, first through fifth, in each category. Sometimes they do not deem any product worthy of the blue ribbon and the second-place red ribbon becomes the best of that year's entries.

Jan is one of six judges who assess canning: jams, jellies, pickles, and canned fruits and vegetables. Ten other judges do the baked goods. "We look at the jars of vegetables and fruits first," she explains. "The canned foods have to be opened to be tasted, of course. The entrants bring two jars of each food, one is opened, judged, and discarded; the second jar is for display. In earlier years, the canned goods were recanned after they were opened for judging and that made for a very steamy judging room, especially when it was a steamy August day." Jams and jellies come after the canned goods. Jan's experience is such that she easily judges 150 jars of jam and jelly in one day.

A University of Minnesota-trained home economist, Jan honed her judging skills as a county agent with the Hennepin County Extension Service. In the years before her children were born and she opted to be at home, she judged the 4-H demonstrations on the county and state level. "I loved that. They were neat kids doing worthwhile things," she says.

"The judges doing the baked goods always start with the breads right away the first day," she continues. "That's because yeast breads stale the fastest. After that, they turn to the quick breads. And the next day they do the cakes, cookies, and bars. Three judges work together to pick the sweepstakes winner for that year."

A day in which you sample 150 jams, along with an array of other preserves, is not a day you're much interested in eating lunch or a snack, Jan admits. "We'll have fruit or some yogurt, something mild, not sweet. And ice water, coffee, and soda crackers." These last, along with celery, are time-honored palate cleansers.

Once judged, the food entries become a massive, colorful display. Entire walls lined with perfectly prepared foods from fluffy angel food cakes to straight-as-soldiers whole green beans in their jars attract slowly shuffling lines of admirers all during the fair. On my own visits to the food exhibits, I've found the people-watching as good as the food-watching. What contortions people will go into trying to read the names on the tags of the winners!

Recipe contests sponsored by food companies on behalf of their products are an offshoot of the food judging. Rather than ribbons, these contests offer cash and personal publicity for the cooks. (Not to mention valuable publicity for the featured food products.) First, Proctor and Gamble ran state contests for pies made with Crisco. Then General Mills started a contest for cakes made with Softasilk cake flour. Soon many of the Minnesota food companies, Hormel to Land O'Lakes, were running contests at the Fair.

The Gedney Pickle Company, based in Chaska, turned its State Fair recipe search into a successful marketing campaign. They set up six categories of jams and jellies, offering sizable cash prizes for the cook's original recipes. Once picked, the women's photographs and their hand-written comments were featured on the labels of the new jam and jelly flavors. It was fun to see my friend Barbara Schaller of Burnsville smiling down from the jar of her peach-raspberry Melba jam at the supermarket. Jan Stroom and her fellow judges often help with picking winners for these contests. "Hormel offered $500 as first prize for a recipe made with their canned chili in 2000. That's getting to be money," she remarks.

Believe it or not, Jan and her colleagues write comments on the entry tags of all the foods they judge. Things like: "needs to be baked longer," "loaf rose too long," or "try adding some garlic or onion for flavor." Fair entrants whom I interviewed say they heed the advice on these critiques and have improved their scoring the next year.

There is no preliminary judging for the State Fair. Nor is there an entry fee. Any resident of the state who gets the food there on the appointed day and hour may enter. "Some of these entries come from excellent cooks," says Jan, "people who produce wonderful food."

Here are ribbon-winning recipes from five of those excellent cooks.

MARJORIE JOHNSON'S APRICOT PECAN OATMEAL MUFFINS

MAKES 12 MUFFINS

1 cup quick-cooking oats
1 cup buttermilk
1 cup all-purpose flour
1 teaspoon baking powder
½ teaspoon baking soda
½ teaspoon salt
¼ cup chopped dried apricots
¼ cup chopped pecans
⅓ cup vegetable oil, preferably canola
1 egg
½ cup firmly packed brown sugar

This Robbinsdale homemaker has long been one of the handful of women who dominate the State Fair food competition, winning sheaves of ribbons. Marjorie is also the food columnist for Rosey's Magazine.

Combine oats and buttermilk in medium bowl; stir to combine. Cover and let stand 20 minutes.

Preheat oven to 375°F.

In a large bowl, combine flour, baking powder, baking soda, and salt. Stir the apricots and pecans into flour mixture.

Add oil, egg, and brown sugar to the buttermilk mixture. Combine well. Pour the buttermilk mixture into the flour mixture. Stir just to moisten the dry ingredients. Divide the batter into 12 greased muffin cups. Bake for 20 to 25 minutes, or until golden brown. Remove muffins from muffin pan and cool on rack.

ELAINE JANAS'S WHOLE GRAIN BREAD

MAKES 2 OR 3 LOAVES

2 packages active dry yeast
½ cup warm water (120 to 130°F)
1 ¾ cup scalded milk
⅓ cup honey
¼ cup soft shortening
1 tablespoon salt
⅓ cup wheat germ
⅓ cup 7-grain cereal*
1 cup whole wheat flour
5 to 5 ½ cups bread flour

*available at food co-ops and natural food stores

Elaine, who lives in Columbia Heights, has been a ribbon-winning baker for many years. Savor the crunchy eating quality of this bread in toast and sandwiches.

Dissolve yeast in warm water. Scald (heat to just below the boiling point) milk and pour over honey, shortening, salt, wheat germ, and 7-grain cereal. Cool to lukewarm. Add yeast mixture, the whole wheat flour and 1 cup of bread flour. Beat until smooth.

Add remaining bread flour gradually to form a stiff dough. Knead on lightly floured board for 8 to 10 minutes. Place in a greased bowl, cover, and let rise until double.

Divide dough into 2 large or 3 small balls and let rest, covered, for 15 minutes.

Shape into loaves** and place in greased loaf pans. Cover with plastic wrap and let rise until light.

Bake in preheated 350°F (325°F for glass pans) oven 40 to 45 minutes, or until loaf sounds hollow when thumped with finger.

**A quick way to shape loaves is to roll ball of dough into a rectangle with rolling pin, then roll up tightly. Seal loaf by pinching edge of dough into roll. Place loaf in pan seam side down.

For dough:

¼ cup scalded milk

2 tablespoons sugar

½ teaspoon salt

¼ cup butter

1 package active dry yeast
  (2¼ teaspoons)

¼ cup warm water (120 to
  130°F)

1 egg

1¾ cups all-purpose flour

For filling:

1 (8-ounce) package cream
  cheese, softened

½ cup sugar

1 egg

1 teaspoon vanilla

For topping:

½ cup butter

¾ cup sugar

1 cup flour

BARB SCHALLER'S CREAM CHEESE COFFEE CAKE

MAKES 12 TO 16 SERVINGS

When Barb Schaller of Burnsville sent this recipe to me, she added this note: "First place, Minnesota State Fair: 1985, 1986, 1989, 1990. Second place: 1987. Not entered: 1988. Bomb, 1991."

Prepare dough: Combine the milk, 2 tablespoons sugar, salt, and ¼ cup butter. Dissolve the yeast in the warm water. Cool the yeast mixture and add to the milk mixture. Add the egg and flour to the yeast mixture—dough will be soft and sticky. Place in a greased bowl and let rise until double, 30 to 45 minutes.

When dough has doubled, roll or pat dough into a circle. Place in a greased 16-inch pizza pan. With greased fingers, shape as a pizza crust with an edge.

Make filling by creaming the cheese and sugar together and adding the egg and vanilla. Pour filling evenly over the prepared crust.

For topping, cut the ½ cup butter into the ¾ cup sugar and 1 cup flour using a pastry blender, working until mixture is crumbly. Sprinkle on top of cream cheese filling. Let crust rise 30 minutes before baking.

Bake in preheated oven at 375°F for 20 to 25 minutes, or until brown. Cut into wedges.

---

6 egg whites

½ teaspoon cream of tartar

2¼ cups sifted cake flour,
  such as Softasilk*

1½ cups granulated sugar

3 teaspoons baking powder

1 teaspoon salt

½ cup vegetable oil

6 egg yolks, unbeaten

¾ cup cold water

1 tablespoon grated lemon
  rind

¼ teaspoon lemon extract

*2 cups all-purpose flour may
  be used in place of cake flour.

PATRICE PAWELK'S LEMON CHIFFON CAKE

MAKES 12 SERVINGS

Patrice, who lives in Annandale, won the baking sweepstakes in 1988 with this light, lovely cake.

Preheat oven to 325°F. In a very large bowl, beat egg whites just slightly. Add cream of tartar and whip until mixture forms very stiff peaks.

Sift together cake flour, sugar, baking powder, and salt into large mixer bowl. Make a well in the center. Add oil, egg yolks, water, lemon rind, and extract. Beat with electric mixer until smooth.

Pour egg mixture gradually over beaten egg whites, folding with a rubber scraper until everything is blended. Pour into a ungreased 10-inch tube pan. Bake 65 to 75 minutes, or until top of cake springs back when touched lightly. Invert and let pan hang until cold. Loosen cake from pan with long spatula; remove from pan.

3 cups granulated sugar

1 ¼ cups butter, softened

8 ounces cream cheese, softened

1 tablespoons fresh lemon juice

1 tablespoon vanilla

1 teaspoon lemon extract

½ teaspoon orange extract

6 eggs

3 cups sifted Softasilk cake flour

½ teaspoon salt

½ teaspoon ground nutmeg

KATHRYN EARNEST'S LEMON CREAM CHEESE CAKE

MAKES 12 TO 16 SERVINGS

One of the biggest bloopers of my food-writing career came when I published this winning Softasilk pound cake omitting, in my haste, the eggs. Six of 'em. Calls about the error lit up the Star Tribune *switchboard. I had to answer all of them.*

Kathryn, who lives in Lindstrom, has won many a ribbon, and took the $175 top prize with this rich, dense cake.

Preheat oven to 325°F. Grease and flour a 12-cup tube pan.

In a large bowl, beat sugar, butter, and cream cheese until light and fluffy. Beat in the lemon juice, vanilla, and the lemon and orange extracts. Add the eggs one at a time, beating well after each addition.

Sift flour, salt, and nutmeg together three times and add to the mixture. Beat until smooth: 2 to 3 minutes. Pour batter into prepared pan.

Bake for 75 to 90 minutes, until a wooden toothpick inserted in center comes out clean. Cool on rack 10 minutes. Loosen cake from pan with a metal spatula and invert onto wire rack to cool. This cake needs no enhancement, but a dollop of lemon sauce or a scoop of orange sherbet would be excellent.

EBERHARD WERTHMANN

THE DEAN OF COOKING TEACHERS

New York has its method actors. Minnesota has its method cooking teacher. His name is Eberhard Werthmann and he's been teaching the chef's art since he was thirty. He taught thousands of aspiring chefs and cooks as head of culinary arts at Saint Paul Technical College. He continues to teach, guiding home cooks through techniques from brothmaking to barbecuing. Eberhard says:

There are three ways to learn cooking. You can learn by habit, as we do from our mothers. That's good, but limited. Or, we can follow recipes. They're wonderful guidelines, but not the law. [This statement gave me pause; I was in the middle of writing 150+ recipes for this book.]

Or, we can learn methods. That's the professional approach. Each food we prepare employs a different method. Soon the students know more than they think they know, because the method can be applied to different foods.

"How many recipes tell you to melt two tablespoons of butter, add flour, cook but do not burn?" he asks. "What are you doing? You are making a roux." Whether the roux thickens fish stock for a sauce or milk for cream soup, the method is the same. Eberhard's point exactly.

He also taught at the Food Fests (no longer being held) at the Kahler Hotel in Rochester. It was there that I saw him in action and marveled at his skill. This man knows cooking inside out. But, more important, he can demonstrate a technique *and,* at the same time, make a point, give a food's history, charm his class with an anecdote. It is a real skill to be able to prepare food with one's hands and, simultaneously, *talk* food. I know; I've taught cooking too. When you

Eberhard Werthmann whips up a batch of hollandaise sauce in the classroom at Cooks of Crocus Hill in St. Paul.

need to concentrate on boning that chicken, it's hard to keep talking, offering variations, describing menus, whatever. And I think Eberhard has a teaching advantage most of us do not have. He speaks with a slight foreign accent— German in his case. And when the teacher has a bit of an accent, the students listen more closely, focus more sharply.

Eberhard's extensive knowledge of food and cooking began in his teens when he apprenticed with a chef in his native Germany. By eighteen, he was a journeyman, traveling from city to city, from country to country. "I learned something valuable from each chef I worked under," he explains. He had the pleasure of cooking for then-chancellor Konrad Adenauer when in Bonn, Germany.

He had twenty jobs in ten years, climbing the ladder of hierarchy in the kitchen, which, he says, is typical in Europe. He moved on to join the Sheraton Hotel chain in Jamaica.

Eberhard, not yet thirty, arrived in Minnesota in 1965, as executive chef of the newly built Sheraton Ritz Hotel in downtown Minneapolis. I still remember my excited anticipation as I passed the huge bouquet in the lovely lobby and headed into the Sheraton dining room. "I had it made at the Sheraton," he admits. It was here, too, that he met his wife, Kathleen. (The hotel has since been torn down.)

In 1966, Eberhard got a call from the technical college in St. Paul, an imposing building near the St. Paul Cathedral. They wanted him to teach would-be chefs. His father had been a teacher and he thought he'd like it too. So, he decided to try teaching for two years. He loved it; he stayed.

The chef's program at now-named Saint Paul College is one of eleven state-supported courses set up to train cook/chefs for the burgeoning food-service field. A new class, about twenty men and women, begins the Saint Paul course each season. They learn basics the first quarter and quantity food-production the second. Eberhard took charge for the third quarter. He worked them hard, teaching them how to organize their many tasks, how to supervise others, how to be responsible for results.

His students ran the school's popular dining room (now the Cityview Grill). Here they showed how well they'd learned their methods. No menu included two foods made with the same technique. For example, when I lunched there, the choices were stuffed game hens (roasting), beef roulades (braising), pork fricassee (stewing), and poached halibut.

The dining room, where you can see the Minnesota History Center and the Capitol's gold dome, packs them in. Not only is the food outstanding, but the value is high. That's because guests pay for food but not labor. For the student cooks and servers, this is a reality program, with a passing grade as the prize.

By the mid-1990s, Eberhard was being called "dean" of Minnesota's chef instructors. That's because so many of his one-time students have worked their way up the professional ladder and are executive chefs and food and beverage directors of some of the top-rated hotels and restaurants in the Twin Cities.

Since retiring from the college at the end of 1999, Eberhard teaches frequently at the two Cooks of Crocus Hill schools, one in St. Paul at the Victoria & Grand food hub, the other at 50th and France in Edina. His class, "Professional Approach to Basics," has been extremely popular. The five sessions cover fish, vegetables, soups, meats, and a complete dinner, each class teaching the different methods. The classes, held over a two-and-a-half-week period, draw students from as far away as northern Iowa.

"First a little bit lecture, using items lined up on a tray," he says of the classes. Then students draw slips to determine which recipe they will prepare. Eberhard and two assistants advise while the students cook. Those interested can move up to an advanced course. "The second course takes it up a notch," he continues. "For example, in the first series of classes, we do pepper-seared fish. In the class on fish in the second series we do salmon with spinach filling in puff pastry." He also teaches a barbecuing course doing four or five entrees in each session along with accompaniments and salsas.

Now that Eberhard is retired (well, semi-retired), he and Kathleen like to donate lunches and brunches to charity silent auctions. "Yes, I cook at home," he says. "My wife cooks too. And we cook together when we entertain."

Chef Werthmann shared these recipes.

PORK FILLET WITH CAPER SAUCE

MAKES 1 SERVING

4 ounces pork tenderloin, cut into 4 slices
Salt and pepper to season
Flour to dredge
½ tablespoon butter
½ tablespoon olive oil

For caper sauce:

½ tablespoon olive oil
1 tablespoon butter
¼ small onion, very finely chopped
½ anchovy filet, rinsed and chopped
1 teaspoon flour
½ tablespoon capers, drained
½ tablespoon parsley, chopped
1 tablespoon wine vinegar
1 tablespoon water
1 tablespoon balsamic vinegar

Capers (pickled flower buds) add piquancy to sauces like this.

Flatten tenderloin slice with a meat pounder (mallet) until thin, season with salt and pepper, and dredge in flour, shaking off excess flour.

In a frying pan, heat butter and oil until hot, add pork slices, and cook until lightly brown on both sides, about 2 to 4 minutes. Remove to a heated plate.

Add olive oil and ½ tablespoon of the butter to the same pan. When hot, add onions and stir-fry for half a minute. Add chopped anchovy and stir well.

Stir in the flour and blend well. Add capers, parsley, wine vinegar, and water, stirring over low heat to thicken the sauce.

Stir in the other ½ tablespoon of butter and the balsamic vinegar.

Pour sauce over cooked tenderloin slices.

BEEF STIR-FRY WITH ARTICHOKES AND CARROTS

MAKES 1 SERVING

5 ounces tender beef, such as tenderloin or ribeye

⅓ cup julienne-cut carrots

⅓ cup frozen artichokes, thawed and quartered

2 green onions, split, cut into 1-inch strips

2 teaspoons soy sauce

1 teaspoon cornstarch

¼ cup beef stock

1 tablespoon oil

Pinch ground ginger

Pinch cayenne pepper

This was excellent with hot white rice, but it would also be good with hot instant couscous.

Cut beef into strips ⅓ inch wide by 1 ½ inches long.

Stir the cornstarch with the soy sauce until smooth. Have the remaining ingredients ready in separate containers before starting to cook.

Heat half the oil in a sauté pan or skillet until very hot. Add carrots, scallions, and artichokes, and stir-fry rapidly for about 2 minutes. Remove from pan.

Add remaining oil to the pan and heat until very hot. Add beef and stir-fry to desired doneness. Quickly stir the cornstarch mixture and add it and the beef stock to the pan. Stir to remove the cooked bits from the bottom of the pan and bring to simmer. Add the vegetables and simmer just until heated through. Taste and correct seasoning.

GRILLED SALMON WITH PINEAPPLE SALSA

MAKES 1 SERVING

4-ounce salmon filet

1 teaspoon lemon juice

½ tablespoon shallot, chopped

½ garlic clove, minced

Ground pepper to taste

For salsa:

1 teaspoon butter

½ tablespoon minced shallot

⅛ teaspoon minced jalapeno pepper

½ teaspoon minced fresh ginger

2 tablespoons orange juice

¼ cup finely diced fresh pineapple

½ teaspoon chopped mint leaves*

½ teaspoon chopped basil*

Pinch of curry powder

*Kitchen shears work well for chopping/snipping fresh herbs like these.

This recipe and the two others here give amounts for one serving, but can easily be doubled, tripled, or quadrupled for more people.

Sprinkle the salmon with lemon juice, shallots, garlic, ground pepper. Let marinate briefly.

Prepare pineapple salsa while the fish marinates. Heat the butter and add the shallots, jalapeno, and ginger. Stir-fry until aroma is released. Add the orange juice and allow it to reduce slightly. Add the pineapple, herbs, and curry powder and warm gently. Do not simmer the salsa.

Grill the salmon over hot coals, until flesh flakes easily with fork, turning once. Total time will be 6 to 8 minutes. If preferred, broil salmon. Serve immediately with warm salsa.

2 tablespoons unsalted butter

1 medium onion, chopped

12 ounces (3 ½ cups) wild and
cultivated mushrooms*

1 clove garlic, minced

2 teaspoons fresh thyme or
dill, chopped (1 teaspoon
dried)

5 cups chicken broth

3 ounces (½ cup) finely
chopped floury potatoes**

14 ounces fresh spinach or
7 ounces frozen chopped
spinach

Salt, freshly ground black
pepper, and nutmeg

4 tablespoons heavy or sour
cream, for serving

*a combination of shiitake,
portabello, or trumpet
mushrooms and white or
brown button mushrooms

**potatoes that cook up mealy
as do baking potatoes such
as russets

SPINACH AND WILD MUSHROOM SOUP

MAKES 4 SERVINGS

An intriguing soup that looks like spinach but tastes like mushrooms and combines the best qualities of both.

Melt the butter in a large pan, add the onion and stir-fry without coloring for 6 to 8 minutes. Add the mushrooms, garlic, and herbs; cover and allow the juices to run.

Add half the broth, potatoes, and spinach. Bring back to a boil and simmer for 10 minutes.

Puree the soup and return to the saucepan. Add the remaining broth and season to taste with salt, pepper, and a little nutmeg. Serve with a dollop of cream stirred into the soup.

APPENDIX
FOR MORE INFORMATION

Please note that if you plan to attend an event or visit a location, call ahead first: dates and availability may change at the last minute.

Books listed may be found or ordered through local bookstores or may be ordered through www.amazon.com or www.bn.com (Barnes & Noble).

CELEBRATIONS AND FESTIVALS

1. BAKE-OFF

Address:
General Mills, Inc.
Post Office Box 1113
Minneapolis, MN 55440
(763) 764-7600

Web address: www.pillsbury.com/bakeoff/

Any cook who meets the Pillsbury Bake-Off criteria and deadlines may enter the cooking contest. However, the Bake-Off contest event—the day that the baking and judging are done—is not open to the public. Only the finalists, judges, Bake-Off staff, and food press may enter the Bake-Off floor.

2. FESTIVAL OF NATIONS

Address:
International Institute of Minnesota
1694 Como Avenue
St. Paul MN 55108
(651) 647-0191

Web address: www.festivalofnations.com
and www.iimn.org

Admission is charged.

3. CINCO DE MAYO

Address:
District del Sol
176 Concord Street
St. Paul, MN 55107
(651) 222-6347

Web address: www.districtdelsol.com, click on Cinco de Mayo

No admission is charged. Food and souvenirs are for sale.

4. NEW ULM'S HERITAGEFEST

Address:
Heritagefest, Inc.
Post Office Box 461
New Ulm, MN 56073
(507) 354-8850

Heritagefest held at:
Brown County Fairgrounds
1200 North State Street
New Ulm, MN 56073

Web address: www.heritagefest.net

Dates: Friday, Saturday, and Sunday, the second and third weekends of July. Heritagefest is held rain or shine.

Admission is charged.

The German-Bohemian Heritage Society. *Deutsch-Bohmische KUCHE*, Edition No. 2. New Ulm, Minnesota: The German-Bohemian Heritage Society.

Address:
The German-Bohemian Heritage Society
Post Office Box 822
New Ulm, MN 56073

5. POWWOW PRIMER

For powwows on Minnesota reservations, contact the Tribal Council of that reservation or the Convention & Visitors Bureau of the local community.

Web addresses:
www.500nations.com/Minnesota_Events. asp. and www.exploreminnesota.com, click on Festivals and Events

6. CELEBRATING PIE

Address:
Braham Pie Day
2nd Street Southwest
Post Office Box 383
Braham, MN 55006
(320) 396-4956

Web address: www.braham.com, click on Pie Day

Date: The first Friday of August.

No admission is charged.

Braham's Pie Cookbook, Revised Edition (2003, spiral bound) can be ordered by sending a check for $15 ($11 + $4 PH) to address above.

Le, Draoulec, Pascale. *American Pie: Slices of Life (and Pie) from America's Back Roads.* New York: Harper Collins, 2002.

7. RONDO DAYS

Rondo Avenue, Inc.
(651) 646-6597

Web address: www.rondodays.org

Festival on grounds of J. J. Hill Montessori Magnet School,
9898 Selby Ave., St. Paul

Senior citizen dinner at Hallie Q. Brown Center, in the Martin Luther King Center, 270 North 10th Street, St. Paul.

8. MINNESOTA STATE FAIR

Address:
Minnesota State Fairgrounds
1265 Snelling Avenue North
St. Paul, MN 55108-3099
(651) 642-2200

Web address: www.mnstatefair.org

Dates: The third Thursday in August
through Labor Day.

Admission is charged. Gate and ride tickets and Blue Ribbon Bargain Books can
be purchased in advance.

9. HMONG NEW YEAR

Sponsor:
Lao Family Community of Minnesota
1433 Franklin Avenue
Minneapolis, MN 55404
(612) 870-1719

Dates: Last weekend in November.

Hours: www.rivercentre.org, click on
Calendar of Events, then November

10. ST. OLAF CHRISTMAS FESTIVAL

Address:
St. Olaf College
1520 St. Olaf Avenue
Northfield, MN 55057
(507) 646-3308

Web address: www.stolaf.edu, click on
Music, then Christmas Festival

Dates: Thursday, Friday, Saturday, and
Sunday of the first weekend in December.

Zempel, Solveig. *In Their Own Words,
Letters from Norwegian Immigrants.*
Minneapolis: University of Minnesota
Press, 1991.

SAVORY SPECIALTIES

11. BERRY PICKING AT THE FARM

Get a *Minnesota Grown Directory* for
details on you-pick farms and farmers
markets. Call (651) 297-2200 in the metro
area or (800) 967-2474 out of state to
obtain your free copy. Or write:
Minnesota Department of Agriculture,
90 West Plato Boulevard, St. Paul, MN
55107. Copies also available at libraries
during fresh produce seasons.

Web address: www.minnesotagrown.com

12. LAND O'LAKES BUTTER

Address:
Land O'Lakes, Inc.
Post Office Box 64101
St. Paul, MN 55164-0101
(651) 481-2222
Consumer Affairs: (800) 328-4155

Web address: www.landolakes.com.
This site offers 600+ recipes, many with
color photos, plus menus and entertaining tips.

13. CABIN TIME

Brubacher, Mary and Margie Knoblauch.
North Country Cabin Cooking. Hopkins,
Minnesota: Garlic Press, 1983.

Address:
Garlic Press
13017 Maywood Lane
Hopkins, MN 55343
(612) 938-5012

14. BETTY CROCKER TAKES THE CAKE

Address:
General Mills
Main Offices
Post Office Box 1113
Minneapolis, MN 55440
(763) 764-7600 or (800) 446-1898

Web address: www.bettycrocker.com

Byrn, Anne. *The Cake Mix Doctor*. New York: Workman Publishing, 1999.

Byrn, Anne. *Chocolate From the Cake Mix Doctor*. New York: Workman Publishing, 2001.

Betty Crocker's Ultimate Cake Mix Cookbook. New York: Wiley Publishing, Inc., 2002.

15. KEN DAVIS BAR-B-Q SAUCE

Address:
Ken Davis Products, Inc.
4210 Park Glen Road
Minneapolis, MN 55416
(952) 922-5556

Web address: www.kendavis-bbq.com

To obtain a copy of Ken Davis News, write to address above.

16. WILD FRUIT

Address:
Minnestalgia
41640 State Highway 65
Post Office Box 86
McGregor, MN 55760
(218) 768-4917 or (800) 328-6731
(218) 768-2533 (winery)

Web address: www.minnesotawild.com
(through 2003, then
www.minnestalgia.com)

17. SCHWAN'S ICE CREAM

Address:
The Schwan Food Company
115 West College Drive
Marshall, MN 56258
(507) 532-3274 or (800) 533-5290

Web address: www.schwansinc.com

18. SOYBEANS

Address:
Minnesota Soybean Council
360 Pierce Avenue, Suite 110
North Mankato, MN 56003
(507) 388-1635 or (888) 896-9678

Web address: www.mnsoybean.org

19. SPAM

Address:
Consumer Affairs Department
Hormel Foods Corporation
36801 Hormel Place
Austin, MN 55912
(800) 523-4635

Address:
SPAM Museum
1937 SPAM Boulevard
Austin, MN 55912
(507) 437-5100 or (800) LUV-SPAM

Web addresses: www.hormel.com and www.SPAM.com

Cho, John Nagamichi. *SPAM-KU, Tranquil Reflections on Luncheon Loaf*. New York: HarperPerennial, 1998.

20. TURKEY

Address:

Minnesota Turkey Research and
Promotion Council
Minnesota Turkey Growers Association
108 Marty Drive
Buffalo, MN 55313
(763) 682-2171

Web address: www.minnesotaturkeys.com

Address:

Jennie-O Turkey Store
Post Office Box 778
Willmar, MN 56201
(320) 235-2622

Web address: www.jennieoturkeystore.com

21. WATKINS VANILLA

Address:

Watkins, Inc.
150 Liberty Street
Post Office Box 5570
Winona, MN 55987

Web address: www.watkinsonline.com

22. WILD RICE

Address:

Minnesota Cultivated Wild Rice Council
4630 Churchill Street, Suite #1
St. Paul, MN 55126
(651) 638-1955

Anderson, Beth. *Wild Rice for All Seasons Cookbook*. Minneapolis: Minnehaha Publishing, 1977.

MEMORABLE PLACES

23. THE AMERICAN SWEDISH INSTITUTE

Address:

The American Swedish Institute
2600 Park Avenue
Minneapolis, MN 55407
(612) 871-4907

Web address:
www.americanswedishinst.org

Dates: Open Tuesday through Sunday.

Admission is charged.

Var Sa God: Heritage and Favorite Recipes & Handbook of Swedish Traditions. Minneapolis: American Swedish Institute, 1980. Available in person or by mail from the Bokhandle, the bookshop on the lower level of the Institute building.

24. BC GARDENS

Address:

BC Gardens
20355 408th Avenue
Belgrade, MN 56312
(888) 884-9766

E-mail address: bcgardens@juno.com

For a directory of local community supported agriculture farms, contact The Land Stewardship Project, 2200 Fourth Street, White Bear Lake, MN 55110, (651) 653-0618, or visit www.landstewardshipproject.org.

25. CARLSON'S APPLE ORCHARD & BAKERY

Address:
Carlson's Orchard, Bakery and
Restaurant
11893 Montgomery Ave. SW
Winsted, MN 55395
(320) 485-3704

E-mail address: pies@tds.net

Carlson's Orchard is one of 450 growers
in the on-line *Minnesota Grown Directory*
at: www.mda.state.mn.us/mngrown. See
print directory order information above.

26. FOREST HISTORY CENTER

Address:
Forest History Center
2609 County Road 76
Grand Rapids, MN 55744
(218) 327-4482

E-mail address: foresthistory@mnhs.org

Cookshack Cooking, a pamphlet of lum-
berjack recipes published by the Forest
History Center, is available at the center.

27. KAVANAUGH'S SYLVAN LAKE RESORT

Address:
Kavanaugh's Sylvan Lake Resort
1685 Kavanaugh Drive
East Gull Lake, MN 56401
(218) 829-5226 or (800) 562-7061

Web address: www.kavanaughs.com

Dates: Restaurant open Memorial Day
through Labor Day, dinner daily except
Sundays. During the fall conference
group meetings are held.

28. CONCORDIA LANGUAGE VILLAGES

Address:
Concordia Language Villages
Concordia College
901 8th Street South
Moorhead, MN 56562
(218) 299-4544 or (800) 222-4750

Web address:
www.concordialanguagevillages.org

29. SCHUMACHER'S HOTEL

Address:
Schumacher's Hotel
212 West Main Street
New Prague, MN 56071
(952) 758-2133 or (800) 283-2049

Web address: www.schumachershotel.com

Dates: Open daily. Both food and lodging
available; reservations required for
rooms, recommended for dining.

Schumacher, John. *John Schumacher's
New Prague Hotel Cookbook*. New Prague,
Minnesota: International Cuisine
Publishers, 1991.

Schumacher, John. *Wild Game Cooking
Made Easy*. New Prague, Minnesota:
International Cuisine Publishing, 1997.

Schumacher, John. *Fish Cooking Made
Easy*. Minnetonka, Minnesota: North
American Fishing Club, 1999.

Schumacher, John and Ron Schara.
Minnesota Bound Game Cookbook.
Cambridge, Minnesota: Adventure
Publishing, 2000.

Schumacher, John and Ron Schara.
Minnesota Bound Fish Cookbook.
Cambridge, Minnesota: Adventure
Publishing, 2000.

30. IRONWORLD

Address:
Ironworld Discovery Center
Post Office Box 392
Highway 169 West
Chisholm, MN 55719
(218) 254-7959 or (800) 372-6437

Web address: www.ironworld.com

Dates: Discovery Center open daily May through September. Admission is charged.

Iron Range Research Center, open daily, May through September; open Monday through Friday, October through April. No admission is charged.

NORTH STAR COOKS

31. LEEANN CHIN

Address:
Leeann Chin, Inc.
3600 West 80th Street
Bloomington, MN 55431
(952) 896-3606

Web address: www.leeannchin.com

Chin, Leeann. *Betty Crocker's Chinese Cookbook*. New York: Random House, 1981.

Chin, Leeann and Katie Chin. *Everyday Chinese Cooking: Quick and Delicious Recipes from the Leeann Chin Restaurants*. New York: Clarkson Potter Publishers, 2000.

32. HOCKEY MOM BETH DOOLEY

Anton, Liz and Beth Dooley. *It's the Berries*. Pownal, Vermont: Storey Communications, 1988.

Dooley, Beth. *Peppers, Hot and Sweet*. Pownal, Vermont: Storey Communications, 1990.

Dooley, Beth and Lucia Watson. *Savoring the Seasons of the Northern Heartland*. New York: Knopf: distributed by Random House, 1994.

Rogers, Jean, ed. *Prevention's Quick & Healthy Low-Fat Cooking Featuring Pasta and Other Italian Favorites*. Emmaus, Pennsylvania: Rodale Press, Inc.

Dooley, Beth. *The Heartland (Williams-Sonoma New American Cooking Series)*. Alexandria, Virginia: Time-Life Books, 2001.

34. AL SICHERMAN

Sicherman, Al. *Caramel Knowledge*. Minneapolis: Pants Press, 1985. New York: Harper and Row, 1988.

37. LYNNE ROSSETTO KASPER

Web address: www.splendidtable.org

The Splendid Table can be heard weekly on public radio stations via Public Radio International.

Kasper, Lynne Rossetto. *The Splendid Table*. New York: William Morrow, 1992.

Kasper, Lynne Rossetto, *The Italian Country Table: Home Cooking from Italy's Farmhouse Kitchens*. New York: Scribner, 1999.

38. BEATRICE OJAKANGAS

Ojakangas, Beatrice. *The Finnish Cookbook*. New York: Crown Publishers Inc., 1964.

Ojakangas, Beatrice. *Scandinavian Feasts*. New York: Stewart, Tabori & Chang, 1992, hardcover no longer in print. Minneapolis: University of Minnesota Press, 2001 paperback re-issue.

RECIPE INDEX

African, Vegetable Mafé, 161
Almonds
  Almond Salami (confection), 12
  Almond-Filled Cookie Cake, 7
  Pistachio Pesto, Linguini with, 213
  Raspberry Almond Shortbread
    Thumbprints, 71
  Walleye Almondine, 154
Amber's Delight, 97
Apples
  Cake, Dried Apple, 149
  Cake, Walnut Bundt, 145
  Cake-Pie, Russian, 146
  Cheesecake, Autumn Harvest, 146
  Cranberry Pudding, 219
  Puff Pancake, 145
  Sauerkraut with Potatoes and, 23
  Varieties, 144
Artichokes, Beef Stir-Fry with, 230
Avocado-Lime Cream Soup, 196
Bagel Spread, Wild Fruit, 92
Barbecue(d)
  Honey Pork, 180
  Pork Sandwiches, 86
  Ribs, Ken's, 86
  Turkey Legs, 41
Bars
  Extreme Brownies, 196
  Frosted Kahlua Creams, 168
  Killer Brownies, 191
  Lemon-Butter, 71
  Marble, 77
  Oatmeal Carmelitas, 6
Beef
  Curry with Eggplant, 54
  Meat Blintzes, 203
  Meat Pasties, English, 172
  Steak Fajitas, 18

Stir-Fried with Pea Vines, 53
Stir-Fry with Artichokes and
  Carrots, 230
Swedish Seaman's, 162
Swedish Meatballs, 133
Taco Salad, 102
Tostadas, 16
Beet Borscht, 11
Berry Sundaes, Double, 93
Beverages
  Lemonade, 41
  Summertime Wine Cooler, 93
Blanc Mange (pudding), 121
Blintzes, Meat, 203
Blueberry
  Grunt (dessert), 66
  Monday (sauce), 66
  Muffins, 65
  Pancakes, 65
Borscht, 11
Breads, quick
  Fry Bread, 29
  Magic Marshmallow Crescent
    Puffs, 6
  Monkey Bread, 76
  Muffins, Apricot Pecan Oatmeal,
    223
  Muffins, Blueberry, 65
  Caramel Rolls, Tiny, 190
Breads, yeast
  Big Big Cinnamon Rolls, 47
  Coffee Bread, Scandinavian, 218
  Cream Cheese Coffee Cake, 224
  Kolaches, Czech, 173
  Schmierkuchen, 22
  Whole Grain, 223
Breakfast
  Caramel Rolls, Tiny, 190

Crepes, Raspberry Cheesecake,
  192
French Toast, Crème Brulee, 191
French Toast, Oven-Baked, 47
Granola, Toasty Nut, 75
Pancake, Apple Puff, 145
Pancakes, Blueberry, 65
Broccoli, Stir-Fried with Red Pepper
  and Tofu, 140
Brownies, 191
Buffalo Burgers, 30
Burgers, Turkey, 114
Byerly's Wild Rice Soup, 126
Cakes
  Apple, Dried, 149
  Apple Walnut Bundt, 145
  Cake-Pie, Russian Apple, 146
  Chocolate Goo, 198
  Fruit-Topped, 150
  Fudge, Triple, 82
  Gingerbread, River Driver's, 149
  Lemon Chiffon, 224
  Lemon Cream Cheese, 225
  Pineapple Upside-Down, 81
  Pumpkin, 81
  Rhubarb Cream, 82
  Spice, Swedish, 134
Calypso Pork Roast, 209
Caper Sauce, with Pork Fillet, 231
Caramel Rolls, Tiny, 190
Caribbean Jerk Chicken, 42
Carrot Salad with Daikon Radish, 54
Carrot Tzimmes, 204
Carrots, Beef Stir-Fry with, 230
Casseroles
  Cheesy Macaroni Bake with Spam,
    110
  Corn Pudding, Fresh, 186

Jansson's Temptation (potato-anchovy), 134
Mashed Potato and Rutabaga, 219
Tzimmes, Carrot, 204
Wild Rice Baron, 126
Cheese Empanadas, 12
Cheesecake, Autumn Harvest (apple), 146
Chicken
  and Barley Soup, 185
  Breasts, Endlessly Easy, 167
  Caribbean Jerk, 42
  Enchiladas, 17
  Parmesan, 76
  Pot Pie, 187
  Salad, 98, 162, 208
  Skewers, 180
  Soup with Matzah Balls, 202
Chinese
  Chicken Skewers, 180
  Green Beans with Cashews, 181
  Pork, Honey Barbecued, 180
  Rice, Fried, Yeung Chau, 181
  Spicy Pork and Tofu, 161
Chippewa Wild Rice Salad, 127
Chocolate
  Brownies, 191, 196
  Cake, Goo, 198
  Chiffon Pie, Crunchy, 35
  Chip Cookies, 48, 72
  Colonial Innkeeper's Pie, 35
  Ganache, 197
Cinnamon Cream Chicken Fruit Salad, 108
Cinnamon Rolls, Big Big, 47
Clarified Butter, 154
Coffee Bread, Scandinavian, 218
Coffee Cake, Cream Cheese, 224
Coffee Cake: Schmierkuchen, 22
Confection: Almond Salami, 12
Cookies
  Almond-Filled Cookie Cake, 7
  Chocolate Chip, Supersize, 72
  Sugar, Louise's, 72
  Macaroons, 121
  Oatmeal Chocolate Chip Cookies, Almost Martha's, 48
  Raisin Oatmeal, Cookees', 149
  Raspberry Almond Shortbread Thumbprints, 71
Corn Pudding, Fresh, 186
Corn, Fried, 88
Cranberry Apple Pudding, 219
Cranberry Salad, Christmas, 60
Cream Cheese Coffee Cake, 224
Cream, Devonshire-Style, 156
Crème Brulee French Toast, 191

Crescent (roll) Puffs, Marshmallow, 6
Czech Kolaches, 173
Desserts, see also Bars, Cakes, Cookies, Pies
  Amber's Delight, Frozen, 97
  Apple Cranberry Pudding, 219
  Autumn Cheesecake (apple), 146
  Blanc Mange, 121
  Blueberry Grunt, 66
  Devonshire-Style Cream, 156
  Fruit Soup, Ole, 60
  Panna Cotta, 214
  Rice Cream (pudding), 59
Dumplings, Spaetzle, 23
Eggplant, Beef Curry with, 54
Eggplant, Ratatouille, 156
Empanadas, Cheese, 12
English Meat Pasties, 172
Extreme Brownies, 196
Fancy Wild Rice (dessert topping), 127
Finnish foods, 218-19
Fish
  Bake, South of the Border, 98
  Herring Salad, Relish Bar, 155
  Lutefisk, 59
  Salmon, Grilled, 230
  Walleye Almondine, 155
French Toast, Crème Brulée, 191
French Toast, Oven-Baked, 47
French, Ratatouille, 156
Fried, see also Stir-Fried and Oven Fries
Fried Corn, 88
Fried Green Tomatoes, 139
Frosting, Cream, 168
Frozen Orange Cream Pie, 97
Fruit
  Bagel Spread, 92
  Cinnamon Cream Chicken Salad, 208
  Double Berry Ice Cream Sundaes, 93
  Filling, Dried, 173
  Soup, Ole, 60
  Soup, Strawberry Chantilly, 204
  Topped Cake, 150
Fry Bread, 29
Fudge Cake, Triple, 82
Garlic Salad Dressing, Sweet, 140
German, foods, 22–23
Gingerbread, River Driver's, 149
Glazed Ham and Sweet Potatoes, 87
Grandma Schumacher's Hash Browns, 168
Granola, Toasty Nut, 75
Green Beans with Cashews, 181

Green Pepper, Ratatouille, 156
Green Tomatoes, Fried, 139
Ham
  Wild Rice and Ham Country Tart, 7
  Glazed Ham and Sweet Potatoes, 87
  Ham Rolls with Zippy Sauce, 208
Herring Salad, 155
Hmong foods, 53–54
Ice Cream Dessert, 97
Ice Cream Pie, 97
Ice Cream Sundaes, Double Berry, 93
Indian Tacos, 29
Italian
  Soup, Marche Wedding, 213
  Linguini with Pesto, 213
  Panna Cotta (dessert), 214
  Porketta, 172
  Roast Potatoes, Romagna, 214
  Turkey Parmigiana, 115
Jambalaya, Minnesota, 87
Jansson's Temptation (casserole), 134
Jerky, meat, 30
Kahlua Creams (bars), 168
Ken's Favorite Ribs, 86
Kibbutz Fresh Vegetable Salad, 203
Killer Brownies, 196
Larrigan Pie, 150
Lemon-Butter Bars, 71
Lemon Chiffon Cake, 224
Lemon Cream Cheese Cake, 225
Lemonade, 41
Lutefisk, 59
Marble Bars, 77
Marche Wedding Soup, 213
Marion Ross's Cheesy Macaroni Bake with Spam, 110
Marshmallow Crescent Puffs, Magic, 6
Matzah Balls, 202
Meatballs, Swedish, 133
Meat Blintzes, 203
Meat, see also Beef, Ham, Pork, and Veal
Mexican
  Beef Tostadas, 16
  Cheese Empanadas, 12
  Chicken Enchiladas, 17
  Salsa Cruda, 16
  Steak Fajitas, 18
  Synchronizadas (snacks), 18
  Taco Salad, 102
Minnesota Jambalaya, 87
Monkey Bread, 76
Muffins, Apricot Pecan Oatmeal, 223

Muffins, Blueberry, 65
Native American foods, 29–30
Norwegian recipes, 59-60
Oats
  Oatmeal Carmelitas, 6
  Oatmeal Chocolate Chip Cookies, Almost Martha's, 48
  Apricot Pecan Oatmeal Muffins, 223
  Raisin Oatmeal Cookies, 149
  Toasty Nut Granola, 75
Orange Cream Pie, 97
Oven Fries, potatoes, 139
Pancake, Apple Puff, 145
Pancakes, Blueberry, 65
Panna Cotta (dessert), 214
Parmesan Chicken, 76
Party-Perfect Stuffed Shells, 102
Pasta
  Cheesy Macaroni Bake with Spam, 110
  Linguini with Pesto, 213
  Salad, Chicken Fruit, 208
  Shells, Stuffed, 102
Peach Praline Pie, 36
Pesto, Pistachios and Almonds, Linguini with, 213
Pies
  Chocolate Chiffon, Crunchy, 35
  Colonial Innkeeper's, 35
  Impossible Pumpkin, 36
  Larrigan (vinegar), 150
  Orange Cream, 97
  Peach Praline, 36
  Sweet Potato, 42
  Wild Rice and Ham Country Tart, 7
Pineapples
  Kabobs, and Sweet Potato, 209
  Salsa, 230
  Upside-Down Cake, 81
Pistachio(s), Almond Pesto, Linguini with, 213
Polish Bigos, 11
Pork, see also Ham
  Barbecued, Honey, 180
  Fillet with Caper Sauce, 229
  Gravy, 209
  Porketta, Italian, 172
  Ribs, Barbecued, 86
  Roast, Calypso, 209
  Sandwiches, 86
  Tofu and, Chinese, 161
Potatoes
  Hash Browns, Grandma Schumacher's, 168
  Jansson's Temptation, 134
  Mashed, and Rutabaga, Casserole, 219

Oven Fries, 139
Romagna Roast, 214
Salad, Old-Fashioned, 77
Salad, Hot German, 22
Sauerkraut with Apples and, 23
Soup, cold (Vichyssoise), 155
Pudding, Vanilla (blanc mange), 121
Pumpkin Cake, 81
Pumpkin Pie, Impossible, 36
Radish, Daikon with Carrot Salad, 54
Raspberry Almond Shortbread Thumbprints, 71
Raspberry Cheesecake Crepes, 192
Ratatouille, 156
Red Pepper, Broccoli and Tofu, Stir-Fried, 140
Red Pepper Soup, 186
Relish Bar Herring Salad, 155
Rhubarb Cream Cake, 82
Rice Cream (Riskrem, pudding), 59
Rice, Fried, Yeung Chau, 181
River Driver's Gingerbread, 149
Robert Moulton's Spam 'N Kraut Soup, 110
Romagna Roast Potatoes, 214
Russian Apple Cake-Pie, 146
Russian Olivier Salad, 162
Rutabaga Mashed Potato Casserole, 219
Salads
  Chili-Chicken, 98
  Cinnamon Cream Chicken Fruit, 208
  Cranberry, Christmas, 59
  Daikon Radish and Carrot, 54
  Dressing, Sweet Garlic, 140
  Herring, Relish Bar, 155
  Potato, Hot German, 22
  Potato, Old-Fashioned, 77
  Russian Olivier, 162
  Seafood with Vanilla Mayonnaise, 121
  Taco, 102
  Vegetable, Kibbutz, 203
  Wild Rice, Chippewa, 127
Salmon, Grilled, with Pineapple Salsa, 230
Salsa Cruda, 16
Sandwich Filling, Turkey, 115
Sauces
  Blueberry Monday, 66
  Custard, 122
  Devonshire-Style Cream, 156
  Vanilla, 122
Sauerkraut, with Apples and Potatoes, 23

Scandinavian Coffee Bread, 218
Seafood Salad, with Vanilla Mayonnaise, 121
Soups
  Avocado-Lime Cream, 196
  Borscht, 11
  Chicken, with Matzah Balls, 202
  Chicken and Barley, 185
  March Wedding, 213
  Ole Fruit, 60
  Pea, Swedish, 133
  Red Pepper, 186
  Spam 'N Kraut, 110
  Spinach and Wild Mushroom, 231
  Strawberry Chantilly, 204
  Summer Vegetable, 218
  Vichyssoise, 155
  Wild Rice, Byerly's, 126
South of the Border Fish Bake, 98
Soy foods, 102–3
Spaetzle (dumplings), 23
Spam recipes, 109–10
Spinach and Wild Mushroom Soup, 231
Spread, Bagel, 93
State Fair recipes, prizewinning, 223–25
Steak Fajitas, 18
Stews, Polish Bigos, 11
Strawberry Chantilly Soup, 204
Stuffing, Wild Rice, 114
Sugar Cookies, Louise's, 72
Summer Vegetable Soup, 218
Swedish
  Jansson's Temptation (casserole), 134
  Meatballs, 133
  Pea Soup, 133
  Seaman's Beef, 162
  Spice Cake, 134
Sweet Potatoes
  Glazed Ham and, 87
  Kabobs, and Pineapple, 209
  Pie, 42
Synchronizadas, 18
Taco Salad, 102
Tacos, Indian, 29
Textured Vegetable Protein (TVP), 103
Tiny Caramel Rolls, 190
Toasty Nut Granola, 75
Tofu
  Chinese Pork and, 161
  Stir-Fried with Broccoli and Red Pepper, 140
  Stuffed Shells, Party-Perfect, 102
Tomatoes, Fried Green, 139
Tomatoes, Salsa Cruda, 16

Tortillas
  Beef Tostadas, 16
  Chicken Enchiladas, 17
  Synchronizadas, 18
Tostados, Beef, 16
Turkey
  Burgers, 114
  Fruit Sandwich Filling, 115
  Legs, Barbecued, 41
  Parmigiana, 115
  Pot Pie, 187
  Roast, 113
  Stuffing, Wild Rice, 114
Turnovers, Cheese Empanadas, 12
Turnovers, English Meat Pasties, 172
Vanilla
  Blanc Mange (pudding), 121

Custard Sauce, French-Style, 122
Macaroons, 121
Mayonnaise, with Seafood Salad, 121
Sauce, 122
Veal, Wiener Schnitzel, 167
Vegetable Mafé, 161
Vegetable Salad, Kibbutz, 203
Vegetable Soup, Summer, 218
Vegetarian, Vegetable Mafé, 161
Vichyssoise, 155
Vienna Cutlets (Wiener Schnitzel), 167
Walleye Almondine, 155
Watermelon on a Stick, 48
Wiener Schnitzel (Vienna Cutlets), 167

Wild Fruit Bagel Spread, 92
Wild Fruit Wine Sauce, 93
Wild Mushroom Soup, Spinach and, 231
Wild Rice
  Baron (casserole), 126
  Fancy (dessert topping), 127
  Ham and, Country Tart, 7
  Salad, Chippewa, 127
  Soup, Byerly's, 126
  Stuffing, 114
Wine Cooler, Summertime, 93
Wine Sauce for Wild Game, 93
Zucchini, Ratatouille, 156

PICTURE CREDITS

Names of the photographers, when known, are either in the full picture caption or in parentheses following the page number on which the picture appears.

Pages i (top), 37–40: Courtesy of the *Minnesota-Spokesman Recorder* © 2003, www.spokesman-recorder.com.

Pages i (middle), 13–15: Courtesy Riverview Economic Development Association, St. Paul, Minnesota.

Pages i (bottom), 163, 165: Courtesy Schumacher's Hotel.

Pages ii–iii, 158–60: Photos by John Borge, courtesy Concordia Language Villages, Concordia College, Moorhead, Minnesota.

Pages vi (left), 19–21: Photo courtesy Heritagefest, Inc.

Pages vi (bottom), 62–64: Photos © Dave Hansen, University of Minnesota Extension Service.

Pages vii (top), 135, 137: Photos courtesy BC Gardens.

Pages vii (bottom), 183: Photo by Kelly Lavin, © 2003.

Pages 1, 32–34: Photos by Valerie Aerosmith.

Pages 2, 4, 79: Photos courtesy General Mills Archive.

Pages 8–10: Photos courtesy of the Festival of Nations®.

Pages 24–26, 123, 125 (Monroe P. Killey), 51 (Michael Kieger), 70 (Charles Hilbbard), 111 (Gilbert Ellestad), 148, 170: Minnesota Historical Society.

Page 28: Photo by Pamela McClanahan, © 2003.

Pages 43, 74: Copyright © Minnesota Office of Tourism photos.

Pages 44–46: Photos courtesy Epiphany Catholic Church, Coon Rapids, Minnesota.

Page 49: Photo by Joey Mcleister, © 2003 *Star Tribune*/Minneapolis-St. Paul.

Page 52: Photo by Richard Tsong-Taatarii, © 2003 *Star Tribune*/Minneapolis-St. Paul.

Pages 55–57: Courtesy St. Olaf College.

Pages 61, 68–69: Courtesy Land O'Lakes.

Page 83: Courtesy Ken Davis Products.

Page 91: Photos courtesy Minnestalgia®.

Pages 94–96: Photos courtesy the Schwan Food Company.

Pages 100–101: Photos courtesy Minnesota Soybean Council.

Pages 104–6: Courtesy of Hormel Food Corporation.

Pages 117–19: Courtesy Watkins, Inc., Winona, Minnesota.

Pages 129. 142–44: Photos courtesy Carlson's Orchard and Bakery, Winsted, Minnesota.

Pages 130–31: Courtesy American Swedish Institute, Minneapolis.

Pages 152–53: Courtesy Kavanaugh's Sylvan Lake Resort.

Page 169: Photo courtesy Ironworld Discovery Center, Chisholm, Minnesota.

Pages 175, 227: Photos by Brian Peterson, © 2003 *Star Tribune*/Minneapolis-St. Paul.

Pages 176–77: Photos courtesy Laura Chin.

Page 188: Photo by Duane Braley, © 2003 *Star Tribune*/Minneapolis-St. Paul.

Page 195: Photo by Catherine Watson, © 2003.

Pages 199, 201: Courtesy of the Jewish Historical Society of the Upper Midwest, St. Paul, Minnesota.

Page 207: Photo provided by Ginny Hoeschen.

Page 211: Photo by Kit Rogers, courtesy of Minnesota Public Radio.

Page 216: Photo provided by Beatrice Ojakangas.

A Cook's Tour of Minnesota was designed by Gail Wiener, Minneapolis; set in type by Wendy Holdman at Stanton Publication Services, St. Paul; and printed by Maple Press, York, Pennsylvania.